조익제 변호사와 함께 영어로 읽는

Introduction to English Civil Law I

for Korean Speaking Lawyers and Law Students

영국 민사법 입문

Vol. 1

Basic Topics, Persons in Law and the Law of Contract

영국법의 기초지식, 인(人) 및 계약법

2008

written by

Prof. Dr. iur. utr. Rainer Wörlen

Translated and additionally commented in Korean

by

Ikze Cho

Attorney at Law(Germany)

Lee International
IP & LAW GROUP

도서출판 법영사

Wörner, Prof. Dr. iur. utr. Reiner
Cho, Ikze

Introduction to English Civil Law
for Korean Speaking Lawyers and Law Students

1. Korean Language Edition 2008

ISBN 978-89-7032-243-8

Published by
BubYoungSa Publishing Co. and Lee International IP & Law Group

Preface

대륙법계 국가인 독일의 법학자가 영어로 영국민사법에 관한 책을 저술한다고 하면 여기에는 특별한 이유가 있을 것이다. 개인적으로 나는 “United Kingdom” 및 “Malta” 등지에서 수차례 체류하면서 영국법의 영향하에 있는 지역의 사람들, 그들의 언어 그리고 그들의 법제도인 영국법에 대한 관심과 호감을 가지게 되었다. 영국법 제도는 외국법 특히 대륙법학자인 나를 매료시켰는데, 내가 느낀 그 감동을 말로 전하기는 쉽지 않다. 그 감동은 직접 느끼고 직접 체험해야 하는 것이다. 그것은 런던 시내 한가운데의 “Royal Courts” 건물에 있는 “High Court”의 재판이나 의회건물 내부의 “House of Lords”의 재판을 “live”로 직접 체험할 때 가질 수 있는 감동이다. 위엄있는 “Inns of Court” 하나를 직접 방문해보고, “Law Society”의 리셉션에 참가하여 생전의 “Lord Denning”(1999년 3월 5일 향년 100세를 일기로 돌아가심)과 직접 악수를 나누었을 때의 감동 등이 바로 말로 설명할 수 없는 것들이다. 본서는 독자 여러분들께서 직접 그 감동을 체험할 수 있도록 길을 예비하는 역할을 할 뿐이다.

본서는 영국법에 관한 교과서일 뿐만 아니라, 영미법의 법률용어를 가르치고자 하는 의도로도 작성되었다. 방주로 작성된 추가의 설명이 독자들의 이해를 도울 것이다. 때로는 그 설명을 반복하기를 주저하지 않았다. Repetitio mater studiorum est (= repetition is the mother of learning)은 특히 법학에 유효한 명언이리라. Understanding is the key of learning!이라는 현대의 격언도 매우 적절한 것이다. 그러나 반복은 Understanding, 즉 이해를 촉진할 것이며, 이로써 고대와 현대의 격언은 아무런 모순없이 그 뜻을 모아 우리에게 배움의 길과 방법을 잘 보여준다고 생각한다.

Schmalkalden, Germany, 2008년 1월　　　　Rainer Wörlen 교수

한국판에 붙이는 글

이미 출간된 미국법 입문 1, 2권에 대한 독자들의 좋은 반응에 힘입어 이번에는 영국민사법 입문 1권도 출간하게 되었음을 기쁘게 생각합니다. 미국법 입문을 출간할 때와 마찬가지로 저는 책을 함께 읽어가는 학생의 마음으로 약간의 설명을 붙여 본서를 독자들에게 소개할 뿐입니다.

국제화되어진 사회의 법률가들에게 영어는 군인의 무기와도 같이 중요한 도구입니다. 이 점은 한국변호사이든지 중국변호사이든지 아니면 저와 같은 독일변호사에게도 마찬가지입니다. 독일에서도 저의 업무의 반은 영어로 이루어졌었는데, 한국에 돌아와서는 영어의 비중을 더 많이 절감하게 되었습니다. 독일에서는 독일 사람과 독일어로 이야기를 나누면 되었는데, 한국에서는 독일인을 만나도 독일어를 모르는 다른 동료들을 위해서, 그리고 기록을 영어로 남기기 위해서 영어를 말해야 했기 때문입니다. 본서는 저에게 항상 큰 도움이 되었습니다. 본서가 독자들께도 영미법 독서의 좋은 출발점이 되기를 바랍니다.

본 출판작업을 적극 지원해주신 독일 Alpmann Schmidt 출판사와 한국 Lee International IP & Law Group의 이승훈 회장님 및 Lee International 법률 사무소의 공동 대표변호사이신 안용덕 전대법관님, 그리고 서영제 전검사장님, 그리고 채정수 대표변호사님께 깊이 감사드립니다.

공동출판을 잘 마무리해주신 법영사 고준영 사장님께 감사드리며, 수년을 한결같이 훌륭한 편집작업을 해주신 정정희 편집장님께도 깊은 감사의 마음을 전하고 싶습니다.

끝으로 본서와 관련된 질문과 토론을 펼칠 수 있는 www.ez-law.co.kr가 준비되어 있기는 하지만, 아직은 다국어 사전의 개발에 역점을 두어 운영되고 있습니다. 본서에 관한 질문 및 토론 게시판도 곧 활성화될 것입니다. 독자들의 많은 관심을 부탁드립니다.

2008년 1월

변호사 조익제

Contents

Part One: Basic Topics

Chapter One Classification and sources of English law

Chapter Two The administration of the law

Chapter Three The legal profession

Chapter Four How to find the law

Part Two: Specific branches of law

Chapter Five Persons in law

Chapter Six The law of contract

Table of cases

Table of statutes

Table of diagrams

Abbreviations

A.C.	appeal cases
All E.R.	All England Reports
Aufl.	Auflage
Bros.	Brothers
c.	chapter
C.A.	Court of Appeal
cf.	confer
Ch.	Chancery (Division)
Co.	company
dies.	dieselben
e.g.	exempli gratia (for example)
E.R.	The English Law Reports
ed./Ed.	edition /Editor
Fam.	Family (Division)
GCSE	General Certificate of Secondary Education
Geo.	(King) George
Hrsg.	Herausgeber
Hon.	(The) Honourable
i.e.	id est (that is)
Inc.	Incorporation/incorporated
J.	Justice
JA	Juristische Arbeitsblätter
lbs.	pounds

L.C.J.	Lord Chief Justice
L.J.	Lord Justice
L.R.	Law Reports
LL.D	Doctor of Laws
Ltd.	limted
M.R.	Master of the Rolls
P.	Probate (Divorce and Admiralty Division)
p.	page
p.l.c.	public limited company
PIL	Private International Law
Q.B.	Queen's Bench (Division)
R.	Regina (Queen)
R.W.	Right Worship
S./s.	section
S.J.	Solicitors Journal
ss.	sections
U.D.C.	Urban District Council
U.K.	United Kingdom
USA	United States of America
UCTA	Unfair Contract Terms Act
v.	versus
Vic.	(Queen) Victoria
Vol.	Volume
W.L.R.	Weekly Law Reports

Bibliography

I. English (and Anglo-American) law in English

Adams	Law for Business Students, 2nd ed., London ... 2000
Adams & Brownsword	Understanding Law, 2nd ed., London 1999
Applebey	Contract Law, London 2001
Bailey & Gunn	(Smith & Bailey on) The Modern English Legal System, 3rd ed., London 1996
Baker	An Introduction to English Legal History, 4th ed., London ... 2002
Barker & Padfield	Law, 11th ed., London ... 2002
Beale, Bishop & Furmston	Contract – Cases and Materials, 4th ed., London-Dublin-Edinburgh 2001
Beale/Hartkamp/Kötz/Tallon	Cases, Materials and Text on Contract Law, Oxford and Portland (Oregon) 2002 [Ius Commune Casebooks for the Common Law of Europe]
Black	Black's Legal Reader – An Introduction to the Anglo-American Law and Legal System, 1. Aufl., Hannover 1998/99
Bradney, Cownie, Masson, Neal & Newell	How to Study Law, 4th ed., London 2000
Brodie (Ed.)	The English Legal System in the Twenty-First Century [The Inner Temple Millenium Lectures], London 2002
Brown	GCSE Law, 8th ed., London 2002
Bruce	Success in Law, 5th ed., London 2001
Cassel	Studying the Law – The Law Students Handbook, 2nd ed., London 2001
Cheshire, Fitfoot & Furmston's	Law of Contract, (by *Furnston*) 14th ed., London-Edinburgh-Dublin 2001
Collins	The Law of Contract, 3rd ed., London-Edinburgh-Dublin 1997;

	AS-Level Law, 3rd ed., London ... 2000
Cooke/Oughton	The Common Law of Obligations, 3rd ed., London-Edinburgh-Dublin 2000
Cownie & Bradney	English Legal System in Context, 2nd ed., London-Edinburgh-Dublin 2000
Cracknell	Contract (Cracknell's Law Students' Companion), 11th ed., London 2000; English Legal System (Cracknell's Law Students' Companion), 5th ed., London 2000
Darbyshire	Nutshells: English Legal System, 5th ed., London ... 2000
Denham	Law – a modern introduction, 4th ed., London 1999
Denning, Lord	The Discipline of Law, London 1979
Dobson/Schmitthoff	(Charlesworth's) Business Law (by *Dobson*), 16th ed., London 1999
Duxburn	Nutshells: Contract Law, 5th ed., London ... 2000
Eddey ...	on the English Legal System (by *Darbyshire*), 7th ed., London 2002
Elliott & Quinn	English Legal System, London-New York 1996; Contract Law, 3rd ed., London 2001
Harris	An Introduction to Law, 6th ed., London-Edinburgh-Dublin 2002
Geldart	Introduction to English Law, 11th ed. (by *Yardley*), Oxford-New York 1995
Goodmann	The Walking Guide to LAWYER's LONDON, London 2000
Jewell	An Introduction to English Contract Law, 1. Aufl., Baden-Baden 1997
Keenan	(Smith & Keenan's) English Law, 13th ed., London ... 2001
Kenny	Studying Law, 4th ed., London-Edinburgh-Dublin 2001
Koffmann/Macdonald	The Law of Contract, 4th ed., Croydon 2001
Lyall	An Introduction to British Law, 2. Aufl., Baden-Baden 2002

Partington	Introduction to the English Legal System, Oxford 2000
Poole	Textbook on Contract Law, 6th ed., London 2001; Casebook on Contract Law, 5th ed., London 2001
Richards	Law of Contract, 5th ed., Harlow (Essex) 2002
Rivlin	First Steps in the Law, 2nd ed., Oxford 2002
Rose	(Blackstone's) Statutes on Contract, Tort & Restitution, 11th ed., London 2002/03
Shears & Stephenson	(*James'*) Introduction to English Law, 13th ed., London-Dublin-Edinburgh 1996
Slapper & Kelly	On English Legal System, 5th ed., London 2001
Smith, J.C.	The Law of Contract, 4th ed., London 2002; (Smith & Thomas) A Casebook on Contract, 11th ed., London 2000
Stone	Principles of Contract Law, 4th ed., London-Sydney 2000
Templeman/Evans	Legal Skills and System – Textbook –, 1st ed., London 1997
Templeman/Krishnan	Obligations: Contract Law – Revision Work Book –, 2nd ed., London 2000; Obligations: Contract Law – Textbook –, 2nd ed., London 2000
Templeman/Read	Obligations: Contract Law – Casebook –, 2nd ed., London 2000
Templeman/Reed	English Legal System – Casebook –, 2nd ed. 1998; English Legal System – Revision Work Book –, 1st ed., 1997; English Legal System – Textbook –, 2nd ed. 2001; all: London
Tayfoor	Law Cartoons: Contract, 1st ed., London 1995
Treitel	The Law of Contract, 10th ed., London 1999
Williams	Learning the Law, 12th ed., London 2002
Whitaker's	Almanack 2002, London 2001

Ⅱ. English (and Anglo-American) law in Korean

이상윤 영미법, 개정판, 2005, 박영사

서희원 영미법강의, 2002, 박영사

김대권 영미법, 개정증보판, 1997, 박영사

김태운 영미법강의, 2004, 신영사

F.G. 켐핀 영미법개론, 1988, 법문사

존 헨리메리만 시민법전통: 대륙법과 영미법의 비교, 1995, 철학과현실사

김봉철 영국법체계의 이해, 2005, 이컴비즈넷

Ⅲ. English legal terminology

Byrd Einführung in die anglo-amerikanische Rechtssprache, 2. Aufl., München-Wien-Bern 2001

Chartrand, Millar & Wilshire English for Contract and Company Law, London 1997

Gibbons Language and the Law, London-New York 1994

Heidinger/Hubalek Anglo-Amerikanische Rechtssprache – Praxishandbuch für Rechtsanwälte, Wirtschaftsjuristen und Wirtschaftstreuhänder –, 2. Aufl., Wien 1996

Riley English for Law, 1. Aufl., Ismaning 1994

Ⅳ. Dictionaries of legal (and commercial) terms

Dietl/Lorenz Wörterbuch für Recht, Wirtschaft und Politik mit erläuternden und rechtsvergleichenden Kommentaren,
Teil I: Englisch-Deutsch, 6. Aufl. München 2000
Teil II: Deutsch-Englisch, 4. Aufl. München 1992

Dietl/Lorenz CD-Wörterbuch für Recht, Wirtschaft und Politik, Teil I und Teil II: Englisch-Deutsch/Deutsch-Englisch. Rund 180.000 Fachbegriffe übersetzt und teilweise erläutert. München 2002

Epstein (General Editor) Law and Commercial Dictionary in Five Languages – English to German, Spanish, French, Italian – Bd. I: A–J, Bd. II: K–Z, München–Paris–Minnesota 1985

Flory/Froschauer Grundwortschatz der Rechtssprache Deutsch–Englisch/ Englisch–Deutsch, 3. Aufl. Neuwied 2002

Köbler Deutsch-Englisches und Englisch-Deutsches Rechtswörterbuch für jedermann, 5. Aufl., München 2001

Lindbergh Internationales Rechtswörterbuch Deutsch–Englisch–Französisch, Neuwied 1995

Romain/Bader/Byrd Wörterbuch der Rechts- und Wirtschaftssprache, Teil I: Englisch-Deutsch, 5. Aufl. München 2000 Teil II: Deutsch-Englisch, 4. Aufl. München 2002

Part One: Basic Topics

Chapter One

Classification and sources of English law
분류 / 법원(法源), 근원

Ⅰ. Introduction
도입, 소개, 서(序)

The English legal system is completely different from the continental legal system. The essential (though certainly not the only) difference is this: Whereas most continental legal systems are characterised by codified statutes, English law is mainly "judge-made law".

법제도, 법제(法制)
(유럽) 대륙의 / 근본적인 차이
법전화된 법률들
판례법(판결로 형성되는 법)

Briefly, this means that English law is case law. It consists of, above all, specific cases whose decisions are based on a series of precedents. Generally, the cases are cited with the names of the persons involved in the case, more commonly known as plaintiff[1] and defendant, for example *Donoghue* v. *Stevenson* (1932). The decisions of actual cases are based on a series of judicial precedents. The precedents are not arbitrary rulings but reasoned judgments.

사례법, 판례법
선례(先例) / 인용하다
관련자
원고 / 피고 / 대(對)
사법적(법원의)
자의적 결정들 / 이유를 단 판결들, 판결이유를 포함한 판결

In no other legal system is the development of the law as closely associated with its historical background as in the English legal system.

밀접하게 연결된 / 역사적 배경

So it is not unusual even today for legal actions to be adjudged on the authority of a precedent dating back to the 14th century [e.g. *Abbots Ripton* v *Can* (1376)].

오늘날에도 드문 일이 아니다 / 소송에 있어서 / 판결을 내리다 / ~의 권위를 들어, ~을 인용하여

Studying English law, therefore, does not only entail gaining a knowledge of its general principles and legal rules,

초래하다
지식습득 / 법규

1) Cf. "*Notation*" on page 70.
70쪽 Notation 참조 요망

but it also requires some knowledge of its development and historical background.

요구하다

II. The classification of English law

As in the continental legal systems in the English legal system we also have to distinguish between various branches of the law.

구별하다 / 법분야

1. Private law and public law

사법 / 공법

Private law is that part of the law which is primarily concerned with the rights and duties of equal ranking individuals. On this basis private law includes all branches of the civil law wherein one individual puts forward a claim against another individual. These branches include amongst others the law of contract and the law of torts.

우선적으로 관련된
동등한 수준의, 동급의
민법 / 청구권을 행사하다, 제소하다
계약법 /불법행위법

On the other hand public law consists of those fields of law which are primarily concerned with the State itself and with the legal relations between the State and the individual who are in a relationship of superiority and subordination with each other.

법분야
상하관계

Public law thus includes constitutional law, administrative law as well as criminal law.

따라서 / 헌법 / 행정법
형법

2. Civil law and criminal law

Another method of classification is to distinguish between civil law and criminal law.

In every advanced legal system a distinction is made between those branches of law which are the concern of private individuals in their relationship with one another, i.e. civil law, and that field of law, called criminal law, which is

선진적, 진보한 / 구별
~와 관련되다, 관계하다

in particular the concern of the State. Criminal law is a code of conduct which the State imposes on all members of its society.

특히 / 행위준칙
부과하다

Thus, civil law includes the law of contract, commercial law, the law of torts, property law, family law, the law of succession and business law.

상법
재산법
상속법 / 경제법

In most civil proceedings one comes across individuals suing one another, e.g., *Donoghue* v *Stevenson*: "*Donoghue*", as the plaintiff is the person who commences the action for the recovery of a claim whilst "*Stevenson*", as the defendant is the person against whom court proceedings are brought.

민사소송
제소하다
원고 / 소송을 제기하다, 제소하다 / 달성, 회복 / 청구권 / 피고(민사소송의) / 법정소송

Criminal law is solely concerned with misconduct defined as a crime or a criminal offence. Criminal cases, known as "prosecutions", are usually brought up by, and in the name of, the State, e.g., *R.* v *Johnson*. This means that nominally the prosecutor is "Regina", the Queen, whilst Johnson is the accused person or defendant. As our book is entitled "Introduction to English *civil* law", criminal law will not be dealt with in any further detail.

전적으로 / 잘못된 행위
(중한) 범죄 / (경한) 범죄
형사절차
이름을 따르면
공소자, 검찰
피고소인 / 피고(형사절차의)
더 많은, 더 깊은

Civil law is sometimes regarded as synonymous with private law. Although strictly speaking it is not incorrect to do so, it would be better to distinguish between civil law as a restricted term and private law covering a much wider area. Civil law is only one branch of private law.

좁은 개념, 협의 / 더 넓은 분야, 광의

Another specific branch of private law is certainly "private international law". Private international law ("PIL") stands as a special field of law in every legal system. PIL is primarily concerned with determining the applicable law which is to be applied by the court in cases involving some foreign elements. Suppose, e.g., that A, in England, makes a contract by correspondence with B, a German, in Germany, and according to the terms of this contract B is to perform certain services for A in the United States of America. Now, suppose that B breaks his contract and that A sues him in England. It would

국제사법
독자적인(독특한, 별도의) 법영역
결정하다
적용되다 / 외국관련성이 있는 사례
계약조건 / 이행하다, 수행하다
제소하다

be clear that the English law of contract is not necessarily the correct law to be applied in all of the facets of this case. So the question which arises is this: which is the applicable law, the German, the English or the American law of contract? In order to determine which is the most applicable law, the court will have to consult the rules of PIL.

반드시, 필수적으로
양상, (다양한) 측면
적용가능한
결정하다
묻다, 연구하다

3. Common law and equity

코몬로, 보통법 / 형평법, 형평칙 (대륙법계의 신의칙에 해당)

The division between common law and equity is historical. These fields of law will be considered in more detail in the following chapter.

구별 / 역사적 배경을 지닌

Common law was the only law applied in the "common law courts" up until 1875, the year in which great legislative reforms took place in English law, as shall be seen later on (for now, remember the *Judicature Acts 1873 1875!*). As its name would imply, common law was common to the whole country and administered in the old Royal Courts. It was particularly concerned with criminal law, the law of contract and the law of torts.

입법개혁
법원조직법
이름이 암시해주듯이
적용되다 / 왕립법원

Equity was the law applied in the Lord Chancellor's[1] "Court of Chancery" before 1875.

로드 챈슬러, 고위법관
챈슬러법원, 형평법원

It was concerned in particular with trusts, aspects of land law and the law of property and grew through the royal power to provide justice where the common law courts had failed to do so.

신탁관계 / 토지법
부동산법 / ~하는 데에 이르다
정의(법)를 제공하다, 규정하다
실패하다

---

1) 정식 명칭은 Lord High Chancellor of Great Britain이다.
2005년 블레어 정부의 Constitutional Reform Act(개헌법) 이전에는 상원(귀족원) 의장, 법무장관(검찰총장 겸임), 사법부의 수장 등 입법, 사법, 행정부를 망라하는 최고의 관직이었다. 2005년 이후에는 상원의장직은 Lord Speaker가, 사법부의 수장은 Lord Chief Justice가 담당하게 되었다. 현재는 내각의 일원(법무장관, Secretary of State for Justice)이며, 국새(Great Seal)의 관리자이기도 하다 (Wikipedia의 Lord Chancellor 참조). 본문에서는 형평법원장의 관직을 가리킨다.

Diagram 1

The Classification of English Law	
Private Law...	**Public Law...**
is that part of the law which is primarily concerned with the rights and duties of equal ranking individuals.	consists of those fields of law which are primarily concerned with the State itself and the individual in a relationship of superiority and subordination.
Civil Law...	**Criminal Law...**
is a part of private law and in detail includes the law of contract, commercial law, the law of torts, property law and business law.	is a part of public law and a code of conduct which the State imposes on all members of its society.
Common Law...	**Equity...**
is common to the whole country and was administered in the Royal Courts. It is particularly concerned with criminal law, the law of contract and the law of torts.	was the law applied in the Lord Chancellor's "Court of Chancery" before 1875 concerned with trusts, land law and law of property.

Ⅲ. The sources of English law

The courts which apply the law are also the interpreters of the law. The "sources" of law are therefore the sources to which the courts turn in order to determine what is lawful.

의뢰하다, 찾아가다 / 적법한, 합법적인

In the English legal system four sources are traditionally identified:

- Legislation — 입법
- Judicial precedents (case law) — 판례법
- Custom — 관습, 관습법
- Books of authority. — 권위있는 교과서, 권위서

The first two are the principal sources, while the other two are subsidiary sources. Considered from the aspect of their sources, laws are generally divided into two main categories according to the solemnity of the form in which they are made. They may be either written or unwritten. In English law these traditional terms are misleading, since the expression "*written law*" signifies any law that is formally enacted, and

으뜸된(주된) 법원(法源)
부차적 법원(法源)
법률들
엄숙한 절차
성문법 / 형식적 의미의 법률

the expression "*unwritten law*" signifies all unenacted law. For example, as we shall see, judicial decisions are often reduced to writing in the form of law reports, but because they are not formal enactments they are considered as "unwritten law".	불문법 / 실체적 의미의 법률 (입법절차를 거치지 않은 법률) 서면으로 기록되다 형식적 (의미의) 법률
Since the fashion was set by the "*Code Napoléon*" (1804) many continental countries have codified much of their law. On the Continent, therefore, the volume of written law tends to preponderate over the volume of unwritten law.	유행이 생기다 법전화하다 양 우세하다
Nevertheless in England unwritten law is predominant due to the fact that most of the English law is derived from judicial precedents rather than from legislative enactments.	우세한 유래하다, 파생하다 입법절차
This does not mean, however, that none of the English law is codified. Having said that though, the English codifications are incomparable with the great continental general codifications such as the "Code Napoléon" or the "Bürgerliches Gesetzbuch"! The English "statute law" is principally related to a particular area of the law, for example, the sale of goods by the *Sale of Goods Act 1893*, which deals with the sale of goods and wares.	비교불가능한 나폴레옹 법전 독일 민법전(BGB) / 법률법 ~에 관련되다 동산매매법 상품
Let us now consider the four sources of English law:	

1. Legislation

a) The supremacy of Parliament

최고권력, 주권

Legislation is, as we should already know by now, enacted law. It is made in documentary form by an Act of Parliament!	문서의 / 의회의 절차를 거친 법률
The Parliament, as in continental countries, is the legislator. The composition of the British Parliament will be mentioned in one of the following chapters.	입법자, 입법부

Legislation can

- create new law, — 새로운 법을 창설하다
- repeal existing law, as well as — 법을 폐지하다
- amend existing law. — 법을 개정하다

A fundamental principle of the English constitution is "parliamentary sovereignty". — 의회의 주권

This means that the law set out in an Act of Parliament cannot be declared invalid by anybody in the State. — 무효로 선언하다

This contrasts, e.g., with the situation in the United States of America. In the USA the Supreme Court has the power to declare legislation "unconstitutional" and therefore inoperative. — 대비되다, 대립하다 / 최고법원 / 위헌의 / 무효의

b) The statutory process

Legislation in England can only be made by "the Queen in Parliament".

This emphasises the fact that Parliament is divided into three bodies: — 강조하다 / 나눠다 / 주체, 부분, 부서

- The Queen
- The House of Lords — 상원(귀족대표)
- The House of Commons. — 하원(평민, 시민대표)

In its preliminary process an Act of Parliament takes the form of a Bill, which is the draft of a proposed statute law. Bills are divided into *Public Bills* and *Private Bills*. — 법률안 / 초안 / 제안된 형식적 법률 / 공공법률안 / 사적 법률안

Public Bills are bills which are to be applied throughout the whole country including *Government Bills* and *Private Members' Bills*. On the other hand *Private Bills* are only to be applied either to a particular locality or to a particular person or group of persons. — 정부법률안 / 의원법률안 / 특정한 지역 / 인적 단체

The Public Bill procedure takes its course in five stages in both Houses, the Commons and the Lords: — 절차 / 5단계의 과정을 거치다

- First Reading – which is a formality; — 제1회 독회 / 형식적인 일
- Second Reading – where the general principles are discussed, — 일반 원칙
- Committee Stage – where the text of the Bill receives detailed consideration, — 위원회
- Report Stage – where any amendments are notified to the House and can be debated, — 수정사항 / 공지하다 / 토론하다
- Third Reading – where final approval is given and only verbal amendments are possible. — 구두 변경

After having been read by both houses, the Commons and the Lords, the Bill is consequently transmitted to the Queen — 전달하다

for the *Royal Assent*.

왕의 동의

The statement which prefaces every Act of Parliament emphasises that the procedural requirements have been observed:

머리말이 되다
강조되다 / 절차적 요구사항

"Be it enacted by the Queen's most Excellent Majesty, by and with the advice and consent of the Lords Spiritual and Temporal, and Commons, in this present Parliament assembled, and by the authority of the same as follows ..."

자문 / 동의 / 종교적 경(卿)들
세속적 경(卿)들 / 평민(대표)들
회합하다

In practice the Royal Assent is given by a committee of three peers, one of which is the Lord Chancellor. Moreover, the Royal Assent is never refused because the Queen has to act on the advice of the Government which, in turn, reflects the will of the electorate.

영국 고위귀족의 일원
거절, 거부하다 / 행동하다
반대로, 자기입장에서는 / 반영하다 / 선거권자

A Private Members' Bill follows the same procedure in Parliament as a Public Bill.

Thus, a Private Members' Bill has also got to be examined and approved by both Houses, though the process it undergoes is quite different.

검토를 거치다
(절차를) 거치다

The preamble and the provisions of the Bill are considered in detail by a small committee from either the Commons or the Lords, and the hearing tends to take the form of a judicial inquiry with counsel and witnesses. If the committee approves the Bill it is almost certain to become law without further difficulty.

전문 / 규정들, 조문들
닮다
법정절차 / 법정자문(변호사) / 증인 / 동의하다

c) Delegated legislation

위임된 입법절차

Most of the Acts of Parliament deal with complicated matters. Consequently the Act itself can only lay down a framework of general principles and the rest of the work lies in the hands of others.

(큰) 틀

This is generally done by civil servants acting in the name of and under the authority of the appropriate Minister.

관리, 공무원
권위하에 / 책임을 맡은, 담당의

Legislation of this kind is called "delegated legislation". The advantage of this delegated legislation is above all the fact that Parliament is relieved from the burden.

(부담을) 벗다 / 짐, 부담

Diagram 2

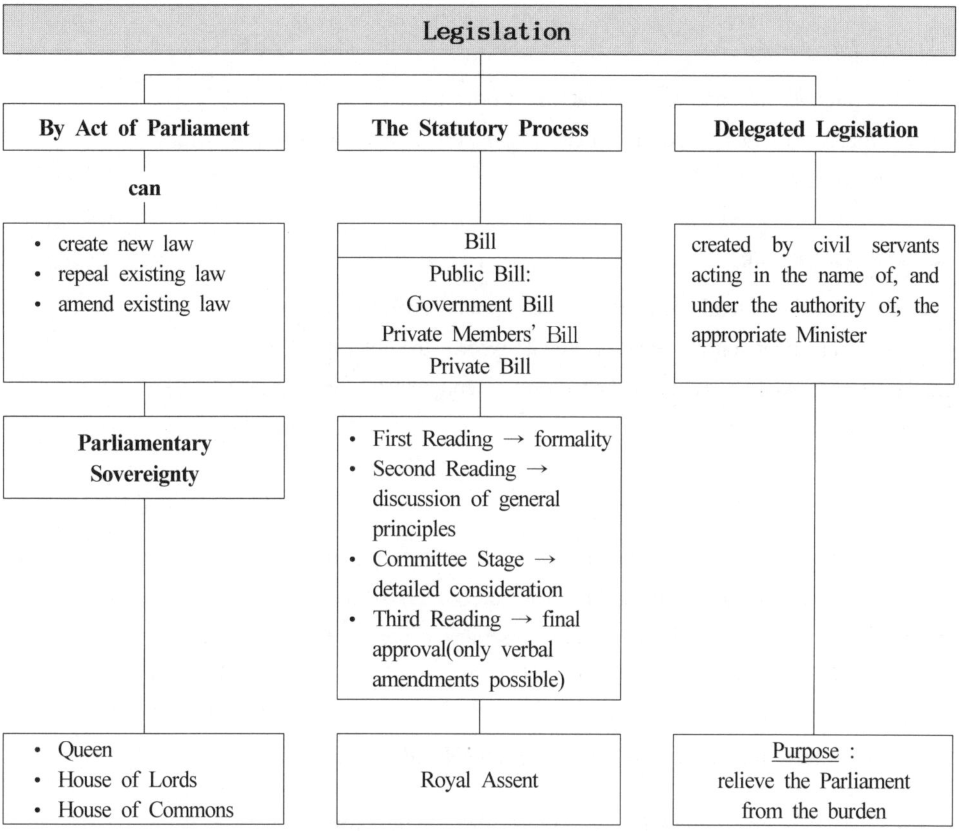

d) The interpretation of statutes

해석

Because of the supremacy of Parliament the judges have no power to declare a statute created by an Act of Parliament to be of no effect. Their task is limited to the interpretation of statutes. They have to interpret the words and phrases used in the legislation. In almost every case presided over by a judge a statute has to be interpreted. There are stacks and stacks of statutes. And "books and books have been written regarding the interpretation of statutes. All for the old hand. "Not one for the beginner" as *Lord Denning* criticises in his famous and best book "*The Discipline of Law*"!

무효의
쌓아둔 것
전문가를 위한

Nevertheless, you, as beginners are bound to acquire knowledge about some major rules involved in the interpreta-

습득하다
주요 규정들

tion of statutes under English law:

(1) *The literal rule:* 문언의

is the cardinal rule and means that the words used in the statute must be interpreted in their *ordinary*, *literal* or *grammatical sense*.

가장 중요한
원래의, 정상적인

(2) *The golden rule:*

states that the literal rule is to be applied whenever possible. You may only depart from it where the literal interpretation would result in absurdity, repugnancy or inconsistency!

벗어나다
엉뚱함 / 모순
비일관성

(3) *The mischief rule:* 손해, 잘못된 상황

is also known as *the rule in Heydon's case* (1584) and states: where the literal or the golden rule are of no result, the judge is entitled to look at the mischief which the legislation in the case under consideration is intended to remedy, and interpret it accordingly.

권한이 있는
당해 사건에서
보상하다, 해결책을 주다

Following this, four questions are to be considered:

- What was the common law before the statute was enacted?
- What was the mischief for which no provisions were introduced by the common law?
- What remedy has been resolved by Parliament to cure the disease? 결의하다, 해결하다 / 치유하다 해악, 잘못된 상황
- What can be the true reason behind the remedy? 법적 해결책, 수단

So judges have to consider: the old (common) law, the mischief and the remedy!

In addition there are a number of other rules which the beginner should know. 그 외에도

(4) *The eiusdem generis rule ("of the same genus" rule):* 동류의

This rule means that where specific words are followed by general words, the latter must be interpreted in the light of the former.

후자 / ~의 의미에서, 고려하에

Example — Evans v Cross (1938) —

The appellant was charged with having driven a car beyond the white line when overtaking on a bend in the road. He was charged under s.49 of the *Road Traffic Act 1930* with ignoring a traffic sign and was convicted by the judges.

He then appealed on the ground that a white painted line was not a traffic sign within the meaning of the Act. Section 48 (1) of the Act defines a traffic sign as "*all* signals, warning signposts, direction posts, signs or *other devices*".

Held: The last three words must be construed as something *eiusdem in generis* with the preceding words and, therefore, a white painted line on a road was not a traffic sign. The appropriate charges would have been for careless or dangerous driving.

항소심 원고 / 고소하다
추월하다 / 커브길
도로교통법
교통신호 / 유죄를 선언하다
다음의 (항소)이유를 들어
정의하다, 설명하다
신호대 / 이정표 / 장치
본 법원은 다음과 같이 판결한다 / 해석하다
적절한 / 부주의한, 과실있는

Considering these four traditional rules of interpretation we can conclude that the English judge is closely bound to the letter of the law. In principal, there is no analogical interpretation, as is most common in continental jurisprudence. The English judge is not allowed to correct the parliamentary legislator.

결론을 내리다
법률의 낱글자 / 유추의
법이론

But there are high authorities — in particular *Lord Denning* — who believe that the English method of interpretation ought to be abandoned in favour of the continental.

고위 권위자
포기하여야 한다

In *Corocraft* Ltd. v *Pan American Airways* Inc. (1969) *Lord Denning* stated: "But the literal meaning of the words is never allowed to prevail where it would produce manifest absurdity or consequences which could never have been intended by the Legislator".

유한 책임회사 / 주식회사 (자본회사)
우세하다 / 명백한 엉터리

Diagram 3

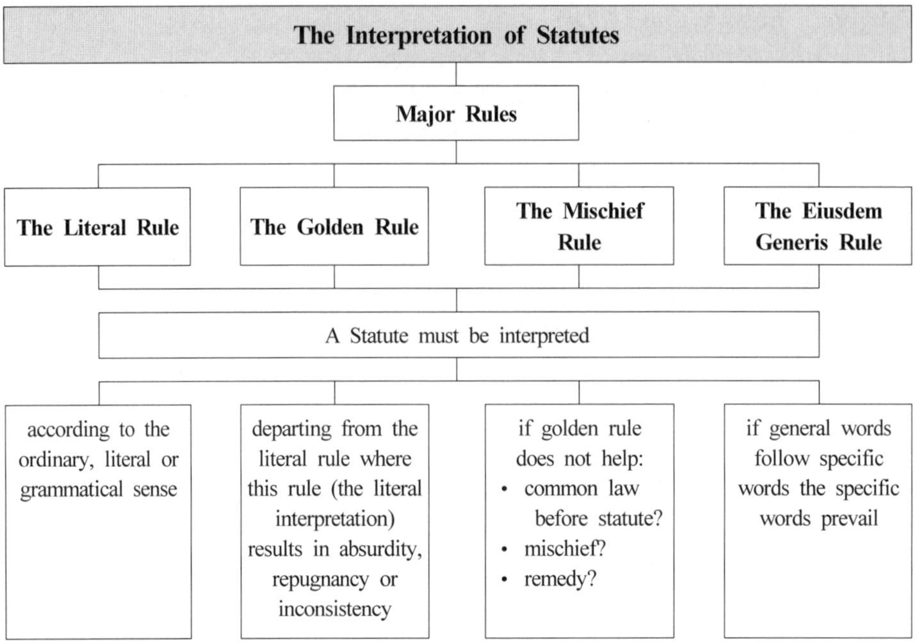

2. Judicial precedents

In the legal systems of all countries at all times, it is usual that the previous decisions of superior courts made in the course of litigation, are treated with respect by an inferior court, when it has to decide a similar case. These previous decisions are regarded as "precedents". If a judge of an inferior court does not follow the decision of such a precedent, he runs the risk that the losing party will file an appeal, and he risks as well that his divergent decision will be overruled by the superior court.

In the same way, courts in all countries will give a special attention to the previous decision of a court of equal authority. The main reason for this practice is that it is clearly desirable that decisions should be uniform. This is a requirement of legal certainty.

It is necessary that citizens should trust the courts in granting equal treatment when deciding similar case.

이전 판결들 / 상급심 법원
소송 / 존중을 받는다 / 하급 법원 / 판결하다
취급되다 / 선례
위험을 감수하다 / 패소자 / 항소하다 / 선례를 벗어난
파기되다
특별히 고려하다, 주의하다
동급법원
바람직한 / 통일적인
법적안정성의 요구
평등한 대우

Moreover, in England precedents are given special attention for other reasons as well.

To become a judge of a superior court it is not sufficient to be a lawyer, it is necessary to be an excellent lawyer! In England there is only a limited number of appointed high judges.

법률가, 변호사
임명하다

Another reason why precedents are given so much importance is that the English superior courts are Royal Courts. Here the judges are "Her Majesty's Judges" who, through their decisions, give direction to the law. These "honourable" judges have an exceptionally important place in English society.

여왕전하의 판사
법의 갈 길을 보여준다 / 명예로운
매우 중요한 지위

Judicial precedents thus play a singularly important role in the administration of justice in England.

독특한
판결을 내림

a) Absolute binding effect

절대적 구속력

Precedents are not only regarded as authoritative pronouncements of the law, but they are absolutely binding for courts which are subsequently called upon to decide similar cases.

권위있는 선언
사후의, 이후의

"Binding" precedents are not merely "persuasive" authorities which *may* be followed if they appear to be correct; they are precedents which must be followed. This doctrine of binding effect forms one of the most distinctive characteristics of English law.

설득력 있는 / 권위
원칙
독특한 성격, 특성

The system may be illustrated by reference to the rules which are applied among the English civil courts.

~을 언급함으로써
~에서 적용되는

The organisation of the courts system in England will be dealt with in the next chapter.

법원조직

The House of Lords is the ultimate appellate court, the highest court in the country. All decisions of the House of Lords are absolutely binding over all other courts. This means that they must be followed by courts called upon to determine similar issues, whether they appear to be correct or not. In other words, a judge who is deciding upon the facts

최종 상소심(상고심)
소가 제기된 법원, 수소법원
결정, 판결하다 / 쟁점
시안, 사실

of a case which are the same or closely related to a former one must apply the same legal principles.

매우 유사한

The House of Lords had been bound by its own precedents up to the year 1966, when a change in attitude was finally announced.

입장의 변화

Below the House of Lords comes the Court of Appeal.

항소법원

Prior to having his case considered by the House of Lords the party would have had his case decided by the Court of Appeal.

Court of Appeal decisions are binding on the inferior courts, but not of course, on the House of Lords.

The Court of Appeal is generally also bound by its own previous decisions, except under the following three conditions, laid down in *Young* v *Bristol Aeroplane Co.* (1944):

하기 세가지 조건을 제외하고

(1) If there are two previous conflicting decisions of the Court of Appeal, the Court has the option to follow anyone of them.

모순되는 판결들

(2) The Court of Appeal may not follow its own previous decision which is in conflict with a later decision of the House of Lords. Hereby it does not matter if its previous decision was overruled by the House of Lords or not.

(3) If a previous decision of the Court of Appeal conflicts with an even earlier decision of the House of Lords or with an earlier enacted statute, then its previous decision has no binding effect, so long as the judges were not aware of the decision of the House of Lords or of the statute. In this case the previous decision of the Court of Appeal, as the saying goes, was given "per incuriam", which means, "through want of care"!

모순되다, 대립하다
더 이전의 판결
흔히 말하듯이
부주의로

In order to better understand this third exemption from the binding effect, it is important to keep in mind the fact that English judges are not obliged to inform themselves of the existence of precedents. It is the job of the barristers to submit to the court those precedents, which are of importance to the litigation in question. (We shall tackle this in the third

예외
의무를 진
법정변호사, 배리스터
제출하다
이것을 상세히 검토할 것이다

chapter!)

Below the Court of Appeal comes the High Court of Justice. A High Court judge is absolutely bound by the decisions of the House of Lords and of the Court of Appeal, but he is not absolutely bound to follow previous decisions of other High Court judges. For the High Court judge High Court precedents are more commonly known as "persuasive authorities", as mentioned above.

상급 민사법원(우리의 지방법원에 해당)

For the sake of certainty of the law, a High Court judge generally follows "persuasive authorities", although he is not obliged to do so.

법적안정성을 위하여

Below the High Court of Justice come the County Courts. Their judges known as "circuit judges", are bound by the decisions of all superior courts.

구법원
순회판사, 구역판사
(circuit=법원의 작은 구역단위)

In legal science the binding effect of previous decisions is called the "doctrine of precedent". In former times this doctrine was known as the "doctrine of stare decisis". The term "stare decisis" means "to stand upon decisions".

법학
선례구속의 원칙
(기존의) 판결을 고수하다

As with every doctrine, the English doctrine of precedents includes both, advantages and disadvantages.

장점 / 단점

- Advantages are:
  (1) The law is made more certain by the building up of principles in every branch of law from the numerous case decisions which have occured over the years,
  (2) the large number of decisions in each area of the law leads to considerable precision arising from the wealth of detail available and
  (3) the system is essentially practical being always based on actual circumstances.

발생하다, 행해지다
신뢰할만한 정교함 / 유래하다
많은 세세한 개별적인 사례들
매우 실천적, 현실적인
실제 상황들

- Disadvantages are:
  (1) Because of the *rigidity* imposed by the "binding" requirement, the discretion of the judge is fettered and sometimes leads to illogical distinctions, and
  (2) the very *bulk of case decisions* over hundreds of years leads to immeasurable complexity.

완고함, 비유연성 / 부과하다
재량 / 사슬에 묶이다
다수, 다량
복잡, 난해함

Especially in connection with the first disadvantage, the doctrine of precedent with its absolute binding effect has caused fierce comment.

> ~와 관련하여
> 격렬한 비판을 부르다

Although since 1966 the House of Lords has not been strictly bound by its own decisions, yet it is still bound in principle.

> 원칙적으로

This fundamental binding of the Court of Appeal was mainly criticised by the legendary *Lord Denning*, the former Master of the Rolls. *Lord Denning* demanded that the Court of Appeal should have the same freedom to overrule its own previous decisions as is awarded to the House of Lords.

> 근본적인
> 전설적인 / 전(前)항소법원 부장판사 / 요구하다
> 달리 판결할 자유
> 허락된

In the "conclusion" of "*The Discipline of Law*" *Lord Denning* expresses his opinion on the "absolute binding effect" of precedents with the following words:

> 결론부
> 언급하다, 표현하다

"Let it not be thought from this discourse that I'm *against* the doctrine of precedent. I am not. It is the foundation of our system of case law. This has evolved by broadening down from precedent to precedent. By standing by previous decisions, we have kept the common law on a good course. All that I am against is its too rigid application — a rigidity which insists that a bad precedent must necessarily be followed.

> 결론을 내려서는 안된다 / 논문
> 근본
> 발전하다 / 확장하다
> 바른 길
> 완고한 적용
> 주장하다

I would treat it as you would walk a path through the woods. You must follow it certainly so as to reach your end. But you must not let the path become too overgrown. You must cut out the dead wood and trim off the side branches, else you will find yourself lost in thickets and brambles.

My plea is simply to keep the path to justice clear of obstructions which would impede it."[1)]

---

1) For you to understand better the wisdom of these "flowery" words, I shall make an exception by giving you the Korean translation of the second half of *Lord Denning's* statement:
"저는 이 문제를 여러분들이 어떻게 숲 속으로 난 길을 걸어가셔야 하는가 하는 것에 비유하여 설명하고 싶습니다. 여러분들이 숲을 지나 목적지에 이르고자 하신다면 반드시 그 숲길을 따라가야 합니다. 그러나 (동시에) 이 길에 잡초가 무성하게 자라서 길을 가리도록 내버려 두어서는 안됩니다. 여러분은 죽은 나무를 잘라내어야 하고, 통행을 방해하는 가지는 쳐주어야 합니다. 그러지 않으면 가시덤불 속에서 길을 잃어버리게 될 것입니다.

> 불분명한, 수식이 많은

In spite of the outstanding authority of Lord Denning among English jurists, and despite the enormous respect which was paid to every word of his, *Lord Denning* did not succeed with his plea. — 뛰어난 / 청원

The rules of the doctrine of precedents, which had been laid down in the decision *Young* v *Bristol Aeroplane Co.* in 1944, on the contrary, were confirmed by the House of Lords in *Davis* v *Johnson* (1979). — (오히려) 반대로 / 확인하다

b) Distinguishing, approving and overruling precedents — 동의하다

What *Lord Denning* had criticised mainly was the fact that the binding effect of precedents can occasionally prevent justice in certain cases. — 때로는 / 구체적 타당성을 결(缺)하게 하다

(aa) *Distinguishing precedents*

Endeavouring to delimit the strict binding effect of previous decisions, the English courts have developed the art of "distinguishing". — 제한하려는 시도의 / 구별의 기술

This "distinguishing" is based on two principles:

(1) A judge is only absolutely bound by a previous decision if the facts of the actual case are identical to the facts of the earlier case. — 사안, 사실

(2) Only those principles of a decision which are the fundamental reasons for the decision are absolutely binding.

Firstly, this means that a judge need not feel bound if the facts of two cases are not congruent. In that case he is "distinguishing on the facts". — 완벽하게 일치하는

Secondly, not everything said by a judge in the course of his judgment creates a precedent, but only his pronouncement of law in relation to the *particular* facts before him. — 판결하는 중에 / 창설하다 / 법의 선언, 중요한 판결이유

This pronouncement is called the ratio decidendi of the case. Ratio decidendi thus means "*the basic reason for the* — 판결이유 / 판결의 기본이유(구속력을 지님)

제가 말씀드리고자 하는 바는 간단합니다. 우리가 정의에 이르는 길에 방해가 되는 것들을 제거해야 한다는 것입니다."

<u>*decision*</u>". In cases where *more* than *one* principle of law is <u>revealed</u> there are said to be <u>*rationes*</u> *decidendi*. In this connection it is worth <u>noting</u> the <u>remarks</u> of *Sir George Jessel* in *Osborne* v *Rowlett* (1880), that "the only thing in a judge's decision binding as an authority upon a subsequent judge is the principle upon which the case was decided".

밝히다, 드러내다 / ratio의 복수
주의를 기울이다 / 언급

Thirdly, judges may, as they often do, let fall so called "<u>*obiter dicta*</u>". These are <u>pronouncements said in passing</u> by a judge in the course of his judgment upon <u>points of law</u> which are not directly relevant to the <u>issue</u> before him. These "*obiter dicta*" may be of great <u>assistance</u> to subsequent courts, particularly if they are made by judges of high <u>repute</u> (such as *Lord Denning*). But they are never binding; subsequent judges are not obliged to follow them.

부수적 의견 / 부수적으로 언급한 이유들 (구속력이 없음) / 법적인 관점 / 쟁점
지지, 지원, 도움
명망

(bb) *Approving precedents*

If a court <u>agrees</u> with a precedent, it is said to "approve" it. The judge will then *follow* the <u>legal reasoning</u> of the previous case. If a court of the *same* status <u>declines</u> to follow a binding precedent, and to follow a *persuasive* precedent it is said to "<u>disapprove</u>".

동의하다
법적 이유, 판결 이유
거절하다
불인정하다

(cc) *Overruling precedents*

If a court of higher status does not agree with the principle of law laid down in a previous case, then it is said to "<u>overrule" that precedent</u>.

해당 선례를 파기하다

A decision is said to be "<u>reversed</u>" when a higher court reaches a contrary conclusion to that reached by the court of first instance in the same case.

파기하다

Diagram 4

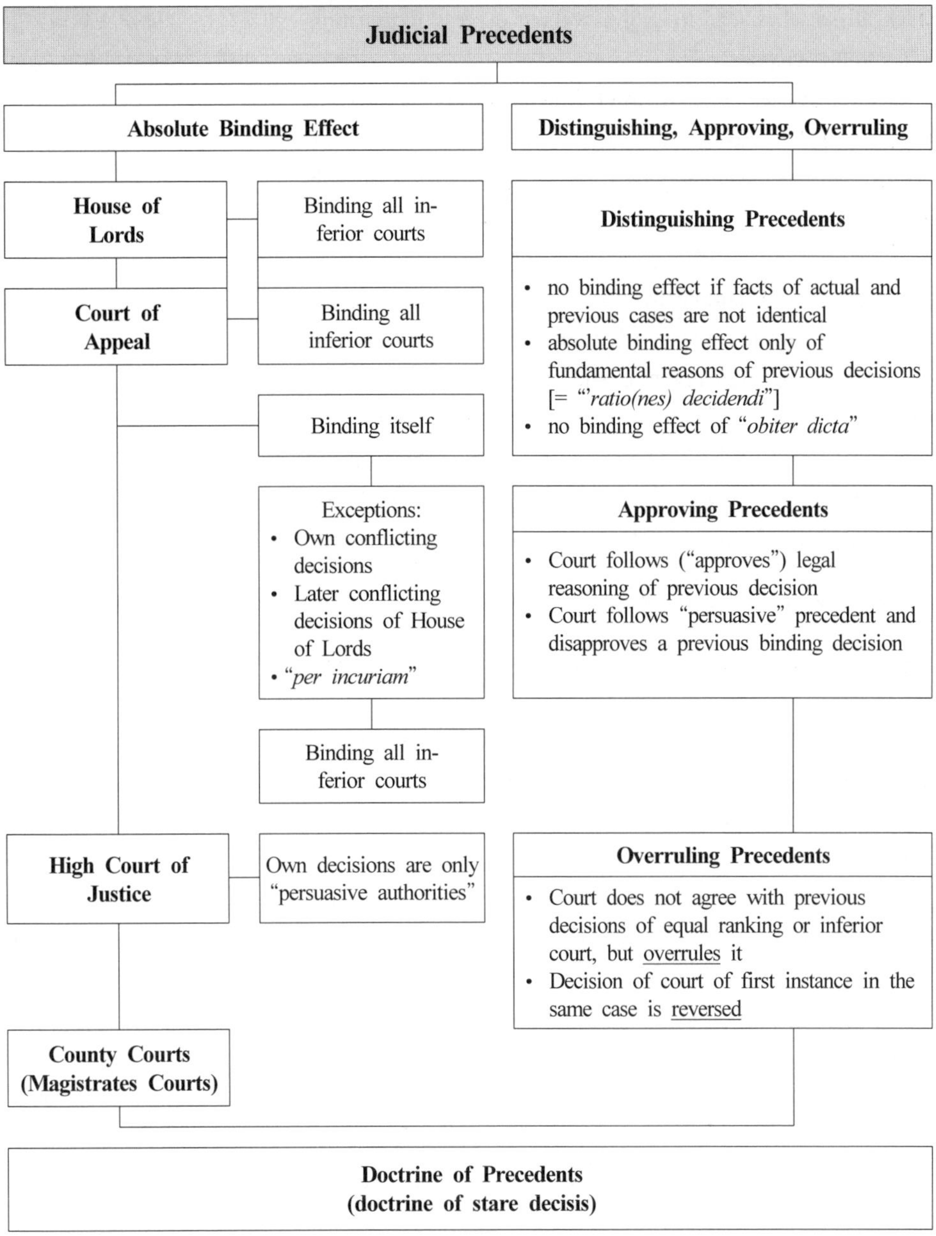

3. Custom 관습

Custom, as we mentioned above, is not one of the principal, but one of the subsidiary sources of law.

<table>
<tr><td>Customs are social habits, and patterns of behaviour, which all societies tend to evolve without express formulation or conscious creation.</td><td>사회적 습관 / 행동양식
발전하는 경향을 보이다 / 명시적인 표현 / 의식적인 창설</td></tr>
<tr><td>Having translated "custom" in German as "Gewohnheitsrecht", one must understand that this translation is only one of the various possible meanings which can be given to the English term "custom".</td><td></td></tr>
<tr><td>In earlier times, custom (in the sense of Gewohnheitsrecht) was taken up by the judges and transformed to the Common Law of England. Actually it is still possible, even today, to argue the origins of custom accepted by the courts [cf. Beckett v Lyons (1967)]. However, its operation is usually restricted to a particular area, or to a particular trade of profession. Such customs may be general, local or conventional.</td><td>~로 바뀌다
논증하다
적용
구역 / 직업분야
계약적</td></tr>
</table>

a) General custom and usage

<table>
<tr><td>Such customs are to be found mainly in mercantile transactions.</td><td>상업적 거래</td></tr>
<tr><td>Many mercantile customs have arisen as a result of international trade and they have, in the course of time, been adopted into the legal system.</td><td>상관습 / 발생하다
무역 / 시간이 흐름에 따라
채용하다</td></tr>
<tr><td>So, for example, many of the rules of the law relating to the sale of goods originated as customs and were adopted by the courts and eventually moulded into a statutory code in the form of the Sale of Goods Act 1893.</td><td>유래하다
점차, 결국 / 형식적 법률로 바뀌다</td></tr>
<tr><td>Thereafter general custom ceased to operate as an important creative source of law.</td><td>그후 / 역할을 다하다
창조적인</td></tr>
</table>

b) Local custom

<table>
<tr><td>A custom can be effective as law in a particular locality although it is now rare for this to be the case.</td><td>유효한 / 특정한 지역
오늘날은 그러한 경우가 드물다</td></tr>
<tr><td>An example of the application of local custom is the famous case of the fishermen of Walmer [Mercer v Denne (1904)].</td><td></td></tr>
<tr><td>In this case the fishermen of Walmer were held entitled, by reason of local custom, to a special (legal) right to dry their nets on a particular beach.</td><td>권리가 있는 것으로 판결하다
지역적 관습에 따라</td></tr>
</table>

For such a right to be recognised as a custom with legal effect, it must fulfil certain requirements.
The custom seeking establishment must

법(률)적 효력
특정한 요구사항을 충족하다
관습법으로 자리잡고자 하는 관습

(1) not be unreasonable,
(2) be "certain" that is to say, the right which is claimed must be proved to adhere to a defined group of people, and
(3) have existed since "time immemorial".

비이성적, 비합리적
속하다 / 특정한 인적 결합
기억 가능한 시간, 즉 매우 오래전부터

c) Conventional custom

Conventional customs are never raised to the level of the common law. However, they may still affect the rights of parties to a contract who, by being members of a certain trade or profession, find that certain customary usages have been incorporated into their contract. Generally, *both* parties must belong to the same trade or profession before the application of a conventional custom will be implied.

보통법의 수준으로 격상된 바 없다 / 영향을 미치다
계약당사자들
무역 / 보통의 관습
계약에 채용되다
암시하다

Diagram 5

Custom

Social habits and patterns of behaviour evolved without express formulation or conscious creation.

General	**Local**	**Conventional**
• mercantile customs: results of trade usages (and international trade) • cf. *Sale of Goods Act 1893*	• Custom as "law" in particular localities → legal effect if custom is • not unreasonable • certain (the right must be proved to apply to a defined group of people) • existing since "time immemorial"	• conventional customs are never raised to the level of law, but • are considered by parties of contract who • belong to same trade or profession
	e.g. "the fishermen of Walmer" case	

4. Books of authority

On the continent textbooks written by famous legal authors form an important source of law. These authors are often cited in decisions of continental courts to prove that a decision is correct. To this extent books of authority are considered as a "source of law" as judges and lawyers make constant use of these books.

증명하다

늘 사용함, 상용

In England, particularly in the past, books of authority, were not so important as a source of law. The former rule was that no writer would be treated as an authority in his lifetime.

저자 / 생존한 당시

Nowadays the courts show much more flexibility using not only leading textbooks by authors of outstanding eminence, but also articles from legal periodicals where these are found to be helpful.

오늘날

지도적 / 매우 중요한

법학 전문지

If a barrister in a case wishes to quote from a book of authority he has to ask the court's permission to adopt the author's argument.

인용하다

허가

Nowadays in practice, however, this etiquette is seldom followed.

에티켓, 예절, 관습

If books of authority are required as a legal source, only books by ancient authors are cited.

요구되다

고대의

The three most famous outstanding authors who are always mentioned in this context in all English legal textbooks are

언급하다 / 법학교과서

- Henry de Bracton's
  "*De Legibus et Consuetudinibus Angliae*", written in the middle of the 13th century which means in English "Treatise on the Laws and Customs of England".

  학술논문
- Sir Edward Coke's
  "Institutes of the Laws of England", which was written between 1628 and 1644.
- Sir William Blackstone's
  "Commentaries on the Laws of England", written in 1765.

  주석서

Diagram 6

Books of Authority

Legal textbooks by authors of outstanding eminence

As a "source of law" in England they are not as important as on the Continent

Judges and lawyers make constant use of books of ancient famous authors to ascertain what the law was in former times

Three classical books of authority

Henry de Bracton's	**Sir Edward Coke's**	**Sir William Blackstone's**
"De Legibus et Consuetudinibus Angliae" = "Treatise on the Laws and Customs of England" −13th Century−	"Institutes of the Law of England" −1628-1644−	"Commentaries on the Laws of England" −1765−

Ⅳ. Further reading[1]

심화학습용 참고서

Baker, An Introduction to English Legal History; *Bernstorff, Graf von*, Einfuhrung in das englische Recht; *Black's* Legal Reader − An Introduction to the Anglo-American Law and Legal System; *Cownie & Bradney*, English Legal System in Context; *Cracknell*, English Legal System ("Cracknell's Law Students' Companion" = cases and statutes); *Darbyshire*, Nutshells: English Legal System; *Denham*, Law − A Modern Introduction; *Denning*, The Discipline of Law; *Eddey*, On the English Legal System; *Elliott & Quinn*, English Legal System; *Harris*, An Introduction to Law; *Henrich*, Einführung in das englische Privatrecht; *Partington*, Introduction to the English Legal System; *Rivlin*, First Steps in the Law; *Slapper & Kelly*, On English Legal System; *Slapper & Kelly*, English Law; *Smith & Bailey*, On the Modern English Legal System; *Templeman & Reed*, English Legal System, Textbook −,

1) Edition, place of publication and year of publication are quorted in the bibliography.

Casebook –, Revision Work Book; *Zweigert/Kötz*, Einfü
hrung in die Rechtsvergleichung.

Chapter Two

The administration of the law

판결을 내림

Ⅰ. Common law and equity

1. Historical background

A very important landmark in English legal history was certainly the Norman Conquest by William the Conqueror which took place in 1066. However, it is not quite correct to maintain that this marked the beginning of English legal history as such!

이정표 / 법의 역사
노르만족의 정복 / 정복자
완전히
주장하다 / 표시하다

Prior to the Norman Conquest, England was divided into several kingdoms and all laws were *local*, and were administered by the lords of the manor in the manorial courts.

이전에
관리, 행정하다
장원(莊園) 영주 / 장원 법원

In those times English legal life was ruled by various written or unwritten laws which had developed from a centuries old legal culture. Already in the 7th century the Anglo-Saxons were beginning to put down in writing their local customs and laws, which had been passed down to them by oral tradition.

법적 생활 / 다양한
수세기 묵은 / 법문화
앵글로색슨족 / 서면으로 작성하다
구전(口傳)

The Norman Conquest of 1066, however, is referred to as a landmark in the history of English law, because it was followed by the spread of Norman law in England. In fact, the Normans, under the reign of William I, strove hard to make the law of England uniform.

~로 표시되다, 일컬어지다
전파
통치 / 노력하다
통일된

And this uniformity finally led to the evolution of a law which was common to the whole country and therefore was called "common law".

통일화 / 발전

So the Norman Conquest of 1066 was the precondition for the beginning of one very important period of English legal history. Following the opinion of *René David* in his famous textbook on comparative law ("*Les grands systèmes de droit contemporains*") the historical development of English law can now be divided into four periods:

전제조건
시기
의견
비교법(우리시대의 위대한 비교법학 체계들 The great systems of comtemporary comparative law) / 역사적 발전

(1) The time before the conquest of the Island by the Normans (Norman Conquest, 1066) — *no uniform law.* 섬(영국)
(2) 1066 until the beginning of the Tudor dynasty in 1485 — *development of the common law* 영국 튜더왕조 가문
(3) 1485 to 1832 — *confrontation* of the common law with equity 대립
(4) 1832 until the present time — the "modern period": *law reforms,* particularly in *procedural law*; *statute law.* 법개혁 절차법 / 성문법률

During the development of the English legal system the two great complexes of rules "common law" and "equity" set up priorities. We will now consider some details concerning the common law. 법규 / 우선적 지위를 수립하다

2. The common law

a) Itinerant justices 여행판사, 순회판사

Common law in its wider sense is understood to be that law which, since the Norman Conquest, has been applied in the whole country and became common throughout the land by the so called "*itinerant justice*".

These judges dispensed royal justice "in Eyre". Appeals against judgments of the itinerant justices could be made to the King's Council ("*curia regis*") on intervention of the Chancellor. The King's Council originally was a body of noblemen who adviced the king. 제왕적 정의(법)를 결정하다 / (판사의 순회)여행 중에 / 항소 왕회(王會), 왕립법원(=King's Court) / 챈슬러의 개입하에 귀족 / 자문하다

b) The common law courts

In the 12th and the 13th century three Royal Courts with different competences were established from the original King's Council. The seat of these three common law courts was at Westminster. 관할권 / 수립하다 소재지

The first, to be established, was the

(1) *Court of Exchequer* — 재무법원

This court was mainly concerned with the administration of the royal revenues. Apart from this financial jurisdiction the Court of Exchequer also had a limited civil jurisdiction.

행정, 관리
수입 / 재무법원 관할권
민사관할

(2) *Court of Common Pleas* — (시민간의) 일반 소건(민사사건)

The Court of Common Pleas was the second court to emerge from the King's Council and dealt initially with disputes between ordinary subjects of the Crown.

유래하다 / 원래는
분쟁 / 보통 신민(臣民)

This court was mainly competent to hear pleas concerning the return of real property or the payment of special debts.

반환 / 부동산 / 채무

(3) *Court of King's Bench*

This court was the last court to emerge from the King's Council and dealt with criminal cases and civil cases in which the Crown was a party.

The judges of these old royal common law courts created the law which is known as "common law" and which was, as said above, fixed from precedent to precedent (cf. "*stare decisis*").

In other words "common law" may be defined as a system of principles which was built up by the common law courts.

We will now consider the basis upon which these principles were evolved. This requires a brief description of the "*forms of action*" or the "*writ system*".

재판절차 / 법원의 명령서, 영장

Diagram 7

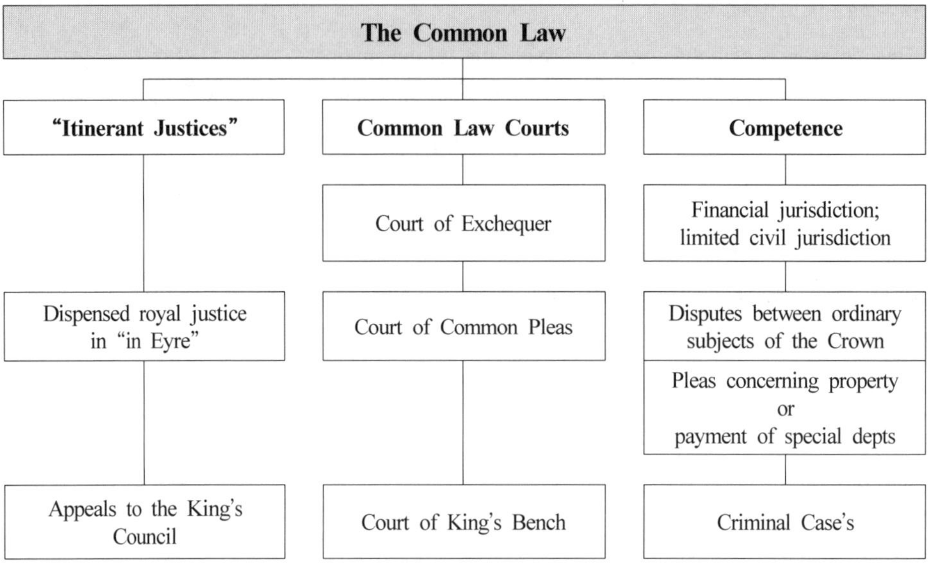

c) The system of writs

Under the old common law system a trial could only be commenced if the plaintiff had a special "writ" which could only be obtained from the administrative offices of the Chancery. For such a "writ" the plaintiff needed the Great Seal from the Chancellor, who acted in the name of the king.

재판
시작하다 / 영장
획득하다
챈슬러 사무처, 관청
직인

A writ, for which a fee had to be paid, was a simple and concise order, emanating from a high authority — in the case of a royal writ it came from the king, through the Chancery, the secretarial department of the state. "Original writs" ("original", because they originated the action) were documents of special rights belonging to their owners. A writ described the exact cause of action, and if an action did not fall within the terms of an existing writ then the common law judges would not allow an action to be brought. The maxim was: "No writ, no remedy!"

수수료
축약적인 / 유래하다
비서부, 사무처
개시하다
소의 기초가 되는 청구권
제소를 허가하다
원칙 / 영장없이는 법적 구제책도 없다

Initially, the writs were composed for particular cases, but as it is natural in every administrative system writs rapidly became formalised.

작성하다 / 특정한 개별사안
재빨리
정형화하다

Actions concerning certain types of misconduct began to be recognised and each type of misconduct or claim had its appropriate writ.

부적법행위 / 청구권
해당하는

Examples of standardised writs are:

정형화된

"Writ of right"[1], "writ of debt"[2], "writ of trespass"[3] or "writ of detinue"[4].

The fact that every action needed its own appropriate (special) writ resulted in the creation of new writs of standard forms so that by the middle of the 13th century there were already about fifty different types of writs in existence.

~로 귀결하다
표준양식

Because of this expansion in the volume of writs the competence and the extent of power in the royal courts naturally increased progressively, whereas, simultaneously, the competence of the local courts (the Earl's Courts and Baron's Courts) became more and more restricted.

확대
권능의 범위
동시에
백작 / 남작(가장 낮은 직위)
제한하다

Behind the scenes, however, lay the conflict between the royal courts and the profitable feudal courts.

무대 뒤에서는
수익성있는 / 봉건법원(장원법원)

The earls and barons rebelled against this restriction and they succeeded in retaining some power, so that the Chancellor was only allowed to issue new forms of writs if the whole King's Council (= "*curia regis*") gave its assent. This was determined by the *Provisions of Oxford* of 1258.

저항하다
유지하다
발급, 발행하다
결정하다 / 옥스퍼드 규정

The *Statute of Westminster II* of 1285 finally provided that the Chancellor (and his officers) had the power to formulate writs "*in consimile casu*" (i.e. in cases of sufficient similarity). But here the common law courts managed to have the last word. The reason for this was that in the 15th century, they acquired the power to decide, whether the writ was valid or not. If the writ was found not to be good, the fact that the plaintiff had the writ himself was not sufficient.

규정하다
작성하다 / 충분한 유사성
획득하다
유효한

1) 토지소유권 확정을 위한 영장
2) 특정채무 변제를 위한 영장
3) 토지점유침해로 인한 또는 인(人)에 대한 상해나 물(物)의 파손으로 인한 영장
4) 점유침해로 인한 영장

In deciding whether the writ was good or not the judges were guided by the previously established common law principles. The machinery of law, the procedure of common law together with their <u>rigid formality</u> could sometimes, in particular cases, result in <u>injustice</u> and <u>hardship</u>.

엄격한 형식성
불의 / 매우 곤란하고 어려운 경우

This evolution led to, perhaps, the most important <u>branch</u> of the English legal system which is called "<u>equity</u>" and which we have already mentioned briefly above.

가지, 영역
형평법(구체적 타당성의 실현을 위한 기준)

Diagram 8

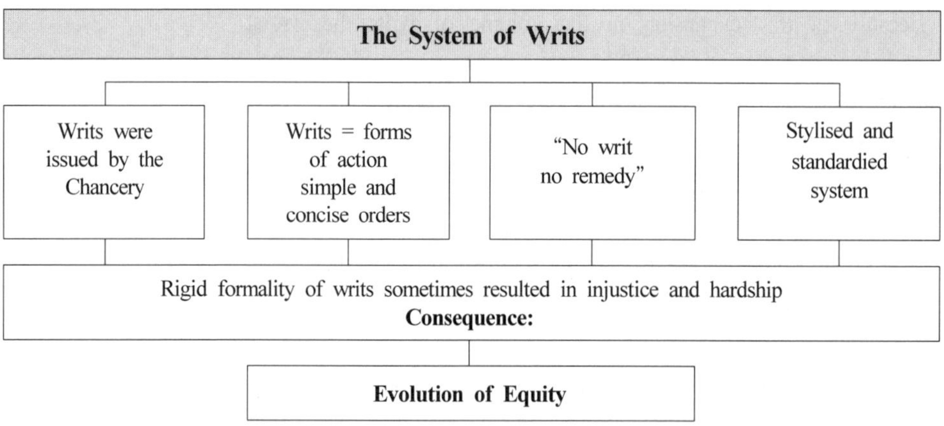

3. Equity

a) The <u>term</u>

용어, 개념

The term "equity" (together with other words corresponding to it) in popular language is sometimes used as if it were something <u>outside of the law</u>. People sometimes speak of a judgment in a particular case as being <u>undoubtedly</u> <u>according to law</u>, but as also being "unfair", "<u>unjust</u>", or "<u>inequitable</u>".

In such cases people would be in reality passing a moral <u>judgment upon</u> the law. Such a moral judgment <u>in no way affects</u> the law. This could be a reason why the law should be <u>amended</u> by statute.

비합법적인
의심할 바 없이 / 법에 따르면
부정당한 / 부적절한, 형평에 어긋나는
(판결을) 내리다 / 결코 영향을 미치지 않는다
개정하다

But when an English lawyer uses the terms "law" and "equity" he does not mean that equity is not law! He is really speaking of two different kinds of law the common law on the one hand, the principles of equity on the other hand which both carry the same legal weight.

The rules of equity are not merely morally but also legally binding: they are corroborated by the courts!

도덕적으로
확인하다, 구체화하다

b) The principles of equity

(aa) *History*

As we have learnt, the common law courts used to sit in Westminster Hall, administering law by following the principles of common law. On one side of Westminster Hall were the three common law courts whilst on the other side was the Court of Chancery. *Equity* was administered in this court, and litigants who could not obtain justice in the common law courts would cross the Hall to seek the Chancellor's aid.

(재판) 기일을 가지다
판결을 내리다
소송의 당사자들 / 얻다
찾다
도움, 조력

But before speaking of the Chancellor as a judge and the Chancery as a real law court, we have to consider that until the end of the 15th century the Chancellor was only an *officer* of the state who acted in the King's name.

In other words, the Chancellor was not originally a judge, nor did he have a court. He was the head of a vast government office — which may be called a secretarial office. The famous legal historian *Maitland* called him "the King's secretary of state for all departments". Whatever writing had to be done in the King's name was done by the Chancellor or through him by his officers.

광범위한
법사학자

The Chancellor as the head of the "Chancery" was responsible for the use and custody of the Great Seal of the realm. He was, moreover, closely associated with the administration of justice, for, as it has already been remarked, the original writs were issued from the Chancery.

보존 / 왕국
사법, 판결
발급하다

Further more, he was an important member of the King's Council whose duty became to consider and adjudicate upon petitions addressed to the Council by subjects who sought

결정하다
청원

justice from it as the body closest to the king himself. Petitions were presented for various reasons. In particular, they were often made by people who had, in one way or another, failed to obtain justice in the common law courts.

실패하다

(1) This failure was usually due to one of three causes: The common law was in some ways *defective*: e.g. the early common law remedies for breaches of contract were grossly inadequate!

결함이 있는
계약위반
매우 부적절한

(2) The only remedy which the common law courts would usually supply was the award of damages, and damages are by no means always a satisfactory form of relief!

제공하다 / 손해배상
충분한 / 회복

(3) Although the law was adequate to meet the case, *justice might not always be obtainable* in the common law courts because of the dominance of one of the parties, who might, in medieval times, often be in a position to over-awe the court itself.

사안에 해당하다
얻을 수 있는
경외심으로 몸이 굳어버리다

The Chancellor could remedy these defects. Being the most important official of the King, he was bound by neither the rules nor the procedure of the common law courts, nor was he likely to be over-awed by any man (as he himself was a very important figure!).

해결하다, 구제하다 / 결함
공무원, 관리
아마도 그는

By hearing the petitions, the Chancellors slowly began to evolve a set of rules which remedied the defects of the common law. The Chancellors decisions were no longer statements of the King's highest *administrative* officers. Gradually they started to administer law as if they were judges themselves.

발전하다 / 일련의 규칙
행정(부의), 행정적

So in the 17th century a "*Court of Chancery*" was formed within the Chancery. The Chancellor actually became a "real" judge and in 1750 he was joined by the "Master of the Rolls", who was his highest ranking subordinate.

신하, 신민

The rules of law applied by the Chancellor and later on by the Court of Chancery and its judges, were called the rules of "equity" (derived from the Latin term "*aequitas*").

파생하다 / 형평

Equity, in a certain sense, is comparable with the German principle of "*Treu und Glauben*" (cf. § 242 BGB). 신의성실의 원칙, 신의칙(한국 민법제2조) / 독일민법전

Before examining the rules of equity in detail I feel it is important here to mention that the conflict between common law and equity reached its climax in the *Earl of Oxford's Case* (1615). In this case the Earl received a judgment in his favour from a common law court, but when he tried to execute this judgment, he was prevented from doing so "by equity", which was represented by Lord Chancellor *Ellesmere*. (조사하다 / 최고점, 정점 / 자신에게 유리하게 / 집행하다 / 방지하다)

King James I (1603-1625) forced the Lord Chancellor and Lord Chief Justice *Coke*, as the representative of common law, to present their conflict to the Attorney General *Sir Francis Bacon* for decision. (강제하다 / 법무장관 / 왕립변호인(69쪽 참조))

Then following the recommendation of *Sir Francis Bacon*, *King James I* decided that in conflicts of common law and equity the courts have to follow the rules of equity. (권고, 추천)

This led to the establishment of the important principle "equity shall prevail". (우선하다)

(bb) *Rules of equity*

If the principles of *common law* and *equity* were in conflict, the following maxims had to be considered by judges:

(1) "*Equity shall prevail*"
The evolution of this rule has just been described above.

(2) "*Equity will not suffer a wrong to be without a remedy*". This principle reflects the main function of equity. Equity grants legal protection also in those cases where there is a deficiency in the (common) law, which is ruled by the maxim "no writ, no remedy". So equity assumes the law: equity was not intended to defeat the common law but to complement and to fill the gaps in. This is also expressed by the next rule of equity. (고통받다 / 불법 / 법적 보호 / 법률상의 흠결 / 전제하다 / 폐기하다 / 보충하다 / 흠결을 메우다)

(3) "*Equity follows the law*"

This means that equity is a supplementary legal protection.

보충적

An example of the application of equity which is usually mentioned in all textbooks on English Law, is the trust. This is a legal term relating to the law of property. We will deal with the matter of trust in more detail in chapter eight. For the time being, I will give a simple illustration of the distinction between the (weaker) "equitable" right and the (universally valid) "legal" right arising out of common law.

적용
신탁관계
관련된, 관계하는
더 약한
일반적으로 유효한

Suppose that A is a beneficiary in respect of certain property which is held by T in trust for him. The legal relationship and the contract upon which it is based, is called a trust. Trusts are a creation of equity. There fore, the right of the beneficiary, A, is an "equitable" one. The trustee, T, as the possessor, however, has the legal title to the property which in conscience he is bound to hold for A, so that A has full use and enjoyment of it. In the old law T was said to hold the property "for the use" of A. This was his obligation "in equity".

수혜자
토지, 재산 / 신탁관리하다 / 법률관계
피조물, 산물
수탁자(신탁재산관리인)
점유자 / 완전한 소유권
양심적으로 / 유지, 관리할 의무가 있는 / 사용 / 수익
관리하다 / ~의 이익을 위하여

Now suppose that T, perhaps for his own profit, sells the entrusted property to B, who does not know anything about the trust between A and T. B is in this case a *bona fide* purchaser for value. The consequence is that B acquires the legal title to the property and it is no longer held on trust for A.

신탁재산을 맡기다
선의의
유상구매자, 유상매수인

The following diagram may help to clarify what has happened here:

Trust

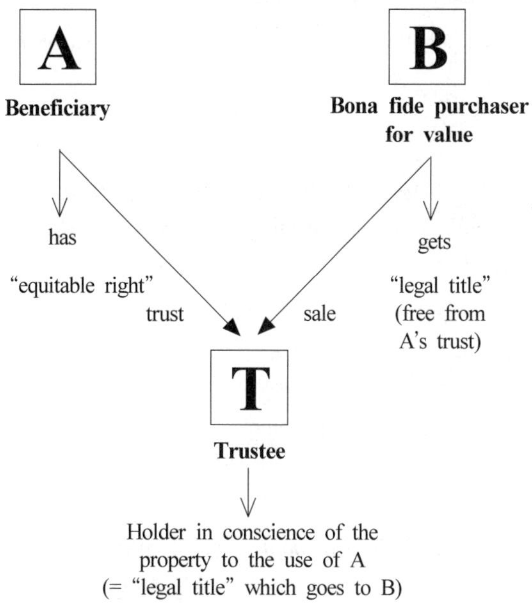

The legal title, acquired by B defeats the equitable right of A. All that A has in this case is a right of action (for damages) against T.

소, 소송

In this case equity has followed the law because two requirements are fulfilled:

두가지 전제조건을 충족하다

(a) B is a *bona fide* purchaser and

(b) B is a purchaser *for value*!

If we change the facts the result will be different:

사안, 사실

(c) B knows of the existence of the trust or

(d) B acquires the property by donation and not by purchase for value.

증여

Now in both cases B's right will cede to A's equitable right. In the first case (c) B's conscience would be affected by his knowledge and the Chancellor would force him to yield it to A.

피하다
영향을 받다
순응하다, 포기하다

In the second case (d), "equity", according to another maxim, "will not assist a volunteer", so that B's gratuitously acquired right gives way to A's equitable right.

돕다 / 무상 매수인 / 무상으로

(4) *"He who seeks equity must do equity" or "He who comes to equity must come with clean hands"* means: A person who demands the help of equity must conduct himself in accordance with law and equity.

행동하다 / 적법하게

Example:

A minor who maintains that he is a person of full age cannot plead his status as a minor against an unsuspecting person [cf. *Overton* v *Bannister* (1844)].

미성년자 / 성년
미성년자의 지위 / 정(情)을 모르는

(5) *"Equity acts in personam"*
means that the procedure in an equity-court always relates to a certain person and not to a specific thing or property.

In this context we speak of the "jurisdiction *in personam*", in contrast to the "jurisdiction *in rem*".

인적 관할
사물 관할

An example may make the difference clearer. Suppose that A receives a judgment in his favour which gives him the right to the recovery of a specific object against B. In such a case, according to the notion of the "jurisdiction in rem", A has only the right to execute power over that specific thing.

개념, 관념
~에 대해 강제집행하다

On the other hand, according to the notion of the "jurisdiction in personam" A has the right to execute the total assets of B.

총자산, 재산

There are still more principles of equity, but in an introductory book we must limit ourselves to the above mentioned five rules.

4. Further development of common law and equity

The conflict between common law (which was applied by the three Common law courts) and equity (applied by the Court of Chancery) came to an end with the (*Supreme Court of) Judicature Acts* (1873-1875). 법원조직법

Through these Acts the superior courts were reorganised and placed concretely upon their present-day footing (with which we will deal with in the following paragraph of this chapter).

설치하다 / 오늘날의 기준으로
단원, 단락

So below the Court of Appeal the new "*High Court of Justice of England*" was established. This new organisation came into being on 1 November 1875, when the High Court of Justice was divided into the following divisions:

개시하다
구성되다 / 부서

(1) the Queen's (King's) Bench Division:
(2) the Chancery Division;
(3) the Common Pleas Division;
(4) the Exchequer Division;
(5) the Probate, Divorce and Admiralty Division.

상속 / 이혼 / 해사법(海事法)

The Judicature Acts empowered the Crown to carry out further reorganisations, and this power was exercised in 1881 when the Common Pleas Division and the Exchequer Division were merged into the Queen's Bench Division. From then on, until 1970, the High Court of Justice was subdivided into the Queen's Bench Division, the Chancery Division and the Probate, Divorce and Admiralty Division. Since 1875 the Court of Appeal and the High Court of Justice have formed the Supreme Court of Judicature. When the Judicature Acts came into force all existing older courts were abolished.

권한을 위임하다 / 수행하다
합병하다
하부조직을 가지다, ~로 구성되다
발효하다 / 폐지하다

The *Judicature Acts* not only provided a new organisation for the courts, but they also laid down that for the future all branches of the Supreme Court should be empowered and obliged to *administer both law and equity*, and to grant both legal and equitable remedies!

부서

It has to be clarified in this context that these Acts did not purport to *fuse* law and equity into one single system of rules! The Judicature Acts merely provided that from then on, the two systems of common law and equity should for

명확히 하다
의도, 의미하다 / 하나로 녹이다

the future be administered by all courts! One should note that the principles of common law as well as the rules of equity still formed two different systems, each having its own history, separately and indepently of one another. 적용하다

And so it is today! In cases where the court has to decide whether there is a conflict between the principles of common law and the rules of equity the Judicature Acts provide a series of *specific rules* as well as the following *general rule*:

"In all matters not herein before particularly mentioned, in which there is any conflict or variance between the rules of equity and the rules of common law with reference to the same subject-matter, the rules of *equity shall prevail*!" 앞서서 차이점

The *Judicature Acts* have been subsequently amended several times. The structure of the Royal Courts today is governed by the *Supreme Court Act 1981*. 개정하다 조직 정해지다

Diagram 9

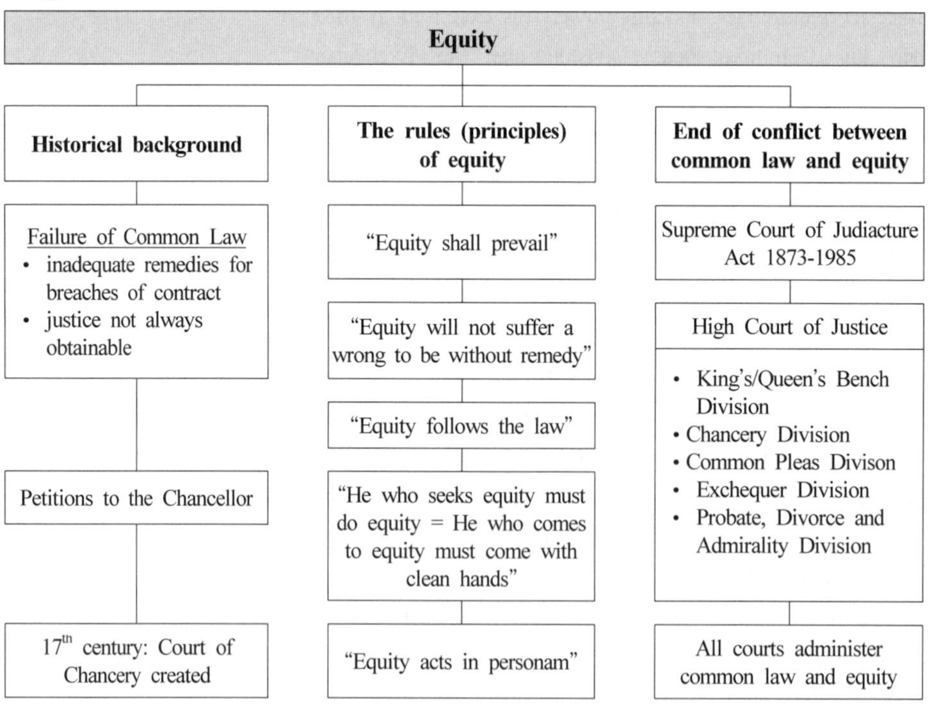

II. The modern organisation of the royal courts

First of all I have to point out that the English <u>law of judicature</u> uses (as you should have noticed already) the terms <u>inferior court</u> and <u>superior court</u>.	법원조직법 하급심법원 / 상급심법원
Although in English law, as is the case in German law, the competence of a civil court is determined by the <u>extent</u> of the <u>value in dispute</u>, there is a general <u>presumption</u> that the superior courts have the <u>local jurisdiction</u> as well as the <u>subject-matter jurisdiction</u>.	정도 소가 / 추정, 짐작 재판적, 지역적 관할 사물관할
So it is <u>admissible</u>, and <u>in this respect</u> different from German <u>procedural law</u>, to start a procedure in front of a superior court, although due to the value in dispute an inferior court would have been the court of first instance. The superior court in such a case can, however, <u>relegate</u> the <u>litigation</u> to the competent inferior court.	허용되는 / 이러한 관점에서 소송법 배정하다, 환송하다 소송

1. The inferior courts

<u>With respect to</u> the inferior courts we have to distinguish between county courts and magistrates' courts. County courts <u>exercise</u> civil <u>jurisdiction</u> whereas magistrates' courts exercise mainly criminal jurisdiction.	~에 관련하여 행사하다 / 사법권

a) The County Courts

The purpose of the County Court is to determine civil litigations of minor importance. The County Courts which were <u>set up</u> by the *County Courts Act 1846* today follow the rules of the *County Courts Act 1984*.	설립하다
The name <u>County</u> Court is <u>misleading</u>, for the new County Courts have nothing to do with the old <u>communal</u> County courts of previous times. Today the organisation of the County Courts is not based upon the geographical division of the country into counties as "<u>shires</u>".	백작 / 혼란을 일으키는 지역적 백작령

For the purpose of the County Court system, England and Wales are divided into judges districts or circuits in such a way as to ensure, that local courts for civil causes of minor importance are readily available throughout the country according to the needs of the population. Nowadays about 400 County Courts exist. County Courts determine procedures by single judges, which are called *Circuit Judges* or *District Judges*. The number of judges is fixed by *The County Court Judges (Maximum Number) Order 1969*. So most of these judges hold their sessions in regular rotation with each other at the various County Courts. Under the provisions of the *County Courts Act 1984* county courts have a wide jurisdiction, including in particular:

구 / 순회구역, 순회구(법원의 행정단위) / 보장하다
준비된, 신속히 / 사용가능한
필요
단독판사 / 구판사
규칙적 순번으로 기일을 주재하다 / 다양한 / ~규정에 따르면

(1) Jurisdiction in most actions concerning breaches of contract or torts,
(2) jurisdiction in actions for the recovery of land,
(3) equitable jurisdiction,
(4) admiralty jurisdiction and
(5) probate jurisdiction.

토지의 반환
유언의 검인(檢認)(cf. 검인법원, 검인관할) / 등기공무원

In every County Court there is a *Registrar* who is responsible for court administration and who has also minor, though in practise important, judicial powers including the power to hear any action in the County Court in which the defendant fails to appear or admits the claim.

사법권
궐석하다 / 청구를 인정하다

In these cases the Registrar renders a judgment by default or a judgment by confession. The Registrar also decides cases in which the value in dispute does not exceed ￡5,000[1].

(판결을) 내리다 / 궐석판결
인낙판결
초과하다

The jurisdiction over the subject of the County Courts at first instance in civil actions is also to be found in the *County Courts Act 1984*. Hereby County Courts are competent to hear claims concerning breaches of contract or torts for which the value in dispute does not exceed ￡50,000. In actions for property the value may not exceed ￡30,000

사물관할
민사소송 / 규정되어 있다
관할권이 있는
계약위반

1) All amounts quoted may be varied.

which is also the limit for actions decided by rules of equity (e.g. trust affairs). There is a right of appeal to the High Court of Justice or to the Court of Appeal against decisions taken by the county courts. 사안, 사건 / 항소하다

b) Magistrates' courts

지방법원 판사

As Magistrates' courts have their importance mainly in criminal law cases they are not dealt with in detail here. 주로

As regards civil law, Magistrates' courts must decide cases concerning maintenance claims between the spouses for their children, adoptions and guardianship proceedings. 부양청구권 / 배우자, 부부당사자 입양 / 후견

2. The Superior Courts

There are two Superior Courts, the Supreme Court of Judicature and the House of Lords.

a) The Supreme Court of Judicature

According to the Supreme Court Act 1981 the Supreme Court of Judicature for England and Wales is composed of

aa) High Court of Justice
bb) the Crown Court and
cc) the Court of Appeal.

(aa) *The High Court of Justice*

From the paragraphs above we have learnt that by the *Judicature Acts 1873-1875* the High Court of Justice was subdivided into the *Queen's Bench Division*, the *Chancery Division and the Probate, Divorce and Admiralty Division.* 나뉜다, 구분되다

Now we should add that a reorganisation was brought about by the *Administration of Justice Act 1970*. The Probate, Divorce and Admiralty was abolished and replaced by a new *Family Division* of the High Court. 첨언하다 / 조직개편 / 행하다 폐지하다 / 대체하다

This new division deals with divorce and other aspects of family law, as well as non-contentious probate, while conten- 상속재산에 관한 비송사건 / 쟁송

tious probate is now assigned to the Chancery Division. Moreover, admiralty matters are assigned to the Queen's Bench Division. 사건 / 배당하다

The High Court of Justice is at first instance competent to hear actions with a value in dispute amounting to no less than £50,000. In actions concerning the law of property or equity the minimum claim is for £30,000. Moreover the High Court of Justice is the appellate instance for all inferior courts. It is at the High Court judge's discretion to accept a claim below the limit of the value in dispute or to relegate it to an inferior court. 항소심 / 재량에 따르다 / 배정하다

At present, according to the *Supreme Court Act 1981* and the *Maximum Number of Judges Order 1999*, the maximum number of *puisine* judges of the High Court of Justice must be 106. This court is the central tribunal for all England and Wales and has its seat in London. The High Court of Justice has several branch offices all over England and Wales, so sittings of the High Court are possible according to convenience. The branch offices are called "Assize Courts". The "Assize Courts" are successors of the "itinerant justices", which we know from the Norman times. 배석판사 / 법원 / 지원 / 심리, 기일 / 필요에 따라 / 고등법원의 지원 / 승계인

Let us now consider the three divisions of the High Court of Justice a bit more thoroughly:

(1) *The Queen's Bench Division* with its seat in the Royal Courts of Justice on The Strand is presided over by the "Lord Chief Justice of England and Wales" who at present is assisted by 72 *puisne* judges. Mainly it has original jurisdiction to try cases at first instance, though it does have some appellate jurisdiction as well. 런던의 거리이름 / (사안을) 심리하다 / 항소 관할권

The jurisdictional competence of the Queen's Bench Division covers all those actions which belonged to the competence of the old common law courts before 1873 and which do not fall under the competence of the Chancery Division or the Family Division. These are, in particular, 사법관할권 / 포함하다, 관할하다

claims for damages caused by breaches of contract or torts. Since 1970 the Queen's Bench Division has had two sub-divisions, the *Commercial Court* and the *Admiralty Court*.

야기하다
상사재판부 / 해사(海事)재판부

The Commercial Court was set up in 1970 and gave official recognition to a long standing practice by which specialised judges had been assigned to commercial cases.

인정 / 오래된
배정하다

The Admiralty Court was also created in 1970. This is not a very busy or active court, for many shipping cases are settled by insurers and they also tend to go to arbitration. A sub-division of the Admiralty Court is the *Prize Court*, which is mainly active in times of war to decide whether the capture of a ship was lawful with respect to the rules of international law.

화해해결되다 / 보험회사 / 중재법원 / 전리법원
압류

(2) The Chancery Division is, in theory, headed by the Lord Chancellor, but in practice, its vice-president, the Vice-Chancellor, presides, and he is assisted by a staff of 18 *puisne* judges at present.

~를 장(長)으로 하다
부의장
의장역할을 하다 / 구성원, 스탭

The Chancery Division has both: original jurisdiction to try cases at "first instance" and appellate jurisdiction.

In the exercise of its jurisdiction at first instance it is the successor of the old Court of Chancery. Although, as we have learnt, all divisions of the High Court (since the *Judicature Acts 1873-1875*) are empowered to administer both law and equity, it is nevertheless still the case that matters concerning equity remain primarily the business of the Chancery Division.

우선

Certain specific matters are, however, expressly assigned to the Chancery Division by the *Supreme Court Act 1981*. These are in particular the execution of trusts, the administration of estates and partnership and company matters. Since 1970 the Chancery Division has dealt with all contentious probate cases; non-contentious probate cases are assigned to the Family Division. A specialised *Patents Court* also forms

부동산 / 파트너회사관계 / 회사관계
특허법원

part of the Chancery Division. Finally we find the *Divisional Court of the Chancery Division* having appellate jurisdiction for cases of bankruptcy from outside of London and other appeal cases, as well as the *Bankruptcy Court of the Chancery Division* which hears appeals of bankruptcy cases occuring within London.

파산사례
파산법원
발생하다

(3) The *Family Division* has a President, who is currently assisted by 17 *puisne* judges. Its jurisdiction at first instance concerns all matrimonial matters including divorce and maintenance claims, proceedings in respect of wardships of minors, adoption and guardianship proceedings. Briefly, as befits its name, the Family Division deals with all proceedings connected to the *Domestic Violence and Matrimonial Proceedings Act 1976*, the *Family Law Act 1986* or the *Children Act 1989*.

현재의
결혼(에 관한)
(재판) 절차
후견관계 / 보호자관계
(이름에) 걸맞다
가정폭력 / 혼인절차법

In addition the Family Division has a divisional court which has appellate jurisdiction for the Magistrates' courts, in cases which concern a number of matters connected to matrimonial disputes and minors.

재판부
혼인관련분쟁

All hearings at the divisional courts of the three divisions of the High Court of Justice are always presided over by two judges whereas most of the sessions at first instance are held by single judges.

(bb) *The Crown Court*

This court was set up in 1971. Criminal cases are its main area of competence. It is sometimes called the Central Criminal Court for England and Wales which forms a part of the Supreme Court of Judicature along with the High Court of Justice and the Court of Appeal. However, this is misleading, as the Crown Court is neither a court of equal rank to the High Court of Justice nor is it a real division of the High Court. In fact it is, on the one hand, a sub-division of the Queen's Bench Division, which has some minor civil

설립하다 / 주(主)관련분야
동일한 지위

jurisdiction but is concerned mainly with all criminal proceedings upon indictments. On the other hand, it is independent from the Queen's Bench Division in so far as it is not controlled by it, but only by the Criminal Division of the Court of Appeal, as we shall see. The Crown Court building in London is known as the "Old Bailey", and the court has branch offices in Manchester, Birmingham, Bristol, Cardiff and Leeds.

고소, 고발
런던 왕립법원의 건물이름
지원

(cc) *The Court of Appeal*

Formerly the Court of Appeal heard appeals regarding only *civil* matters, but since 1966 it now consists of a Civil Division and a Criminal Division. The Civil Division at present has a staff of 35 Lord Justices of Appeal. The quorum for a hearing is usually three judges.

이전에는
항소법원 판사
결정가능한 최소인원수

To become a Lord Justice of Appeal it is necessary, according to the *Supreme Court Act 1981*, for a judge to have served for 10 years at the High Court of Justice. Then, following that and if proposed by the Prime Minister and the Master of the Rolls, he will be appointed by the Queen.

임명하다

(1) The Civil Division

In practice the president of this division is the Master of the Rolls. His position dates from the Middle Ages when the Master of the Rolls was the Chancellor's highest ranked officer and deputy in the Chancery.

대리자

Since the 17th century, he has administered documents of the state and the registers of royal records, which were written on parchment and rolled up (and were therefore called "rolls"). From that time to now his activities have changed more and more from those of an administrative officer to those of a judge. The jurisdiction of the Civil Division of the Court of Appeal includes the power to hear appeals of civil matters from all three divisions of the High Court of Justice as well as of the County Courts and the Magistrates' courts.

국가문서
색인, 목록 / 법원서류
양피지 / 감아올리다

The purpose of an appeal is to ensure only the correct interpretation and application of the law, but not to check the validity of the facts of the case. 보장하다 유효성

Thus, the Court of Appeal is usually bound by evidence given in the inferior courts. A new hearing of evidence is only permitted if the circumstances of the case reveal new, previously unknown facts. 증거 증거조사(기일) 밝히다

(2) The Criminal Division

This division of the Court of Appeal was set up by the *Criminal Appeal Act 1968* to replace the former "Court of Criminal Appeal". Its jurisdiction is defined in this *1968* Act with amendments by the *Criminal Appeal Act 1995*. 확정, 결정하다

The Criminal Division mainly hears appeals from the Crown Court.

(dd) *The House of Lords*

The House of Lords to most people is known as the Upper House of Parliament in contrast to the House of Commons. But the House of Lords is also the highest judicial court of the United Kingdom. The background to its development is once more historical: In earlier times the king was the highest judge in the land, particularly in the medieval period. 상원 / 하원

As such, he was advised, as we have seen, by the King's Council ("curia regis") which was a central governing body and existed before Parliament evolved. This body exercised all the powers of the King, including his judicial powers. Thus, when Parliament became established the Upper House retained these judicial powers. Judicial procedures took place in the Upper House, headed by the King assisted by the Lords without the Commons who, for the greater part, sat in their own chamber dealing with political, but not judicial matters ... So when a *lawyer* today speaks of the "House of Lords" he will normally have in mind not the parliamentary (political) Upper Chamber, but the (law) court which goes by the same name. Technically, and in practice, the House of Lords as a court is not identical to the House of Lords as 단위, 기구 유보, 보유하다 의사를 가지다 상원

the Upper House of Parliament. The House of Lords as a (law) court is a committee of the Lords and is actually separate from the political Upper House. In this sense the House of Lords is the highest court not only for England and Wales but also for Scotland and Northern Ireland which, incidentally, have their own legal systems and separate administrations of law.

그밖에도

The House of Lords is, apart from the European Court of Justice (Luxembourg), the ultimate court of appeal. It consists of the Lord Chancellor as its president and between nine and twelve peers the "Lords of Appeal in Ordinary" (who should not be confused with the "Lords Justice of Appeal" of the Court of Appeal). Two of those so called "Law Lords" as members of the House of Lords are usually from Scotland.

별도로 하고 / 유럽대법원
최종 상소심
상원의 판사
혼란하다, 착각하다

Normally five judges sit in court which requires a majority vote to reach a decision.

다수
투표

As the ultimate appeal authority the House of Lords hears appeals from the Court of Appeal if this court admitted it as reversible or if a special Entrance Qualifications Committee of the House of Lords allowed the appeal.

항소심
상고가능 / (상소)허가위원회

An appeal from the High Court of Justice to the House of Lords without a hearing in the Court of Appeal — known as "leap-frogging" — is only admitted in cases of outstanding general importance. Moreover, in this situation, the House of Lords will only agree to consider the case, if the decision will create new jurisdiction, or if the judge of the High Court feels bound by precedents of the Court of Appeal or the House of Lords.

즉시상고
창설하다

3. The Judicial Committee of the Privy Council

법사위원회 / 추밀원(樞密院)

This committee, which is usually called the "Privy Council" in short, is not a real court. It does not dispense justice but only makes recommendations and gives advice to the monarch.

법을 결정하다, 판결하다
권고안을 결의하다 / 국왕

The importance of the Privy Council rose with the expansion of the Commonwealth and fell with its decline.

상승하다
하강하다

The reason for the existence of the Privy Council is that the House of Lords only has the power to pronounce binding decisions for the United Kingdom only. It is not empowered to administer law for the colonies and the members of the Commonwealth. However, most of the Commonwealth states have recognised the Privy Council as an ultimate instance for appeals against decisions of their highest courts. This is, for example, the case in Malaysia, New Zealand, the Channel Islands, the Isle of Man and Gibraltar; but not Australia and Malta which are exceptions.

선포, 공포하다
통일왕국, 대영제국
인정하다

The Judicial Committee of the Privy Council does not only apply English law in its decisions, but also the law of the state from which the case originated. For this reason, decisions of the Privy Council are not considered precedents for English courts or the Privy Council itself.

적용하다
~에서 유래하다

Diagram 10

System of Courts Exercising Civil Jurisdiction

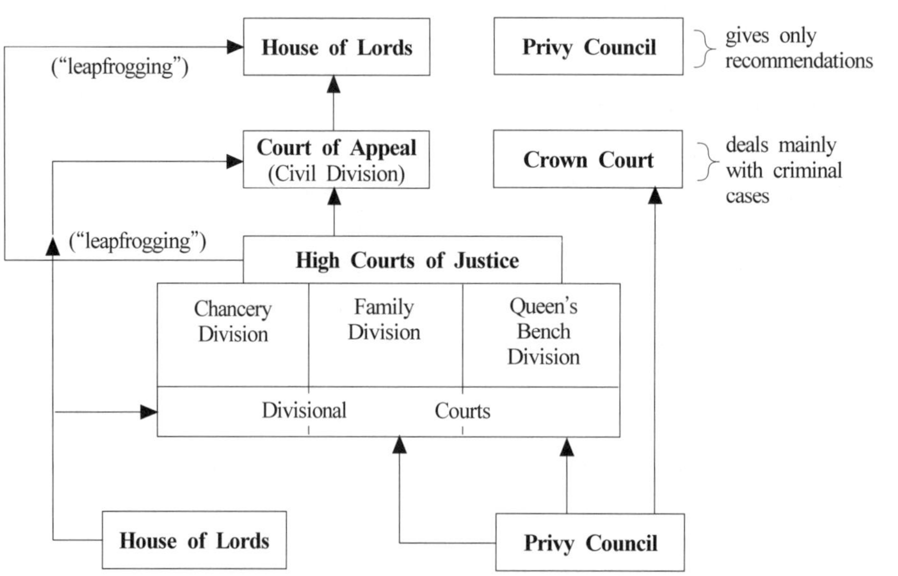

Note: Appeals are indicated thus ——►)

III. Further reading[1)]

Baker, An Introduction to English Legal History; *Bernstorff, Graf von*, Einführung in das englische Recht; *Black's* Legal Reader – an Introduction to the Anglo-American Law and Legal system; *Cownie & Bradney*, English Legal System in Context; *Darbyshire*, Nutshells: English Legal System; *David/Grasmann*, Einführung in die großen Rechtssysteme der Gegenwart; *David/Spinosi*, Les grand systèmes de droit contemporains; *Cracknell*, English Legal System ("Cracknell's Law Students' Companion" = cases and statutes); *Denham*, Law – A Modern Introduction; *Eddey*, On the English Legal System; *Elliott & Quinn*, English Legal System; *Harris*, An Introduction to Law; *Henrich*, Einführung in das englische Privatrecht; *Partington*, Introduction to the English Legal System; *Rvlin*, First Steps in the Law; *Slapper & Kelly*, English Law; *Slapper & Kelly*, On English Legal System; *Smith & Bailey*, On the Modern English Legal System; *Templeman & Reed*, English Legal System, Textbook –, Casebook –, Revision Work Book; *Zweigert/Kötz*, Einführung in die Rechtsver

1) Cf. footnote on p. 23.

Chapter Three

The legal profession

법률가 직업

Ⅰ. History

The organisation of the English courts, as was described in the previous chapter, owes its origin and evolution to a professional group of lawyers. This group had its flowering period in medieval times and all along was in actual fact organised in corporate bodies.

~에서 유래하다
직업군 / 법률가 / 개화기
그 이후에
법인체(=body corporate)

It cannot be over-emphasised that the career of a judge in England has always been quite different from that in Germany, France and other continental countries.

아무리 강조해도 지나치지 않다

As has already been indicated, in England a lawyer can only become a judge after having practised as a barrister or solicitor[1] for a considerable amount of time, during which he should have acquired the reputation of being an excellent and successful jurist.

시사하다
상당한 양
얻다 / 명망

Precursors of the present English professional lawyers, however, were the above mentioned "itinerant justices" who were members of the curia regis and who either administered justice at the Royal Courts or travelled through the country for this purpose. In fact, it was they who first had the idea of institutionalising the legal profession.

전임자

The professionalisation of the advocates was preceded by the professionalisation of the judges. As a consequence judges and advocates joined together to form a unified professional group of lawyers. A trend was initiated in the 13th century, as a result of which judges were chosen from among practising advocates. This trend established itself as a rule in 1400 and is still in force today.

(주도적으로) 시작하다

The first advocates like the first judges were ecclesiastical authorities. They dominated the judicial practice until a

성직자
지배하다, 지배적이다

---

1) Cf. footnote on page 59!

secular legal profession was formed. which gradually led to a clear separation and classification of the various judicial activities and professions.

세속적(교회에 대한 대립어) / 점차

This classification, which goes back to Roman law was based on a distinction between legal advisers. On one side there were advisers, who assisted a person and voiced his opinion in court (*advocatus*); on the other side were advisers, who made or accepted legally binding statements on behalf of a person and thus acted as a party to the process (*procurator*).

법률자문가
말하다

As in Roman law there was never any doubt in English law, that the profession of advocates should be divided into two different fields of activity.

활동분야, 영역

This was the basis from the English legal profession evolved. In the modern English system, of course, the allocation of tasks is different in detail from Roman times.

기초
발전하다
업무분담

Initially, however, the division of functions did not follow strict rules, and therefore it was not unusual for legal advisers in previous times to exercise the dual function of both "*attorney*" and "*pleader*".

처음에는
변호사(대리인) / 변호사(법정 변론인)

The first regulation of the exercise of the legal profession was formulated at the end of the 13th century. In 1275 a statute was issued whereby professional lawyers found guilty of collusion should be punished.

유책한
통모, 공모 / 벌하다

Five years later, the City of London ruled in an enactment, that lawyers admitted to the Bar for the first time had to take an oath. Moreover the fields of activity of attorneys and pleaders were declared strictly separate.

규정하다
선서하다

During this time the profession of *attorney* developed into an independent profession. His tasks included, amongst others, the management of clients' correspondence in cases of minor difficulty. Representation at the Bar, however, was the exclusive privilege of the *pleaders*.

독립적인 / 과제 / 무엇보다

The differentiation between attorneys and pleaders was, if you like, a distinction between "serving" and "intellectual" lawyers, a distinction, on which the present day difference between solicitors and barristers is based.

섬기는

After 1215 the Common Bench developed into the first

public court of Common Law. The first mention of lawyers appearing at the Bar is found around 1280. They were called "*narratores*" and performed the same role as the pleaders.

언급
등장하다

In the 14th century these "narratores" formed a corporation which was regulated by the "Order of the Coif" and from then onwards they became known as "serjeants at law" ("*servientes ad legem*").

법인
변호사법, 변호사령 / 그 이후로는 / 왕립법률관

Lawyers wishing to become members of this corporation had to take an oath, declaring that they would faithfully serve their king as serjeant. Moreover, the new members had to organise a celebration, in which, occasionally, the king participated. During this celebration they were fitted out with fine robes and donned as a special sign of rank, a white headgear, the "coif". Later a small piece of white cloth on the wig was retained as a symbol of the coif.

충성스럽게
축제를 주최하다 / 때때로
치장하다
값비싼 법복 / 받다 / 서열 표식
두건
가발

After this admission ceremony the new serjeant was introduced to the Court of Common Pleas by two established serjeants. Then, for the first time, he was called to the Bar.

입회의식

In the 15th century these "serjeants at law" were said to be the richest advocates in the world!

~라고들 하였다

As the importance of the Court of Common Pleas declined, inevitable so, too, did the importance of the "serjeants at law".

축소되다 / 피할 수 없는

From this time on, the "serjeants at law" began to appear also at the Court of King's Bench and the Exchequer Court.

In these Courts, however, there were already other practising lawyers who were not members of the "Order of the Coif". Therefore, the serjeants had to share their earnings with these lawyers.

개업 법률가(변호사)
나누다 / 수입

The decline in their status led to a loss of the serjeants' privileges in connection with the appointment of judges. Then, being a member of the "Order of the Coif" was no longer a prerequisite to becoming a judge, but rather the qualification was being a lawyer of outstanding eminence. This could be achieved by excellent pleadings at the Bar or by being an author of a "Book of Authority".

몰락 / 손실
우선권, 특권 / 임명
전제 / 오히려
대단한 명성
도달하다 / 변론

Famous English jurists such as, for example, *Coke* and

Blackstone became judges without ever having practised as "serjeants at law", in the "Court of Common Pleas".

So it was not surprising, that the number of serjeants diminished steadily, especially as their privileges at the Bar were lost completely when under King James I (1603-1625) the "King's Counsel" was created.

줄다 / 지속적으로
고위변호사, 왕의 자문관

This institution was created to honour excellent lawyers of outstanding merit and it has been preserved to the present day. The emblem of a King's Counsel is a silken robe, which is handed over to him during a solemn ceremony. Even today, when a lawyer is appointed to be a Queen's Counsel it is said that "he has taken silk".

명예롭게 하다
대단한 공로 / 보존하다
엠블럼, 상징 / 비단 법복
전달하다 / 화려한 의식
임명하다

One of the first famous lawyers in King James' time, who was appointed to be King's Counsel, was *Sir Francis Bacon* (1561-1626).

The decline of the serjeants was finally sealed by an enactment of 1846 which provided that every lawyer who was a barrister should be admitted to the Court of Common Pleas. The Order of the Coif, it is true, has never been officially abolished, but since *Lord Lindley* who died in 1921 there have been no more serjeants. Their corporation building, the "Inn", was sold in 1877.

봉인하다
폐지하다
법인(단체) 건물

Diagram 11

History of the Legal Profession

Roman Law		**Middle Ages**	**King James I (1603-1625)**
"advocatus" assisting at the court	→	"attorneys" with	"King's Counsel" was created
"procurator" acting as a party to the process	→	"pleaders" → "narratores" → "sergeants at law" ↓ "Order of the Coif"	→ excellent lawyers → Sir Francis Bacon

II. Barristers

1. Development

In the meantime the profession of barrister reached its flowering period. The term barrister owes its origin to the permission given to lawyers to appear at the Bar. The barristers established their own Inns in London.

허가

These Inns developed as a result of practical requirements. Usually judges and serjeants – since the 14th century – had their own houses, in which their students, the "apprentices of the law", also lived. The students, however, thought it useful, to join in groups to learn and study, sometimes meeting in guest houses of a magnate who had space to spare on his premises.

실제적 필요
도제
가입하다
유력자 / 여유공간
집, 장소

About 20 such houses are known to have existed, of which four were predominant in the subsequent period and still exist as "Inns of Court" in London today: the "*Honourable Society of Lincoln's Inn*", " ... *of the Inner Temple*", " ... *of the Middle Temple*" and " ... of *Gray's Inn*".

주도적 / 그 이후의 시기
명예로운

2. The Inns of Court

a) Origin

These "Inns of Court" were never officially founded but they arose spontaneously out of a need to complement the studies at the universities. In the middle ages only Roman law and Canon law were taught there, but no common law.

설립하다
보충하다
(중세) 교회법

Each Inn had a chapel, a library, a dining hall and a garden. The two older Inns of Court are the *Inner Temple* and the *Middle Temple*. Their names go back to the "Temple", which was (until 1313) the house of the "*Order of the Templars*".

Famous members of the Inner Temple, include *Blackstone* and Chaucer and of the Middle Temple *James Boswell* and *Lord Halsbury*.

The earliest documents of *Lincoln's Inn* date back to the year 1422. This Inn presumably owes its name to the *Earl of Lincoln*. He was an administrator for the Bishops of Chichester, whose city palace had previously been situated on the same site in London. Famous members of Lincoln's Inn were *Sir Thomas More*, *Cromwell*, *Pitt*, *Disraeli* and *Gladstone*.
짐작하건대
주교

Gray's Inn, in existence since 1371, was named after the former owner of the buildings *Lord Gray de Wilton*. Well known students of Gray's Inn include *Sir Francis Bacon*, *Lord Burghley* and *Lord Denning*.1)

b) Organisation

Members of the Inns of Court are either barrister-students or practising barristers. The management of the Inns is exercised by benchers, highly esteemed and experienced barristers (mostly Queen's Counsel) who are not elected by the members, but co-opted. This means that they are directly appointed by the bench and the Bar for life.
경영
이사(회) / 인정받다
호선하다, 천거하다
임명하다 / 판사회와 변호사회

Their tasks include the acceptance of new students who intend to become barristers as well as the admission of graduate students as barristers.
포함하다 / 수락
허가
대학졸업생

Besides the Inns themselves there are institutions which are supported by and responsible for these four "Inns":
지지하다

- The Council of Legal Education 법률교육
  organises the professional training and studies of the student members of the Inns. 직업훈련
- The General Council of the Bar (*Bar Council*) 변호사회
  represents the professional interests of barristers against the legislative and the public. Furthermore it lays down rules and regulations pertaining to professional duties and it passes preliminary judgments on complaints against barristers (e.g. "breaches of professional duties").
  직역이익
  입법부 / 규정하다
  ~에 관하여 / 직업적 의무
  가처분 결정 / 불평, 이의제기
  위반
- The Senate of the Inns of Court and Bar
  deals with the investigation of charges of professional 조사 / 고소 / 반직역행위

1) Lord Denning was perhaps the most distinguished judge of the 20th century (*Goodmann*, p. 169).

misconduct. So it represents a disciplinary tribunal of the "Inns of Court". The Senate decides on complaints passed on by the Bar Council. Its decisions may be appealed in the High Court of Justice.

직역자치법원
넘기다
항소하다

Diagram 12

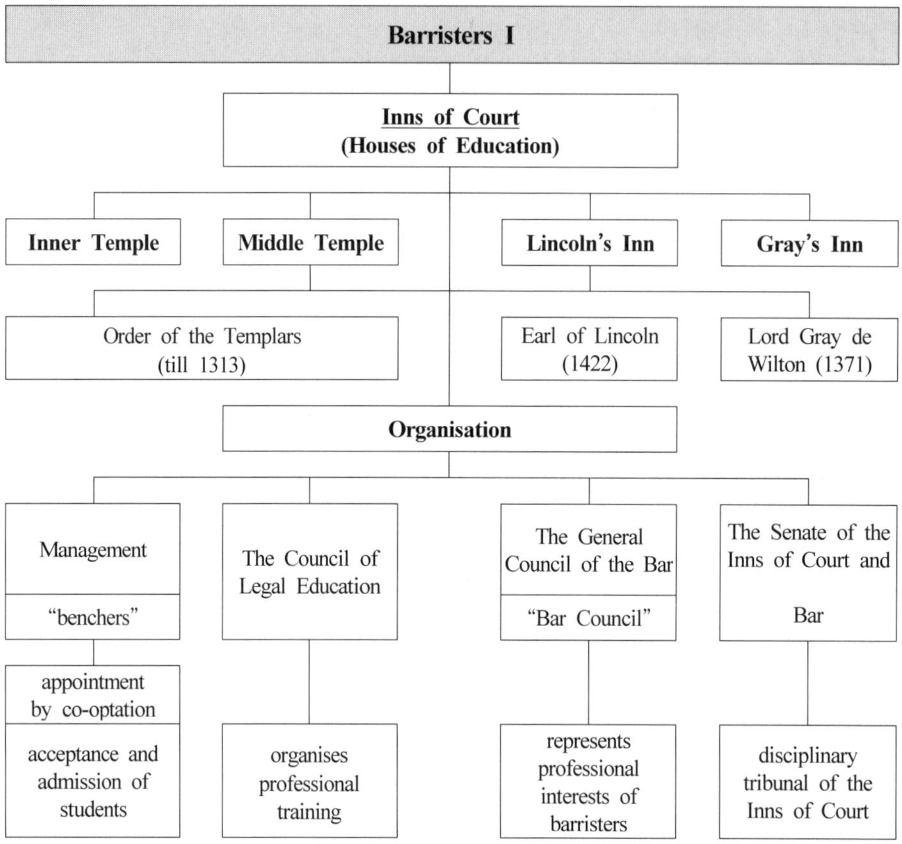

3. Education

After having learnt the basic principles of law at university, students who intended to become barristers, requested admission to an "Inn of Court".

허가를 구하다

There they spent about seven years, frequenting the courts to exercise their skills in practice, learning to engage in legal argument and nurturing social contacts with the other members of their Inn.

방문하다
법률적으로 논증하다
돌보다

The education and career of today's barrister has not changed essentially[1] from that of previous times:

커리어, 직업

After having studied law for about three years at a university (which is not obligatory at law) and graduated as a Bachelor of Laws or a Bachelor of Arts, the graduate applies for admission to an Inn. Usually his application is accompanied by a reference from a practising barrister who is a member of the Inn.

법적인 의무가 있는
법학자 / 문학사
첨부하다
추천서

In principle any lawyer – regardless of nationality – can become a barrister if he possesses the required qualifications (and if he is able to finance his education).

소유하다 / 필요한 자격

First and foremost, the applicant must show a broad general education to university entrance requirement standard. Furthermore he must be of good character, clean conduct, and enjoy a good reputation. During his period of education the candidate has to pass a number of minor examinations before he can sit his final examination. This examination consists of two parts, and candidates who are graduates are usually exempted from the first part.

지원자
일반교육 / 대학입학자격
예절
명성 / 교육기간
졸업시험을 치르다
면제하다

For the second part of this examination all candidates must attend lectures of the "Bar Vocational Course" (BVC) given at the "Inns of Court School of Law".

강의를 듣다 / 직업적

This school (situated in "Gray's Inn") is an institution common to all the Inns and is overseen by the "Council of Legal Education".

감독하다

Moreover Bar students have to attend several "dinners" held at their Inn. These dinners, held in sessions called "dining terms", take place at least every three weeks in the Inn's dining hall. This "Dining in Hall" provides an opportunity for students to have conversations about general and legal matters with other students and experienced practising barristers.

저녁식사, 정찬
제공하다

To become a barrister a student has to participate in at least 24 dinners[2].

After solemn admission as a barrister (the "calling to the

허가의식 / 법정변호사로 임명하다

1) There *have been* some changes which will not be discribed here.
2) This ist different for those studying outside London (since 1997).

bar") by the benchers, the junior barrister has to spend his first year practising with an experienced barrister. This year is referred to as his year of "pupillage". To attain the ~로 본다 / 수련기간 / 얻다
position of a judge he is usually required to practise as a barrister for five to fifteen years, depending upon the importance of the court to which he is then appointed.

Diagram 13

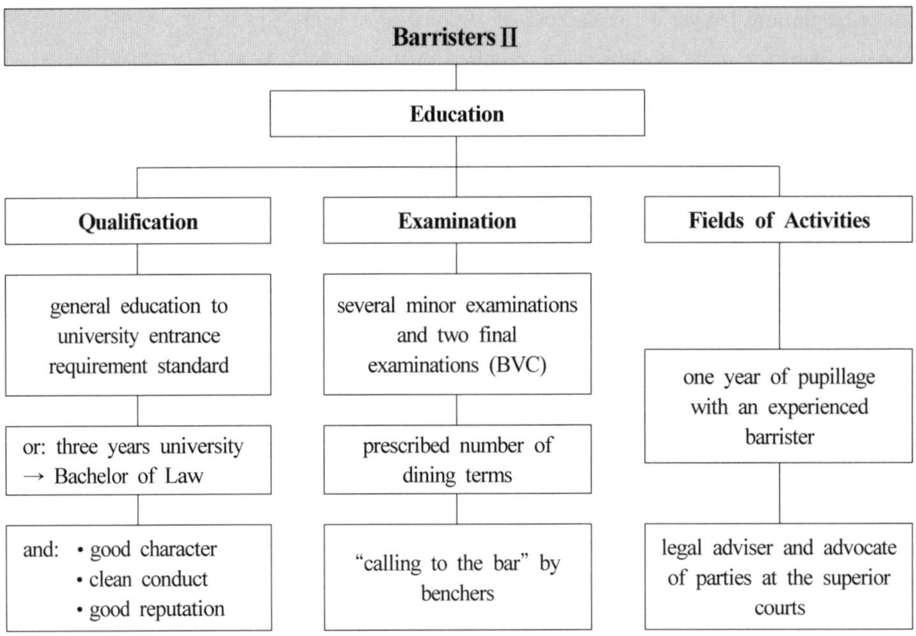

4. Fields of Activities

The field of activities of barristers extends above all to the practice at the Bar of the High Court of Justice and its 실무
superior courts. Here they enjoy privileges, which are not statutorily set up, but based on time-hallowed custom and 법률로 정하다 / 오래된
tradition, which has its origin in the medieval monopoly of the "serjeants at law".

Their position as legal advisers to a party, who in principle can appear personally at the bar, goes back to that of the Roman *advocatus* or the medieval "pleader".

The activities of a barrister also include the drafting of 초안작성

written pleadings especially in fundamental and difficult legal cases.

준비서면(변론서면) / 근본적인

At present there are about 10,000 barristers; their elite is still formed by the "Queen's Counsel" (about 10%), who are qualified to be appointed as a judge of the County Courts or the superior courts. The highly sophisticated professional law of the barristers formerly precluded them from direct contact with clients. Every person who sought law at a superior court had to contact a solicitor. Therefore it was very important for every barrister to have good relations with approved solicitors' offices which brought him clients.

엘리트

매우 복잡한 / 직업법(변호사회 자체 규정) / 배제하다

법을 구하다, 권리를 찾다

좋은 관계 / 인정받은

Although barristers may nowadays contact clients directly a good relationship with approved solicitors whose offices are known to the general public, is still of importance.

III. Solicitors

The essential difference between barristers and solicitors was[1] that a solicitor is not allowed to represent clients in superior courts. The position of a solicitor is comparable with the position of the *procurator* at Roman law or the medieval "attorney".

1. Fields of activities

The field of activity of the modern solicitor is very intricate and can not easily be described comprehensively.

다양한 / 포괄적으로

He maintains good relations with his clients and assists them as a personal legal adviser. The solicitor prepares the proceedings for the party he represents in a County Court or in a Magistrates' Court. In a case where a decision is within the competence of a superior court the solicitor procures the services of a barrister for his client.

유지하다

중개하다

1) Cf. the *Courts and Legal Services Act* 1990 as well as the *Access to Justice Act* 1999: Under these Acts approved solicitors now have rights of audience before every court in relation to all proceedings.

Moreover, solicitors effect conveyances of property, prepare wills, advise on trusts and matrimonial matters and handle the defence of accused people. 실행하다 / 부동산 이전 유언 / 변론을 담당하다 고소하다

Solicitors formerly enjoyed a monopoly in conveyancing, which formed about 50% of their activities. This monopoly was, however, removed by the *Administration of Justice Act 1985* and the *Building Societies Act 1986*. The effect of these Acts was to inaugurate a new profession of licensed conveyancers under the control of the "Council for Legal Conveyancers". 독점 / 부동산 양도를 위한 문서작성 제거하다 도입하다 / 부동산 양도 전문인

Nevertheless solicitors still dominate in conveyancing. To a certain extent their activities are comparable with those of German notaries. 공증인

Although an English solicitor may be a good lawyer, above all he is a businessman, and therefore he may often find it more "efficient" to employ a barrister. This does not mean that the solicitor takes no further interest in the case, for it is his function, acting upon the barrister's "advice on evidence", to prepare the witnesses and get the case ready for trial. 효과적인 입증에 대한 조언 증인 / 기일을 준비하다

English solicitors predominantly work in law offices with several partners and it is not unusual for big and renowned solicitors offices to consist of more than 50 partners and "assistant solicitors". These partnerships are called "law firms". Approximately one third of the more than 8,000 solicitors offices are managed by a single lawyer. A small percentage of solicitors work as employed lawyers in the legal department of business enterprises. 주로 / 법률회사 유명한 대략 운영되다 사업체

In total in England and Wales there are about 80,000 solicitors, of whom around 63,000 hold practicing certificates. 허가증

2. Organisation

The professional organisation of the solicitors is embodied in the Law Society (previously "Incorporated Law Society"), which was founded in 1826, although ever since 1719 the professional activity of solicitors has been regulated by various 지역조직 / 법인을 조직하다

enactments and statutes.

The Law Society's centre is their Hall in *Chancery Lane* in London, and it works through a Secretary-General and a permanent staff under the ultimate control of its council of representative solicitors and its (annual) President.

런던의 거리이름
사무총장
직원 / 평의회

The Law Society is authorised by virtue of the law to establish rules on the education and admission of solicitors with the consent of the Lord Chancellor and of other superior court judges. This society exercises a large professional jurisdiction through a particular disciplinary board.

법률에 따라
규정을 수립하다
동의
징계위원회

The efforts of the Law Society since the 19th century have considerably helped the profession of solicitors to achieve a reputation similar to that already enjoyed by barristers, thereby raising its members' standards.

명성
기준을 높이다

3. Education

Every student with a university education is, in principle, eligible to join the Law Society.

자유롭게 ~ 할 수 있다

To become a solicitor he has to undertake a four to five year period of apprenticeship as "articled clerk"[1] with a practising solicitor. For a graduate this period can be shortened to two or two and a half years.

이수하다
교육 / 사무변호사 시보
축소하다, 단축하다

Moreover, solicitor students attend lectures organised by the Law Society and like barrister students sit for a final examination consisting of two parts.

University graduates are exempted from the first part. After having succeeded in his examination and having completed his contract of apprenticeship, he asks the Master of the Rolls for admission to the "Supreme Court Roll of Solicitors" (which is the official list of admitted solicitors administered by the Master of the Rolls).

대학졸업자
합격하다
이행하다 / 직업훈련계약

1) Nowadays: "trainee solicitor".

Diagram 14

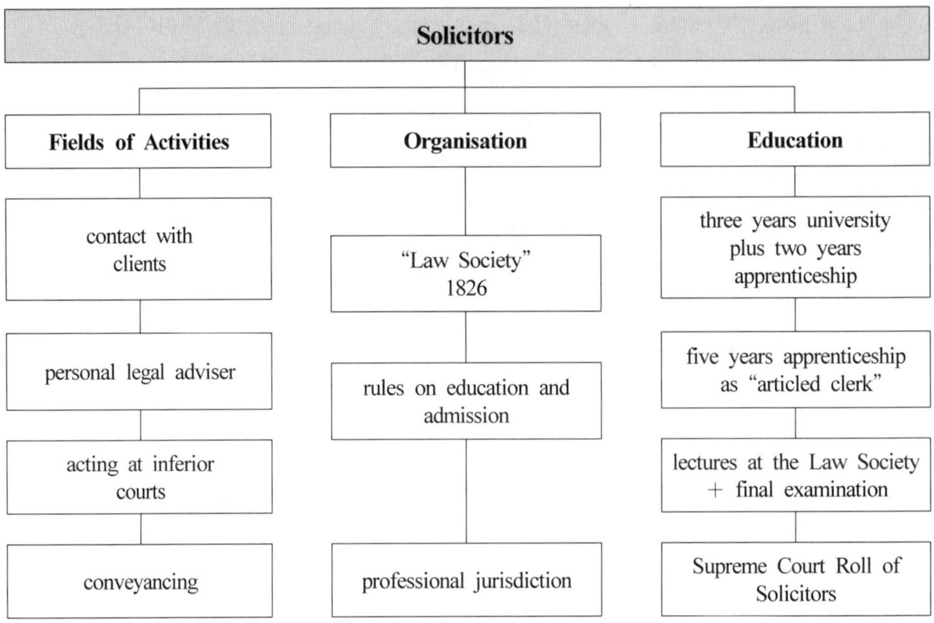

Ⅳ. Judges

As has already been indicated the judges' career does not form its own branch of the legal profession in England. There is no judges' career in an institutional sense as in most continental legal systems. Herein the English system contrasts with the position found in continental countries where judgeship can be a career on a civil service basis.

법관경력, 이력, 법관의 진로
기구적인 의미
여기에서
판사직
공무

The English legal profession has only two branches: barristers and solicitors. Each profession, as previously explained, has developed independently, and each has its own controlling body. No person may practise in both capacities concurrently. All judges of superior courts are required to be barristers and before appointment should have had many years practical experience.

독립적인
감독기구 / 분야
동시에 / 법정변호사이어야 한다

Although judges are not civil servants, the regulations for the different courts (inferior and superior courts) are established precisely by law. In the same way the fields of

규정, 규칙
법률로 상세히 규정하다

activity of the judges, their appointment, their salaries and the conditions of their dismissal are defined by law. 임명 / 월급 해임

1. Appointment

Except in the case of the *Justices of the Peace* at the Magistrates' Courts, an individual who works on an honorary basis can only become a judge after extensive legal education as well as several years' practice as a barrister or solicitor. 명예직으로 광범위한

County Court judges are appointed by the Crown (Queen) on a proposal by the Lord Chancellor. 제안, 제정에 따라

They must be lawyers of seven years' standing. As "His/Her Honourable Judge (surname)" they are directly addressed as "Your Honour". 7년 경력의 명예로운(판사 앞에 붙이는 경의 호칭) / 성(姓) / 호칭하다

The *High Court judges* are also appointed by the Crown on the advice of the Lord Chancellor. They must be barristers of ten years' standing. 자문에 따라

As "The Honourable Mr./Mrs. Justice (surname) they are addressed as "Your Lordship" or "My Lord". A knighthood is bestowed on appointment. 기사의 작위를 받다

The *Court of Appeal judges*, called "Lord Justices of Appeal", are appointed by the Crown at the suggestion of the Prime Minister.

They must either be barristers of fifteen years' standing or already be High Court judges. As "The Right Honourable Lord/Lady Justice (surname)" they are also addressed as "Your Lordship" or "My Lord". 매우 명예로운

Finally the *House of Lords judges*, called "Lords of Appeal in Ordinary" (= "Law Lords"), are also appointed by the Crown on the advice of the Prime Minister. On their appointment they are simultaneously created "Life Peers". 동시에 / 종신으로 고위귀족이 되다

To become "Law Lords" they must either be barristers of fifteen years' standing or have held a high judicial office for two years. Usually they are elevated from the Court of 고위 판사직 승진하다

Appeal.

The senior appointments in the system, i.e. the offices of the Lord High Chancellor[1], the Lord Chief Justice[2], the Master of the Rolls and the President of the Family Division of the High Court, are also decided by the Crown on the advice of the Prime Minister.

고위직 임명
결정하다

2. Salaries[3]

County Court judges receive an annual salary ranging between £99,420 (circuit judges) and £107,346 (senior circuit judges) and are entitled to travel allowances. On retirement a pension is payable (*Administration of Justice Pension Act 1950*).

그 중간에 위치하다
권한을 가지다 / 여행비용 / 은퇴 / 판사연금법

High Court judges receive an annual salary of £132,603. The President of the "Family Division" receives £157,699 annually.

The "Lord Chief Justice of England and Wales", who is the president of the "Queen's Bench Division" receives £171,375 annually.

Court of Appeal judges ("Lord Justices of Appeal") earn £149,897 per year, whilst the "Master of the Rolls" as its president receives £163,213.

수입을 가지다
~동안

"The Lord High Chancellor" as the president of the *House of Lords* (who is also the president of the "Chancery Division" of the High Court of Justice) receives £167,760. Each "Lord of Appeal in Ordinary" in the House of Lords gets £152,072.

Moreover, as *parliamentary* chairman of the House of Lords the Lord Chancellor receives nearly half of his judge's salary.

의장

All these judicial salaries are charged to the "Consolidated

판사월급 / ~의 부담이다 / 국고

1) Who is also President of the Chancery Division (part of the High Court of Justice).
2) Also President of the Queen's Bench Division (part oft the High Court ...).
3) *Whitaker's Almanack*, 2002, p. 368-376 (£1 = 1,59 €<약 1900원>).

Fund" which means that they are not subject to annual review by Parliament as is the case with the salaries of civil servants. Nonetheless Parliament does fix the salaries of the judges. 감사

3. Immunity 면책특권

All judges enjoy immunity. For superior court judges this means that they may not be sued in a civil action for things said, or acts done, in the course of their work. This immunity enables judgments to be given freely, without the possibility of subsequent civil action and the endless prolongation of litigation. Consequently the superior court judges enjoy this immunity even if they act maliciously or in bad faith.

고소하다
자유로운 판결을 가능하게 하다
연장
고의, 악의로 / 악의로

There is a presumption that the acts of a superior court judge fall within his jurisdiction and it is unusual and difficult to visualise such a judge acting outside his jurisdiction, County Court judges have a similar immunity, but only when acting within their jurisdiction.

추정
관할권 내에서
상상하다

4. Dismissal

County Court judges are liable for acts done or things said outside or in excess of their jurisdiction. Therefore, they can be removed from office by the Lord Chancellor for inability or misbehaviour.

재판권을 위반함
면직하다 / 무능력

A County Court judge's retirement age is 72, or at the Lord Chancellor's discretion up to 75.

은퇴연령 / 재량에 따라

This is laid down in the *County Courts Act 1959.*

The *Judicial Pensions Act* of the same year (1959) provides that the retirement age for superior court judges was 75.

법관연금법

The *Judicial Pensions and Retirement Act 1993* lowered the normal retirement age of all judges to 70, but inferior judges may be permitted to work until 75 if it is considered to be in the public interest. Their appointment may be

낮추다

renewed on a year by year basis by the Lord Chancellor. As for Supreme Court judges appointed from 1995 and Law Lords who were not High Court judges by 1995, they must retire at 70.

The reason behind this relatively high pension age is the fact that, before being appointed, judges must have indulged into long and intense legal studies. 인내하다

Indeed, if we had to consider the figures of the present[1] twelve "Lords of Appeal in Ordinary" (+ The Lord High Chancellor) in the House of Lords we would come out with the following ages of appointment (present age in brackets: 57 (62), 67 (69), 62 (72), 61 (69), 63 (70), 61 (68), 58 (64), 64 (70), 66 (71), 61 (66), 66 (70), 66 (70), 66 (68). 괄호속에

The Lord High Chancellor, "The Right Honourable *The Lord Irvine of Lairg* was born in 1940 and — when fairly young — was appointed in 1997! The age structure in the Court of Appeal and the High Court of Justice is very similar.

As already mentioned this is common to all judges. They enjoy high reputation and respect in public not only for their high office, but usually also for their personal charisma. 직위, 직책 / 개인적 카리스마

If, e.g., there is a public discussion on a decision of the "Master of the Rolls", you will never hear or read "The Master of the Rolls has decided" but "*Lord Denning*[2] has decided" or — at present — "*Lord Phillips* has decided".

Every person in England who has a certain relationship with the law knows that "The Right Honourable *The Lord Phillips of Worth of Matravers*" is at present the "Master of the Rolls".

(Do you, as a Korean reader, know the name of the present president of the Korean Supreme Court?)

---

1) Whitaker's Almanack 2002, p. 368.

2) *Lord Denning* retired at the age of 83.

5. Function

과제, 임무

In contrast with the German legal system, in England, trial conduct is not a matter for the judges but for the advocates who have to submit all precedents which can support their arguments.

재판진행
변호사
제출하다

The task of the judge is quite limited. He is bound to hear what is submitted by the advocates and to pay judicial respect to it. However, he is not bound to ascertain the truth.

제한된
법적판단을 하다
진실을 조사하다

So it is not unusual for a decision of an inferior court to be overruled by an appellate court, due to the fact that the judge of the inferior court had asked too many questions, thus hindering the ordinary course of proceedings.

항소법원
방해하다 / 재판과정

Lord Denning expressed what is expected of a good English judge as follows [*Jones* v *National Coal Board* (1967)].

기대하다
석탄이사회(석탄 관청)

"In our law ... the judge is not allowed in a civil dispute to call a witness whom he thinks might throw some light on the facts. He must rest content with the witnesses called by the parties .... So also it is for the advocates, each in his turn, to examine the witnesses, and not for the judge to take it on himself lest by so doing he appears to favour one side or the other .... Lord Bacon spoke right when he said that "patience and gravity of hearing is an essential part of justice, and an overspeaking judge is no well-tuned cymbal."

민사쟁송
~으로 만족하다
각자 순서대로
증인을 심문하다
그리하여 ~않도록 / 편애하다, 일방에 유리하게 하다
인내 / 위엄, 권위
끼어들어 말하기 / 잘 조율된

Diagram 15

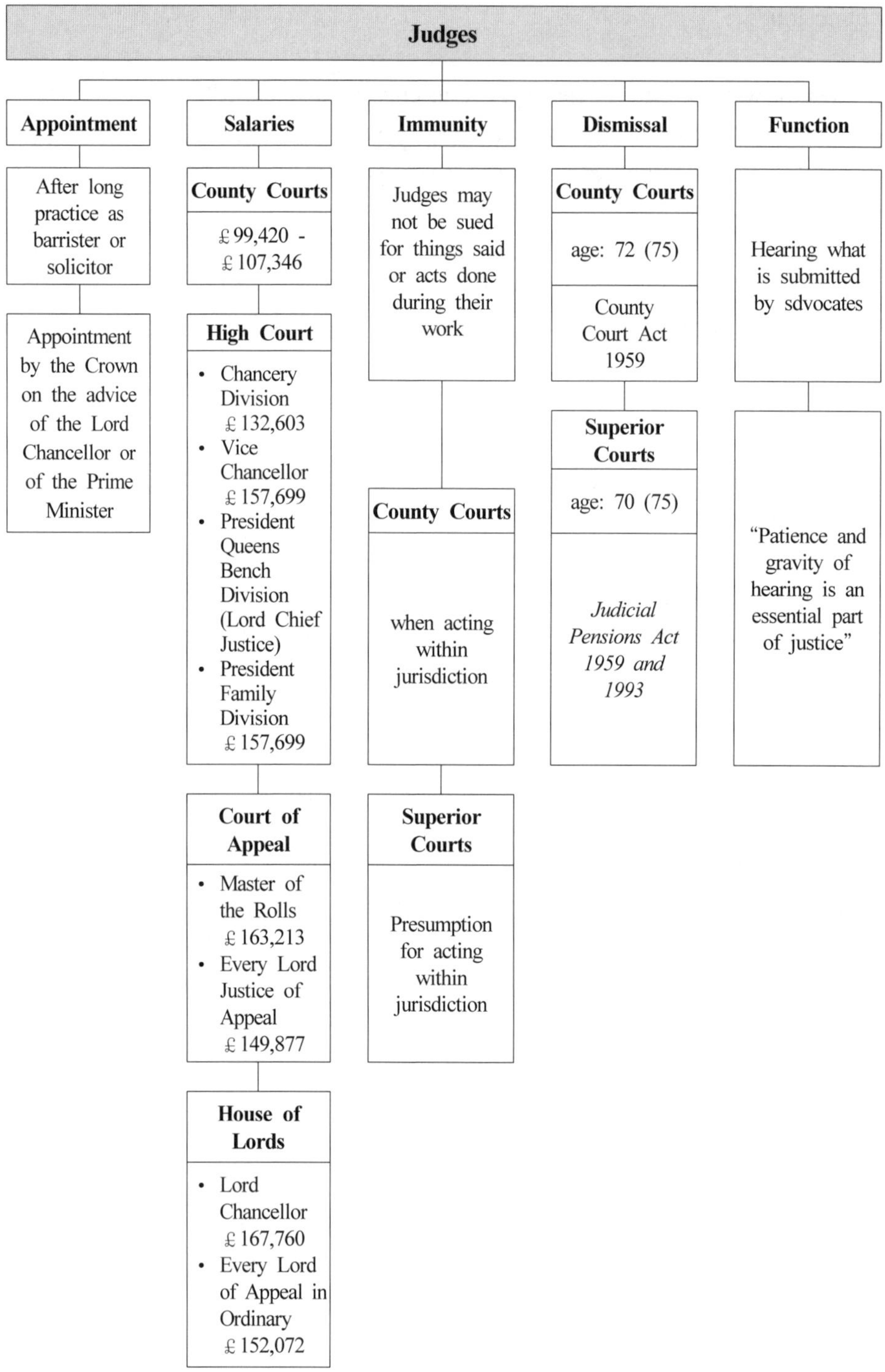
Judges
Appointment
After long practice as barrister or solicitor
Appointment by the Crown on the advice of the Lord Chancellor or of the Prime Minister
Salaries
County Courts
£99,420 - £107,346
High Court
• Chancery Division £132,603
• Vice Chancellor £157,699
• President Queens Bench Division (Lord Chief Justice)
• President Family Division £157,699
Court of Appeal
• Master of the Rolls £163,213
• Every Lord Justice of Appeal £149,877
House of Lords
• Lord Chancellor £167,760
• Every Lord of Appeal in Ordinary £152,072
Immunity
Judges may not be sued for things said or acts done during their work
County Courts
when acting within jurisdiction
Superior Courts
Presumption for acting within jurisdiction
Dismissal
County Courts
age: 72 (75)
County Court Act 1959
Superior Courts
age: 70 (75)
Judicial Pensions Act 1959 and 1993
Function
Hearing what is submitted by sdvocates
"Patience and gravity of hearing is an essential part of justice"

Ⅴ. Other personnel of English law

1. The Attorney-General and the Solicitor-General

왕립변호인
부(副)왕립변호인

The Attorney-General is an elected member of the House of Commons who is also an eminent barrister. The same applies to the Solicitor-General, who is his deputy. Both belong to the majority party in Parliament and are appointed by the Prime Minister. Consequently they both resign with a change of the government of which they form part. The principal duty of the Attorney-General is to act as legal adviser of to government departments and to represent the Crown whenever a case involves public rights.

선출위원
뛰어난
대리인, 부(副)
여당
사임하다

2. The Director of Public Prosecutions

형사소추

As there is no official in England and Wales comparable with the continental public prosecutor, the Director of Public Prosecutions (created by the *Prosecution of Offences Act 1879*, amended by the *Prosecution of Offences Act 1985*) is concerned essentially with *giving advice* to the police and other bodies on the conduct of prosecution.

검찰
범죄
관청 / 형사소추

The Director of Public Prosecutions should be an eminent lawyer, solicitor or barrister of ten years' standing, but not an elected politician.

10년 경력의

As his activities belong to criminal law they are not further described here.

3. Magistrates

평화판사

Magistrates, or as the older term goes "justices of the peace" can be either unpaid lay judges or professional salaried lawyers.

평화판사
명예직 일반인 판사 / 월급을 받는

Professional magistrates, known as "stipendiary magistrates", are appointed by the Crown upon the recommendation of the

유급의
추천에 따라

Lord Chancellor, from among barristers or solicitors of at least seven years' standing.

As already mentioned the majority of magistrates' work relates to criminal law.

Civil cases which are treated in Magistrates' Courts concern such varied matters as domestic proceedings, licensing, rating and affiliation.

가사소송 / 인허가
지방세 / 친부인지

Notation

부가설명

The operation of the civil courts has now been affected by the implementation of the "*Woolf Report*": in July 1996, *Lord Woolf* M.R., published his blueprint for radical reform of the civil justice process. The precise way in which the jurisdiction on the civil courts will be altered remain to be seen.

시행
초안
변경하다 / 기다려볼 일이다

VI. Further reading[1)]

Baker, An Introduction to English Legal History; *Bernstorff, Graf von*, Einführung in das englische Recht; *Cownie & Bradney*, English Legal System in Context; *Cracknell*, English Legal System ("Cracknell's Law Students' Companion" = cases and statutes); *Darbyshire*, Nutshells: English Legal System; *Denham*, Law — A Modern Introduction; *Eddey,* On the English Legal System; *Elliott & Quinn*, English Legal System; *Goodmann*, The Walking Guide to LAWYER's LONDON; *Harris*, An Introduction to Law; *Henrich,* Einführung in das englische Privatrecht; *Partington*, Introduction to the English Legal System; *Rivlin*, First Steps in the Law; *Slapper & Kelly*, English Law; *Slapper & Kelly*, On English Legal System; *Smith & Bailey*, On the Modern English Legal System; *Templeman & Reed*, English Legal System, Textbook —, Casebook —, Revision Work Book; *Wörlen*, Grundlagen und Entwicklung der juristischen Berufe, in England, JA 1978, 165 ff. und 384 ff.; *Zweigert/Kötz*, Einführung in die Rechtsvergleichung.

1) Cf. footnote on p. 23.

Chapter Four

"How to find the law"

In Chapter One, dealing with the classification and the sources of English law, the importance of cases and statutes as sources of law was explained.

To further your studies in English law you should know how to find reports of cases and copies of statutes. What follows in this chapter is an attempt to introduce you to the major series of law reports and to the consolidated statutes.

To further: 지속하다, 확대하다
reports: 보고문
attempt: 시도
law reports / consolidated statutes: 판결모임집, 판례집 / 법률모음집

Ⅰ. Law reports

1. Introduction

A full law report nowadays generally includes the following information:

- The names of the parties
- (Appeals to the House of Lords have since 1974 carried the same title as in the court of first instance. It is important to note here that previously it was the name of the appellant which appeared first, but now that is no longer the case.
  Example: If *Smith* was the plaintiff at first instance and *Johnson* the defendant, the case was called *Smith* v *Johnson*. Now suppose that *Johnson* appeals against the judgment of the court of first instance, he becomes automatically the appellant. Before 1974 the name of the case would have changed to *Johnson* v *Smith*. Since 1974 its name remains *Smith* v *Johnson*);
- the court in which the case was decided;
- the name of the judge or judges;
- the date or dates of the hearing;
- the headnote

appellant: 항소원고
hearing: 기일, 재판
headnote: 판결의 요지

(a summary of the decision given by the reporter); 배석판사(보고자)
- a list of precedents cited and discussed;
- the history of the case in litigation
(including a summary of the claims made and the result of proceedings in lower courts);
- the facts
(the facts stated in the judgments may be unedited or the reporter may set out the facts separately); 미출판의
- the name(s) of counsel (= barristers);
- the arguments of counsel
(these are only regularly printed in a few sets of reports, e.g. "The Law Reports"; interjections from the bench may also be included); 초안
- the judgment or judgments
(in full reports these are printed verbatim, otherwise only summaries are given); 말을 그대로 옮긴
- the order of the court and an indication of whether leave to appeal was granted or refused; 법원의 구성 / 언급 항소의 허가
- the names of the solicitors;
- the name of the barrister (or other reporter) who reports the case.

As indicated by the term "report", law reports are not an official collection of case decisions published by a court or a judge, but private editions made by lawyers, who are usually barristers. This is due to the fact that no English judge is obliged to write down his decision. ~에 기인하다

2. Law reporting

Law reports are reports of the more important cases decided by the superior courts. Not all cases are reported, rather only those of legal interest. Most of the reported cases are decisions of the House of Lords, which are, as you have learnt, absolutely binding on all lower courts. Of the decisions of the Court of Appeal only about 25% are published and only about 10% of those of the High Court of Justice. 법적 이해, 법적 이익

There are no reports of the cases decided by the inferior

courts (which make up about 95% of all English judgments)!

The reports may be divided very roughly into "the old" and "the new". The old run from the time of *Henry VIII* (1491-1547) to 1865 and the new from then to the present time.

대략의

a) Pre-1865 Reports

The earliest law reports — before *Henry VIII's* time were contained in the "Year Books", compiled annually between the thirteenth and sixteenth centuries.

모으다

These reports concentrated upon points of procedure and pleading rather than the final decisions of the courts, and were written first in Norman French and later in "law French" (a mixture of English, French and Latin). They are today mainly of interest to legal historians, and it is highly unlikely that you — studying English law — will ever need to consult them!

소송의 요점과 변론

법사학자 / 매우 개연성이 낮은

자문을 구하다, 참고하다

Between the sixteenth and nineteenth centuries a large number of "private" or "nominate reports" appeared. They were produced chiefly by private reporters in their own names. They varied widely in their style and content, their accuracy and their reputation. Some, such as those of *Coke*, *Plowden* and *Saunders* were of high authority. Others were regarded as of little value, in particular those of *Barnadiston* and *Espinasse.*

주로

구별되다 / 내용

정확성

In the eighteenth century, *Barnadiston* reported some of the decisions of the King's Bench (ranging from 1726 to 1734) in two volumes. When this reporter was cited by a barrister (named *Preston*) before Lord *Lyndhurst*, the latter exclaimed: "Barnadiston, Mr. Preston! I fear that this is a book of no great authority; I recollect in my younger days, it was said of Barnadiston, that he was accustomed to slumber over his notebook, and wags in the rear took the opportunity of scribbling nonsense in it".

소리치다

기억을 하다, 되돌아 보다

익숙하다 / 선잠이 들다

엉덩이의 꼬리

낙서하다

Also Espinasse who reported between 1793 and 1807 Nisi Prius cases did not escape judicial condemnation. The famous

아직 최종적으로 결정되지 아니한 사례들 / 법원의 / 비난

English jurist *Pollock* (1783-1870) said of him that he heard only half of what went on in court and *reported the other half*! *Espinasse* got another kick by Justice *Maule*, who, when a case in which Espinasse was referred to, said with some emphasis that he did not care for Espinasse "or any other ass"!

(무슨 일이) 있었는지
공격을 받다
강조 / 신경쓰다
멍청이(욕설의 하나)

Stories such as those of *Barnadiston* and *Espinasse* are related in English law textbooks to put the student on his guard when dealing with some of the old reports.

보고되다 / (학생들에게) 주의를 주다

In the eighteenth century the focus of attention switched from pleadings to court decisions and the best reports included the full reasons. Many of these reports are of high quality. The first to be published in more or less the form we have today, although not verbatim reports, in this period were *Burrow's* reports. The first that regularly published reports of recently decided cases were *Dunford and East's* "Term Reports".

관심의 중심 / 바뀌다
문자 그대로의
최근

The private reports are cited by the name, usually abbreviated, of the reporter or reporters the volume and the page. (The year is not technically part of the reference but is normally included.) A series of reports of the nineteenth century, for example, of *Barnewall and Adolphus*' is abbreviated "*B. & Ad.*" If, for instance, your reference is "1 B. & Ad. 289, it means volume one of *Barnewall and Adolphus*' *Reports* at page 289. If you use one of the older reports you will regularly find a corresponding list of abbreviations at the end of the report or its last volume.

축약한
서류번호
약어

Most of the cases in the private reports were reprinted in "*The English Reports*" (abbreviated E.R.) published in 178 volumes between 1900 and 1930; volumes 177 and 178 contain a complete index of all cases in the reprint.

다시 인쇄한
재쇄

Together with "The English Reports" is supplied a chart, indicating the volume of the "E.R." in which some old

공급하다 / 챠트

reports are to be found in a slim volume at the end of the series of the "E.R.".

Should you ever be lucky enough, for example during a scholarship of studying English law in the United Kingdom you will surely find the chart hanging in the library of your law school or university.)

장학금 / 연합 왕국(Great Britain 전체를 지칭)

b) "The modern period" (since 1865)

The modern period of law reporting began after 1865, when, as the result of a general demand from the legal profession, the "General Council of Law Reporting" was set up. The reason was that the patchwork coverage of private (enterprise) law reports was seen to be unsatisfactory. The Council formed in 1865, consisted of the Attorney-General, the Solicitor-General, two barristers from each of the "Inns of Court", two seargants and two solicitors. This body was constituted as a self supporting commercial enterprise whose function has always been that of issuing a series of "Law Reports" (L.R.) which are 'authorized' as semi-official reports.

누더기, 짜깁기
간주되다
단체, 구성체, 몸
설립하다
반(半) 공식적인

The old private reports ceased soon after this Council came into being. In 1870 the Council was incorporated as "The Incorporated Council of Law Reporting of England and Wales". Its primary object was to be:

> ... "the preparation and publication in a convenient form, at a moderate price, and under gratuitous professional control of reports of judicial decisions of the Superior and Appellate Courts of England."

발효하다, 시작하다 / 통합되다, (회사로) 등록설립되다
주된
적절한
저렴한 / 무상의

The Council is not funded by the state and is non-profit-making. Its reports are, as mentioned above, semi-official, because judgments appearing in *The Law Reports* are checked by the judges. Therefore this series should be cited in preference to any alternative. Today *The Law Reports* are classified into the following divisions:

지원받다
우선적으로
~로 분류되다

- Chancery Division (Ch.) – reports of cases in the Chancery Division of the High Court and cases appealed from there to the Court of Appeal.

- Queen's Bench (Q.B.) — reports of cases in the Queen's Bench Division of the High Court and cases appealed from there to the Court of Appeal.
- Family Division (Fam.) — reports of cases in the Family Division of the High Court and cases appealed from there to the Court of Appeal.
  — Until 1972 the Family Division was Probate, Divorce and Admiralty Division (P.) —
- Appeal Cases (A.C.) — reports of cases in the Court of Appeal, the House of Lords and the Privy Council.

The first three series contain judgments at first instance in the three Divisions, and also judgments on appeal to the Court of Appeal. If a further appeal is taken from the Court of Appeal to the House of Lords, the decision of the Lords will be reported in the fourth series called the Appeal Cases.

In addition to these semi-official "Law Reports" there is, nowadays, a wide range of privately-published law reports. Most of these series concentrate upon a particular area of legal developments (e.g., the law concerning industrial relations or the law relating to road traffic).

~이외에도
폭넓은, 다양한
특별한 영역
노동법
도로교통법

However, there are two series which publish cases dealing with decisions affecting a wide field of legal issues. The general series, with which most students of law will quickly become familiar, are the "*Weekly Law Reports*" *(W.L.R.)* and the "*All England Law Reports*" *(All E.R.)*

~에 관한

Each of these series reports cases with full reasons.
There are, in addition, some sources which provide a short summary of, or extracts from judgments given.

생략하지 아니한 판결이유
초록

Moreover it is possible to find short reports of case developments in a variety of sources. The most up-to-date of these sources are those newspapers which print law reports. Most of the quality daily newspapers contain law reports as well as news items on matters of legal interest. *The Times* has

판례의 발전, 경향
다양성 / 최신의
진지한 일간지(흥미위주 일간지에 대칭하는 말) / 주제들

contained such reports for the longest period and is regarded as being the most authoritative source of such reports.

This survey should be enough for Korean and German students. Maybe it was already a bit too much! But I hope that some readers may be interested to know more than just what is compulsory. 개략

Those students wishing to know more about law reports and about "how to find the (English) law" (should read the relevant passages on "Law Reports" in *Glanville Williams, Learning the Law*, who suggests (on page 37 – see "Further reading") useful handbooks of law reports. Even from this "Introduction to English Civil Law" itself you should gain information about finding references and using law reports. 원하는 / 추천하다

3. How to use law reports

Every case which is reported in a series of law reports can be referred to by way of the names of the parties concerned in the action. Thus, where a court action is brought by someone called *Johnson* in dispute with someone called *Smith*, the case is referred to as *Johnson* v *Smith*. Referring to a case in this way, however, is of limited usefulness. The reference does not tell the reader the date of the case nor does it indicate the series of reports in which it can be found. It does not even tell us which case involving a *Johnson* and a *Smith* the reader is being referred to. Thus, in addition to its name, each reported case possesses a unique reference indicator. This normally (although not always in the same order) includes: ~을 통하여, (이름을) 인용하여 / 분쟁중인 / 어느 정도만 유용한 / 언급하다, 언급되다 / 가지다 / 독특한 사건번호

(1) A date (year) reference. Some series have a volume number for each year. Where the date reference tells you the year in which the case was reported the date is normally enclosed in square brackets. 대괄호
(2) A reference to the volume number (if there is more than one volume of the particular law reports series in

the year concerned).
(3) A reference to the (abbreviated) title of the series of law reports in which the report is to be found.
(4) A reference to the page or paragraph number at which
the report of the case may be located. 위치하다

If the case of *Johnson* v *Smith* is reported in the first volume of the *Weekly Law Reports* for 1962, at page 739, the reference would be:

Johnson v *Smith* [1962] 1 W.L.R. 739.

This is usually called the citation for the case. 인용(방식)

Knowing this reference or citation, it is possible to go to
the shelves of the law library, which house the volumes of 포함하다, 가지고 있다
this law report series, and to turn directly to the report of the case.

If you know only the names of the parties in the case you
will need first to ascertain the specific reference. Although 조사하다
indexes may help in such instances, still the approach could 접근하다
be said to be quite inefficient and time-consuming. Normally, 비효율적인 / 시간을 낭비하는
therefore, recourse is had to a general reference manual, ~을 사용하다, 의지하다 /
which is known as a case citator. Such a case citator is 참고서 / 사례인용집
provided by the commercial reference service known as
Current Law. 최신법(서비스의 명칭)

The Current Law system of citations for cases works
through a combination of three separate reference items: 참고서

(1) Two (hard-bound) volumes covering the periods 1947-1976 and 1977-1988. 하드커버로 제본된
(2) A laminated volume covering the period from 1989 (one volume for every year). 플라스틱 파일철
(3) "Monthly parts", which are issued regularly in 월간지
pamphlet form, for the current year. 팸플릿, 얇은 책자

The importance of using all three items to complement one 부분 / 서로 보충하다
another will appear when we consider the problem of
locating up-to-date references: Entries in the *Current Law* 찾다 / 등록정보들
Case Citator are listed by the titles of cases, arranged

alphabetically. Thus, to find the law reports reference to the case *Johnson* v *Smith* you need to turn to the alphabetical heading under "Johnson". There you can find: 표제

> *Johnson* v *Smith* [1962] 1 W.L.R. 739; 106 S.J. 507; [1962] 1 All E.R. 225, C.A. – Digested 62/1249: Referred to 72/2355. 요약된

What can we discover from this information? 읽어내다, 찾아내다

We discover not only the law reports reference to the first volume of the *Weekly Law Reports* for 1962, at page 739, but also that there are reports of the same case in:

> 106 S.J. 507 – which means the 106th volume of the *Solicitors' Journal* at page 507, and [1962] 1 All E.R. 225 – meaning the first volume of the *All England Law Reports* for 1962, at page *225.*

We are also informed that the court which delivered the decision was

> C.A. – which means the Court of Appeal.

Furthermore, we are told that a digest of the case has been included in a companion volume to the *Current Law Case Citator* at: 요약본

> 62/1249 – which means the companion year volume of *Current Law* for 1962 at paragraph 1249.

Finally we learn that the case was "referred to" in another case and that this other case is to be found at:

> 72/2355 – which means the companion year volume of *Current Law* for 1972 at paragraph 2355.

II. Statutes

The second principal source of English law (besides precedents) is undoubtedly statute law.

1. Statute collections

English statutes have been published since 1483, partly in annual volumes, partly in single issues. As the statute books of previous years are difficult to find, it is convenient to use the official publication "Statutes in Force". This is arranged in encyclopaedic form and in loose-leaf binders, where some statutes are reprinted with amendments from time to time.

법률모음집
편리한, 적절한
현행법(공인 법령집의 명칭)
여러 권으로 된 백과사전식 / 낱장 파일철 / 개정사항들

The defect of the official "Statutes in Force" is that it does not provide proper annotations to the statutes. For these you have to use *Halsbury's Statutes of England*, consisting of 50 volumes, which are updated in loose-leaf-binders.

하자
적절한 주석
최신상태로 만들다

In both publications (the official "Statutes in Force" and Halsbury's), statutes are divided alphabetically into subject-groups.

주제별 분류

If, for example, the statute you are looking for obviously belongs to a particular subject, like "contract", take the corresponding volume of the collection and open it at the title "contract".

For the names of statutes that have received the royal assent since the last supplement of "Statutes in Force" and "Halsbury's", consult the current numbers of the "*Current Law Statute Citators*", one from 1947-1971 and one from 1971 onwards.

Statutes since 1947 are better consulted in the annual volumes of "*Current Law Statutes Annotated*" than in the official annual edition. This is published in parts which are

찾을 수 있는
주석이 달린

subsequently bound into a volume for the year. Amendments, etc., can be traced through the above mentioned *Current Law Statute Citators*. 추적하다

2. Methods of citation 인용방법

Statutes are cited in three ways:

(1) By the short title which includes the calendar year (e.g. *Fatal Accidents Act 1846* – which was, by the way, replaced by the *Fatal Accidents Act 1959*). 사망사고에 관한 법률

(2) By the regnal year or years and the chapter (e.g. "9 & 10 Vict. c. 93", which is pronounced as "the statute nine and ten Victoria, chapter 93" or "the ninth and tenth Victoria, chapter 93". The meaning of this citation is that the Act received the royal assent in the session of Parliament beginning in the ninth year of Queen *Victoria's* reign (1837-1901) and concluding in her tenth year, being the ninety-third statute passed in that session. 통치년 완료하다, 매듭짓다 회기
Another example: "14 & 15 Geo. VI, c. 15" is the fifteenth statute in the session of Parliament beginning in the fourteenth year of King *George* VI's reign (1937-1952) and concluding in his fifteenth year. Since not everybody knows by heart the regnal years of the English queens and kings, this method of citation often requires a time-consuming search.

(3) By a compromise of the first two methods (e.g. the *Fatal Accidents Act 1846* (c.93) this method has been preferred since 1963. Statutes are only cited with the short title and the year and chapter numbers referring to the year. So the *Fatal Accidents Act 1846* (c. 93) is the ninety-third statute passed in the year 1846, or the *Administration of Justice Act 1960* (c. 65) is the sixty-fifth statute passed in the year 1960.

The text of a statute consists of sections which are divided 조(條)

into sub-sections. The sections have numbers but are not denoted by section marks as they are in German statutes. Sub-sections are also numbers and are usually cited within round brackets. Thus, a special provision is cited for instance: *Family Law Reform Act 1969, s. 1 (2)*, which means section one, sub-section two.

항(項)
조(條)표식 = §

Ⅲ. Further reading[1)]

Black's Legal Reader – an Introduction to the Anglo-American Law and Legal System; *Bradney/Cownie/Masson/Neal/Newell*, How to Study Law; *Templeman/ Evans*, Legal Skills and System – Textbook –; *Williams*, Learning the Law.

1) Cf. footnote on p. 23.

Part Two: Specific branches of law

Chapter Five

Persons in law

Ⅰ. Introduction

Persons are regarded in law as subjects who possess certain rights and owe certain duties.

권리의 주체가 되다
의무를 가지다

Generally speaking an adult human being is a legal person and may be referred to as a "natural person".

성인 / 법적 주체(주의: "법인"이 아님) / 언급되다, 취급되다 / 자연인

It is also possible, however, that a legal person may not be a single human being. In fact various corporations and incorporated associations attach to themselves similar rights and duties as are attached to ordinary human beings. These legal persons are called "juristic persons". In English law such corporations are formed by charter, statute or registration under the *Companies Act 1985* or previous Acts; there is also the common law concept of the corporation sole.

법인회사, 법인체
자본회사 / 요구하다
법인
설립허가서 / 등기, 등재
법인격을 가진 1인(人) 인적회사

Moreover it should be noted that even with regard to human beings the law distinguishes between certain classes, and ascribes to some a "status" which may carry with it a more limited set of rights and duties than are ascribed to the normal adult.

~에 관하여
~에 속하는 것으로 하다 / 법적 지위

These classes are unborn persons, minors, persons of unsound mind, bankrupts and aliens.

태아 / 미성년자 / 정신지체자 / 파산자 / 외국인

Animals are not legal persons but legal objects (things). However, animals may be protected by the law in certain respects, e.g. against cruelty.

법적 객체
보호하다
잔혹함

II. Natural persons

1. Unborn persons

As in continental legal systems, in English law, too, even before birth a human being is not without legal recognition. In England antenatal life is protected by the *Infant Life Preservation Act 1929.*

법적 인정
출생전
보호

In the law of property and the law of succession a child conceived, but not yet born will be treated as if it has been born. At any rate it should be so treated for its own sake.

수태한 상태의
이익, 유익

For example, even a bequest to children "born previously to the date of my death" will include a child conceived before this date and born within due time afterwards. However, if the child is not born alive, things will remain as if it had never existed.

유증
시한 내에, 적시에

2. Infants and minors

a) Minority and majority

From the moment of birth till the age of 18, a child is considered to be an infant or a minor. Thus, minority ceases at the age of 18.

멈추다

The age of majority was reduced from 21 to 18 by the *Family Law Reform Act 1969.* Section 1 (1) of this Act provides that as from 1 January 1970, a person

> "shall attain full age on attaining the age of eighteen instead of on attaining the age of twenty-one; and a person shall attain full age on that date if he has then already attained the age of eighteen but not the age of twenty-one."

가족법개정법
규정하다
도달하다
성년

(From this formulation you may conclude that English statutes like continental-european ones are very "precise".)

(문장)표현
정치(精緻)하다

The *Family Law Reform Act 1969* section 9 (1) provides

further that

> "the time at which a person attains a particular age expressed in years shall be the <u>commencement</u> of the relevant <u>anniversary</u> of the date of his birth". 시작 / 기념일

That means, as indicated above, for instance: a child born on 26 July 1982, will reach his or her majority at the very first moment of 26 July 2000.

b) Rights and liabilities of minors under the civil law

(aa) *Law of contract*

A contract between an adult and a minor is binding on the adult, but is not binding on the minor, unless it is for <u>necessaries</u> (e.g. food, clothes) or for the minor's <u>benefit</u> (e.g. <u>training and education</u>). 생필품 / 이익 / 직업훈련과 학업

A minor may make contracts to <u>acquire movable personal property</u> (CD-players, books, etc.), but a minor cannot legally buy or <u>dispose of</u> land. 동산소유권을 취득하다 / ~을 처분하다

Thus, under English civil law, <u>legal capacity</u> is a <u>basic precondition</u> of making contracts. But the consequences of <u>lacking legal capacity</u> are quite different from German or Korean civil law. We will deal with this subject in our next chapter on "The law of contract". 행위능력 / 기본 전제조건 / 행위능력을 결함

(bb) *Law of <u>torts</u>* 불법행위

Torts are civil <u>wrongs</u> which are not breaches of contract or <u>trust</u>. 불법 / 신탁관계

Minors are not so well protected with regard to liability in tort. <u>In principle</u> a minor is <u>liable</u> for all the torts he or she <u>commits</u>. 기본적으로 / 책임이 있는 / 범하다

Usually a minor is without <u>means</u>, and – unless a parent or <u>guardian</u> is directly and personally involved in the <u>commission</u> of the tort an <u>injured</u> party is left without remedy since <u>a parent</u> or guardian as such is not liable. Details about the position and liability of minors in respect 수단 / 보호인, 후견인 / (불법행위를) 범함 / 피해받은 / 부모 일방

of torts will be considered in Chapter Seven.

(cc) *Property rights* 물권

A minor may own all kinds of personal or movable property, but cannot legally own land (*Law of Property Act 1925*, s. 19).

소유하다

(dd) *Litigation right* 재판수행권

A minor may not personally bring a civil action, but must do so through a "next friend" (usually a parent). Where a minor is sued he must defend an action through a responsible person acting as his *guardian ad litem*. Minors under 17 may not apply for legal aid, but their parents or guardians may do so on their behalf.

민사사건을 제소하다
제소를 당하다, 피소를 당하다
소송후견인
법률규제를 신청하다
그들(미성년자)의 이름으로

(ee) *Marriage* 혼인, 결혼

Minors under 16 years of age cannot marry – as under German law – and may only do so under 18 if they have the written consent of their parents or a magistrate.

후견판사

(ff) *Wills*

Minors have no legal capacity to make a valid will. Where, however, they are serving as a member of H.M. Forces on military service, or as a mariner or seaman at sea they may make an informal will.

유효한
선원

c) Miscellaneous rights and liabilities of minors outside civil law

다양한

(aa) *Voting* 선거권, 투표권

Under the *Representation of the People Act 1969* (since consolidated within the *Representation of the People Act 1983*) young people cannot vote at a local or parliamentary election until they are 18 and their names appear on the electoral role.

합쳐진
선거인 명부

(bb) *Criminal law*

A child under 10 years of age is not criminally liable for any offence or crime, and cannot, therefore, be convicted.

형사적 책임을 지는
(경한) 범죄 / (중한) 범죄 / 유죄판결을 빋

Between 10 and 14 a child is presumed incapable of forming the intention of committing a crime or an offence.[1] But this presumption may be rebutted, if the court finds that such a child knew his conduct to be wrongful.

짐작하다, 추정하다 / 무능력한
고의를 가지다
추정 / 반증하다
불법성을 인식하다

Children over the age of 14 are in principle liable for criminal acts, but special procedures are taken with regard to their trial and punishment.

범죄 / 특별한 절차를 취하다
재판 / 처벌

(cc) *Passports*

A British passport may be obtained at the age of 16. Children under this age are usually enlisted in their parent's passport. This rule has been changed recently: if parents obtain a new passport they must obtain passports for each child.

여권
열거하다

(dd) *Driving*

Persons under 17 may not hold a driving licence to drive a car or motorcycle on the road. A minor aged 16, however, may obtain a licence to drive a moped.

운전면허증

(ee) *"Enjoyments" (civil liberties)*

유흥

- Persons under 14 are not allowed in public bars or restaurants where *alcoholic drinks* are offered (= licensed premises). Where food is served, younger children maybe admitted.
- Persons over 14 and under 18, although allowed to enter a bar may not be served with, or drink alcohol.
- It is not an offence for persons under 16 *to smoke*, but shopkeepers may not sell cigarettes or tobacco to persons apparently under that age.
- Persons under 18 may not see *films* certified as "18" and minors under 15 may not see films certified as "15".
- Persons under the age of 18 are not allowed in betting shops, *gambling* clubs or casinos, and they may not gamble in bars of licensed premises. A person under 16 may not buy a National Lottery ticket.

주류판매가 허용된 음식점
명백한
인증받은
내기
도박
도박하다
국영 복권

1) This rule has changed by s. 34 of the *Crime and Disorder Act 1998*.

Diagram 16

Infants and Minors

Minority and majority: Minority ceases at 18 = children born on 26 July 1982 will reach majoritiy at the very first moment of 26 July 2000

Rights and Liabilities of Minors under Civil Law

Law of Contract

- Minors are only bound by contract for necessaries or to their benefit.
- Minors may make contracts on movable property, but not dispose of land.
- Legal capacity is different from German civil law.

Law of torts

- Minors are in principle liable for all torts, unless a parent or a guardian is in-volved.

Property Law

- Minors may own all kinds of movable property, but not land.

Litigation/Process

- Minors can only bring civil actions through a "next friend" (parent, guardian)
- Defence by *guardian ad litem*

Marriage

- not under 16
- 1618: with written consent (parent/ma-gistrate)

Wills

- no legal capacity
- exception: military service or mariner

Miscellaneous Rights and Liabilities of Minors outside Civil Law

Voting

- not before having reached majority

Criminal Law

- under 10 no criminal liability
- 10-14: conduct to be wrongful is decisive
- 14-18: liable, but special trial and punishment

Passport at age of 16

Driving: 16: mopeds; 17: cars

Civil Liberties

- no visit to licensed premises ("pub") under 14
- 1418: allowed to vistit pubs, but not to drink alcohol
- smoking: shopkeepers may not sell cig. or tobacco to minors under 16
- films: limits are "15" and "18"
- Gambling: not allowed for minors

3. Persons of unsound mind

The legal capacity of the mentally ill varies between the different branches of law and, in many ways, it is similar to the capacity of children.	정신지체자
Regarding civil rights and liabilities, insanity has a very restricted operation. In general the *contract* made by a mentally disordered person is fully binding on him or her unless the other party was aware of the mental illness. This will be dealt with in more detail in Chapter Six concerning the law of contract.	정신병 제한적인 효과 정신장애가 있는 ~에 관한
Unless intent is necessary, a person of unsound mind would be liable in *tort* because the aim of the law of torts is to compensate the injured person, not to punish the person who committed the tort.	고의 보상하다
Litigation action on behalf of a person of unsound mind must be brought in the name of the next friend, or defended by a *guardian ad litem*.	소송행위 소송후견인
A *marriage* contracted by a person so insane at the time as not to appreciate the nature of the obligations of married life may be set aside at the suit of either party. The marriage of a person who has been judicially declared insane is totally void, and the same is said to be true of any *disposition of property* made by such a person.	평가하다 무효화하다 / 소를 통하여
As regards *criminal law* a person who can show that he or she did not understand, or did not know that he was doing wrong may plead insanity. In that case the English courts will decide using the so-called "McNaghten rules" Thereafter an accused person is presumed to be sane, until he or she can prove the contrary.	~에 관하여는 (재판정에서) 주장하다 피소된

Although criminal law is not the subject of this book I

will explain this point briefly because the formation of the "McNaghten rules" is a good example of the nature of common law as case law: In 1843, Daniel McNaghten, motivated by an insane delusion of persecution by Sir Robert Peel, killed Edward Drummond who was Peel's secretary.

발생

추격을 당한다는 병적 망상

McNaghten was acquitted on the grounds of insanity, and the House of Lords produced several rules, which are still applied today in criminal cases where insane persons are involved. As the rules were produced in the case *R.* v *McNaghten* (1843) they are known as the "McNaghten[1] rules".

무죄선고하다

Diagram 17

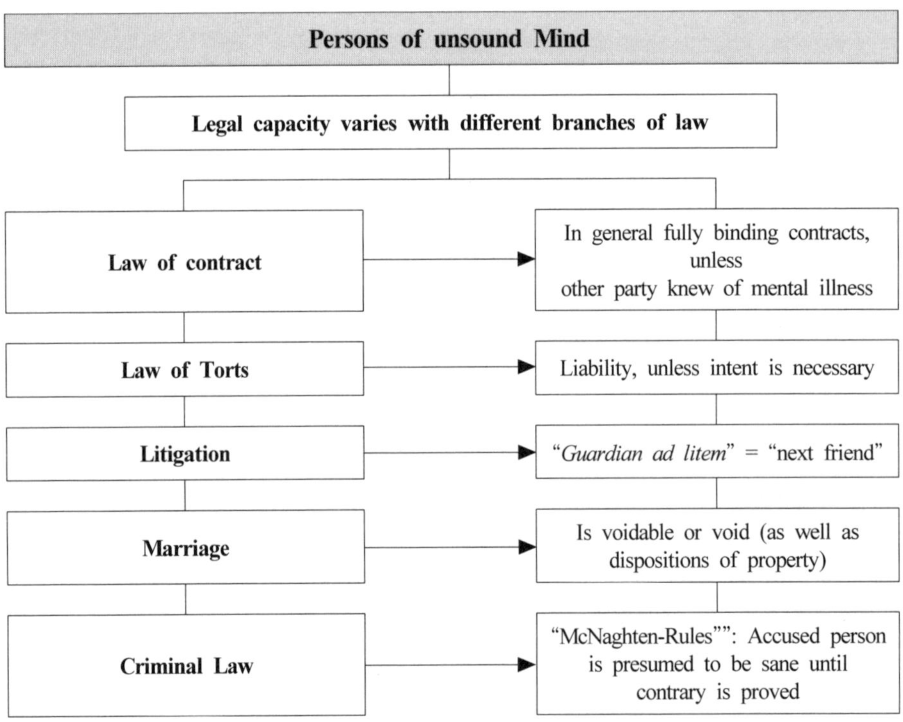

1) You can also find cited the name as M'Naghten: The spelling of the defendant's name has been almost as controversial as the state of his mind.

4. Bankrupts

파산자 / 지불불능자

The law relating to bankruptcy is now governed by the *Insolvency Act 1986*, but bankruptcies prior to 29 December 1986 still fall under the *Bankruptcy Act 1914*.

파산 / 규율하다
파산법 / 지불불능

The *Insolvency Act 1986* provides that an individual may be bankrupt if he cannot pay the debt claimed in the creditor's bankruptcy petition.

채권자의 / 파산신청

If the debt cannot be paid the courts will make a bankruptcy order, by which an outsider or the official receiver will determine the total amount of assets.

파산선고
파산관재인 / 자산

As in German law the assets, namely nearly everything owned privately or in business, are then distributed in a special order of preference. If there are no assets left for the unprivileged creditors, they receive nothing. When debtors are adjudicated bankrupts, they are disqualified from enjoying certain rights which they may have previously exercised:

우선순위, 서열
특혜가 없는 / 채무자
판결하다

- They cannot sit or vote in Parliament.
- They cannot become members of a local councils or justices of the peace. (지방의회)
- They may not be directors of a company or take part in its management.
- They may not obtain a loan over a certain amount or make a contract without declaring their bankruptcy. (대출)

Diagram 18

Bankrupts

An individual is bankrupt if he can not pay his debts to his creditors.

Bankrupts are disqualified from certain rights. They cannot

- sit or vote in Parliament.
  become a member of a local council or become a justice of the peace.
- be a director of a company or take part in its management.
- obtain a loan over a certain amount.
- make a contract without declaring their bankruptcy

5. Aliens

외국인

Aliens are persons who are not British citizens. Citizens of the Republic of Ireland are not treated as aliens. The following restrictions apply to aliens[1]:

- Aliens may not vote at local or parliamentary elections.
- They may not become Members of Parliament.
- They may not work in the United Kingdom without special permission.
- They must register with the police and notify changes of address to them. 경찰에 등록하다 / 알리다
- They are liable to deportation if they engage in crime. 추방

III. Juristic persons

As we have mentioned already, the concept of persons in law is not restricted to human beings. In every day life when one speaks of a "person" one means an individual human being, but in legal terminology the word has a different, and an older signification. 법률용어 의미

"*Person*" is derived from the Latin "*per*" (= "through") and "*sonare*" (= "to sound"), because in ancient times "*persona*" signified an actor's mask through which the sound of his voice came to the audience. According to *James* one can compare a lawsuit with a drama: "By a gradual transference" "*persona*" came to mean first the actor himself, as identified with his part, then in a legal sense it came to signify the subjects of legal rights and duties. In the course of this transference the word lost nothing of its original force because it came to denote, not an individual litigant as a *human being* but anybody or anything permitted to assert legal claims or be subjected to legal duties: on a legal "stage" the mask of personality does not therefore necessarily have to be worn by human beings. Thus, in a legal sense the word has come to mean something wider than simply a

배우의 / 관객 / 민사소송 / 점진적인 이행 / 역할 / 법적인 의미 / 의미하다 / 재판당사자 / 법적청구권을 주장하다 / 종속적인 / 무대 / (마스크를) 쓰다, 입다

1) Exceptions are made to EU nationals and Commonwealth citizens.

human individual. It means any individual, group, or even thing which the law will recognise as a bearer of legal rights and duties." (권리의무의) 주체, 담당자

This explains the existence of "juristic persons" in a very sophisticated, but at the same time clear manner. 정교한 / 동시에 / 분명한

Juristic persons, being subjects with "artificial personality" have to be distinguished from natural persons with "ordinary personality".

Artificial personalities in English law are sometimes also called corporations.

1. Corporations

A corporation is an artificial person, a legal entity, with a distinctive name, perpetual succession[1]) and a common seal. Corporations have a corporate legal existence completely separate from the human beings who created and administer them. There are two main classes of corporations: corporations "*sole*" and corporations "*aggregate*". 법적단위 구별가능한 이름 / 독자적인 법인격 / 일반적인 직인 / 법인의 설립하다, 창설하다 / 유지, 관리하다 / 1인 법인, 단독법인 / 집합법인, 다수인으로 구성된 법인

a) Corporation sole 단독법인

A corporation sole consists only of one person at any time. Examples include the Queen, and all bishops and parsons, all in their public capacity. It is, therefore, the title or the office which is the legal person, and the natural person holds the property and carries out the relevant duties while in office. When the holder dies, loses office, resigns or retires from office, the title passes to a successor and the corporation sole continues. The property and powers are vested in the new holder of the office. 목사 / 국가기관(의 자격)으로 수행하다 그만두다, 사임하다 은퇴하다 이전하다

b) Corporation aggregate 집합법인

A corporation aggregate consists of groups of people, such

1) 직역을 하자면 "끊임없는 계승" 정도로 이해할 수 있다. 법인이 그 구성원의 변동에도 불구하고 권리와 의무의 주체로서 지속적인 존재능력을 가지는 것을 강조하는 용어이다.

as the dean and the chapter, the chairman and members of public boards or the members of trading companies. 사제장과 사제회의 / 의장 공공이사회 / 상사회의

The corporation has a legal existence separate from the human membership, which may change from time to time, while the corporation remains unaffected. 영향을 받지 않는

c) Creation of corporations

(aa) *By Royal Charter*

Under common law the monarch has the power to create corporations at the royal pleasure. The monarch may grant a Royal Charter to groups of subjects who petition for purpose. Trading companies, in days of colonisation, such as the "Hudson Bay Company" and the "East India Company" were formed in this way, as well as the "British Broadcasting Corporation" (B.B.C.) in 1926. The method of creating new corporations by Royal Charter is also used to give corporate status to educational, charitable or scientific bodies, for example newly founded universities. 부여하다 왕의 문서 / 청원하다 교육의 / 공익적인

(bb) *By specific statute*

Some corporations are created by a specific Act of Parliament. The "National Coal Board" (which is now the "British Coal Corporation") for instance, was created by the *Industry Nationalization Act 1946*, and the "British Railways Board" by the *Transport Act 1962*. And unlike the B.B.C. the Independent Television Authority was established by the *Television Act 1984*. Another example is "British Telecom" which owes its existence to *British Telecommunications Act 1981*. 국립화, 국유화 ~와는 달리

(cc) *By registration under the Companies Acts*

(1) *Public limited company*

The *Companies Act 1985*, which replaced earlier Acts provides the means for a group of persons to create a corporation. Most registered corporations are trading companies wishing to acquire the advantages of limited liability. They are easily recognised by the last word of their name being 수단, 돈 획득하다

"Limited" (abbreviation: "Ltd."), e.g. "Johnson & Smith Ltd.".

The *Companies Act 1985* (s. 25) requires all new public companies of England as well as those already in existence to include at the end of their names "public limited company" or the abbreviation p.l.c. A public company must have a share capital of at least 50,000 of which not less than 25 % must be paid before the company is incorporated. A public company must have a minimum of two shareholders.

기초자본, 주식자본
자본회사로 등록하다
주주

(2) *Private company limited by shares* — 유한회사

A private company is a company also registered under the Companies Act without being a public company. The main difference from a public company is that its shares are not offered to the public. The shares are owned by a specific number of shareholders such as the members of a family or employees of the company.

근로자

Private companies must have a minimum of two members (there is no maximum), but there is no minimum capital required. They are guilty of an offence if they offer their shares or debentures to the public.

유책한 / (경한) 범죄
채무증서, 회사채, 사채(증서)

d) Effect of incorporation — 법인설립

Every corporation, whether a public or a private company, must be set up in accordance with the provisions of the Companies Act, and must therefore fulfil certain formal requirements.

설립하다 / 규정
형식적 요건

Registered companies' activities are regulated by two documents: The *Memorandum of Association*, which is the foundation document, and the *Articles of Association*.

정관
설립문서 / 회사설립계약

The Memorandum of Association, as the basis of a company's existence, governs the company's external activities. Its main clauses provide information on the name and address of the registered office of the company. In England and Wales (also in Scotland), the objects of the company, the members' limited liability and the company's share or capital structure.

규정하다 / 외부적 법률관계 (법률행위)
유한책임

These are the preconditions for the distinct existence of a corporation which has a legal personality separate from the individuals (members) who compose it. In English textbooks this is usually illustrated by reference to the following leading case.

***Example* — *Salomon* v *Salomon & Co. Ltd (1879)* — :**

Aaron Salomon, a boot manufacturer and leather merchant, incorporated his business as a limited company. The Memorandum of Association was signed by Salomon, his wife and five children, each holding one share. Salomon and his family held practically all the shares of the company and Aaron Salomon acted as its managing director. The company borrowed money from Salomon in his private capacity and issued debentures to him. The company failed and went into liquidation. The liquidator claimed that the company and Salomon were the same person and that the debenture held by Salomon should be set aside.

Held (by the House of Lords): that the company was a separate legal entity, different altogether from the members. So the company was an artificial person independent of Salomon, and the relationship between the company and him was one of debtor and creditor.

구두 생산자 / 가죽 상인
빌리다 / 개인자산
실패하다 / 청산하다
청산인
별도로 구별하다
채무자 / 채권자

The Articles of Association govern the internal administration of the company, on such matters as e.g. procedure of (shareholders') meetings, the appointment of directors and the amount of share capital including all rights and liability attached to the shares.

주주총회의 절차
이사들
결부된

Diagram 19

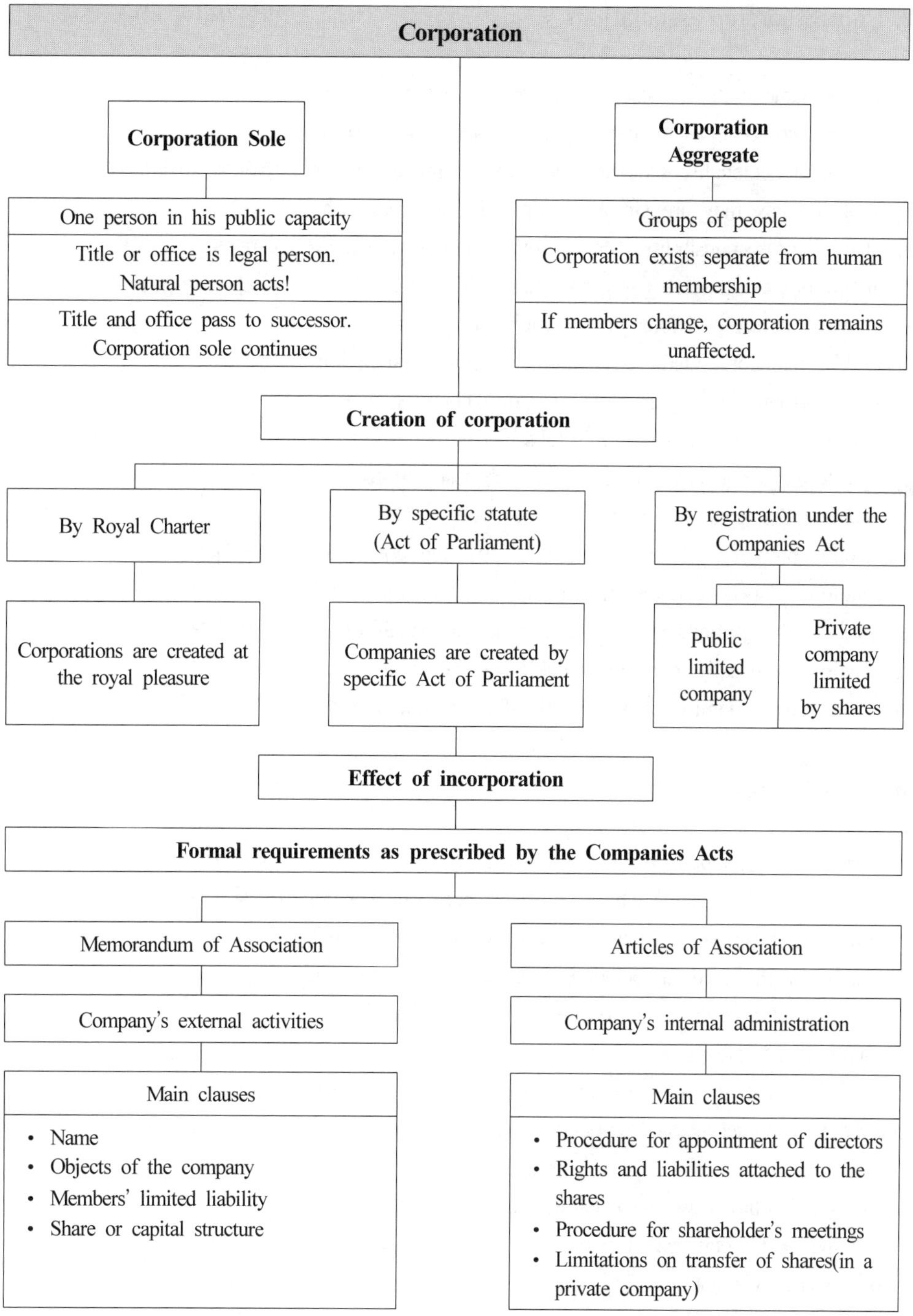
Corporation
Corporation Sole
One person in his public capacity
Title or office is legal person. Natural person acts!
Title and office pass to successor. Corporation sole continues
Corporation Aggregate
Groups of people
Corporation exists separate from human membership
If members change, corporation remains unaffected.
Creation of corporation
By Royal Charter
Corporations are created at the royal pleasure
By specific statute (Act of Parliament)
Companies are created by specific Act of Parliament
By registration under the Companies Act
Public limited company
Private company limited by shares
Effect of incorporation
Formal requirements as prescribed by the Companies Acts
Memorandum of Association
Company's external activities
Main clauses
• Name
• Objects of the company
• Members' limited liability
• Share or capital structure
Articles of Association
Company's internal administration
Main clauses
• Procedure for appointment of directors
• Rights and liabilities attached to the shares
• Procedure for shareholder's meetings
• Limitations on transfer of shares(in a private company)

2. Unincorporated associations

법인격없는 사단, 조합

As the name implies, these associations of natural persons differ from corporations in that they (the associations) do not have a legal personality separate from their members. In the eyes of the law they are simply groups of individuals who all share legal responsibility. Many groups of natural persons or institutions exist which carry out their affairs in much the same way as corporations, but which are in fact non-charitable unincorporated associations. These associations consist of groups of people operating with a common interest. Examples are tennis clubs, golf clubs and other sports or clubs catering for leisure activities. As such associations have no independent legal personality, their property is treated as the joint property of the members. An unincorporated association as such cannot own property. On the other hand, a member who purports to make a contract on behalf of his association is usually personally liable to the other party. And generally a member is also liable if he commits a tort.

법적인 의미에서
나누다
사업을 수행하다
공익의
여가클럽
공동의
의도하다

3. Partnerships

인적회사

A partnership is defined by the *Partnership Act 1890* (s. 1) as "the relationship which subsists between persons carrying on business in common with a view of profit", although incorporated associations are excluded. By the *Partnership Act 1890* s. 45 "business" includes every trade, occupation or profession.

정의하다
존재하다

The fact that the purpose of a partnership is business precludes an unincorporated association, such as a sports club for instance, being classed as a partnership.

목적
분류하다

The relationship between the partners may be created orally, in writing or by conduct. A partnership may therefore come into existence without a formal agreement. In practice, however, it will usually be constituted by a formal partnership agreement. This agreement only governs the relationship between the partners and do not affect the rights of third parties.

묵시적(인 행동)으로
인적회사설립계약

4. Differences between corporations and partnerships

The main distinctions between a partnership, which is collectively known as a "firm" [s. 4 (1) *Partnership Act 1890*], and a registered corporation are the following:

공동으로

a) Personality

A partnership has no legal personality apart from its constituent members whereas a corporation is considered as a separate legal entity.

정관의 규정에 따른 회원, 사원

b) Management

If there is no contrary agreement, all partners are entitled to participate in managing the business. The members of a corporation have no such right, because the right of management of the company is vested in its directors.

반대의 합의

무역하다, 양도하다

c) Contractual capacity

계약능력, 법률행위능력

Partners have the authority to enter into contracts on behalf of the partnership in the ordinary course of its business. Members of a corporation, however, are not allowed to make contracts on behalf of their corporation.

계약을 체결하다

d) Liability

책임

Because a partnership as such has no separate legal entity, all partners are liable, both individually and collectively, for legal liabilities of the firm.

e) Profit

A partnership must have the intention of making a profit. This is not necessary with a company.

이익획득의 의사, 의도

f) Members

A partnership may not generally have more than 20 members, but exceptions have been granted for certain

보장된, 부여된

professional groups, e.g. for solicitors!

g) Termination or dissolution

A partnership is dissolved by
- death or bankruptcy of a member,
- agreement, 계약, 합의
- expiry of the agreed period of its duration, 기간만료 / 합의한 기간
- the completion of the particular purpose for which the firm was formed, 이행
- order of a competent court, if it (the court) considers it "just and equitable" to do so. 정당하고 형평에 맞게

Companies are wound up either compulsorily or voluntarily. 청산하다 / 강제로 / 자발적으로

Compulsorily when creditors demand in court the dissolution of the company because it may be the only way of recovering the debts. Voluntarily, when the company decides to discontinue its existence. 중단하다

Diagram 20

Differences between **Corporation and Partnership**

Corporation		Partnership
Separate legal entity	**Personality**	No distinct legal personality from its members
Vested in directors	**Management**	Unless otherwise agreed: All members entitled
Corporation as a legal person	**Liability**	All partners are liable
Not necessary	**Profit**	Intention of making a profit
No maximum	**Members**	Not more than 20 – Exceptions admitted –
• Compulsory: at the suit of unpaid creditors • Voluntary: when the shareholders decide to wind up the company	**Termination/Dissolution**	• death or bankruptcy of a member • expiry of the agreed duration • order of court

5. Conclusion

In introductory English legal textbooks one may find various other types of associations, some that have their own legal personality (e.g. the registered joint stock company) others not (e.g. trade unions).

개론적인, 소개하는
주식회사
노조

Here it is not necessary to name them all, since we are mainly dealing with English *civil* law in general, not with its special branch *company* law in detail.

명명하다

Some associations have been selected for this chapter and presented to you to make clear the difference between the rights and duties of the different persons in law: natural persons, legal (juristic) persons and other (unincorporated) associations.

선발하다

Ⅳ. Further reading[1)]

Adams, Law for Business Students; *Barker & Padfield*, Law; *Brown*, GCSE Law; *Boucher & Corns*, GCSE Law Casebook; *Dobson & Schmitthoff,* Business Law; *Geldart*, Introduction to English Law; *James*' Introduction to English Law; *Kenny*, Studying Law; *Lyall*, An Introduction to British Law; *Sim & Scott's*, A Level English Law; *Rivlin*, First Steps in the Law; *Slapper & Kelly*; English Law; *Smith & Keenan*, English Law.

1) Cf. footnote on p. 23.

Chapter Six

The law of contract

Ⅰ. Introduction

The law of contract probably lies at the very heart of contemporary civil law. Therefore, this chapter will be more extensive than the others. On the other hand, due to the limits of such a book as regards its nature and length, one cannot enter deeply into the detail of all the complexities of such a vast branch of English civil law.

핵심
현대
포괄적인

If this work whets your appetite for more information you are advised to consult the books which are mentioned under "Further reading".

(구미를) 당기게 하다

Ⅱ. Historical background

In the first chapter it was stated that in no other legal system is the development of the law as closely associated with its historical background as in the English legal system. It was also stated that English law is based on legal rules which were first developed in the Middle Ages. Surprisingly enough, when considering the history of the law of contract one comes to the conclusion that a contract in the modern sense did not exist in early medieval times.

Nowadays a contract is defined as an agreement between two or more parties, who promise to give and to receive something from each other and who intend the agreement to be legally binding.

합의
법적 구속력이 있는

Under medieval English law a claim based on such a contract was not possible. Of course even in medieval times goods were exchanged and the buyer had to pay for them. However, when he refused to pay for delivered goods, the "contract" was not enforceable by the seller.

재화 / 교환하다
배송된
계약에 기초하여는 강제 또는 제소할 수 없었다

The action could only be brought for two reasons:

- The plaintiff (here seller) asserts that the defendant owes him a certain amount of money, because he received goods from him (the seller). In this case the plaintiff got a *writ of debt*, whereby the defendant was ordered to render the goods or pay a sum of money.
- The plaintiff asserts that the defendant has made to him a solemn covenant to do something special, that is a promise made under seal. Then he obtained a *writ of covenant*, whereby the defendant was ordered to keep the covenant.

주장하다
반환하다
(엄격한 형식의) 약속, 보장
약속 / 직인을 찍음

The *writ of debt* was issued when the goods had already been delivered.

The *writ of covenant* was issued because a *formal* promise from the defendant existed.

Thus, in both cases there was no agreement between the parties, no mutual consent, which today characterises a contract.

상호합의

Only in the course of the 15th and 16th centuries did it become possible to sound an action upon a breach of an informal promise. In this case the plaintiff got a *writ of assumpsit* (which is Latin meaning "he undertook"), whereby the defendant was ordered to effect performance, if the plaintiff could prove that damage had arisen from the breach of promise.

무형식의
"그가 (그것을) 부담하였다"
급부를 제공하다

By about the year 1600 the action for a writ of assumpsit had expanded to take over the work of the older actions based on debts and covenants, and gradually the term *contract* began to acquire its looser modern sense of agreement.

확대하다 / 부담하다
느슨한

However, we can still find this medieval differentiation in modern English law, where two classes of contracts exist: simple (informal) contracts, which must be supported by consideration, and formal contracts, which must be written, and also "signed, witnessed and delivered" (and do not need consideration).

지지하다(여기서는: 이행하다)
약인, 반대급부
증인이 서명하다 / 전달하다, 넘겨주다

This will be discussed in some of the following paragraphs.

Diagram 21

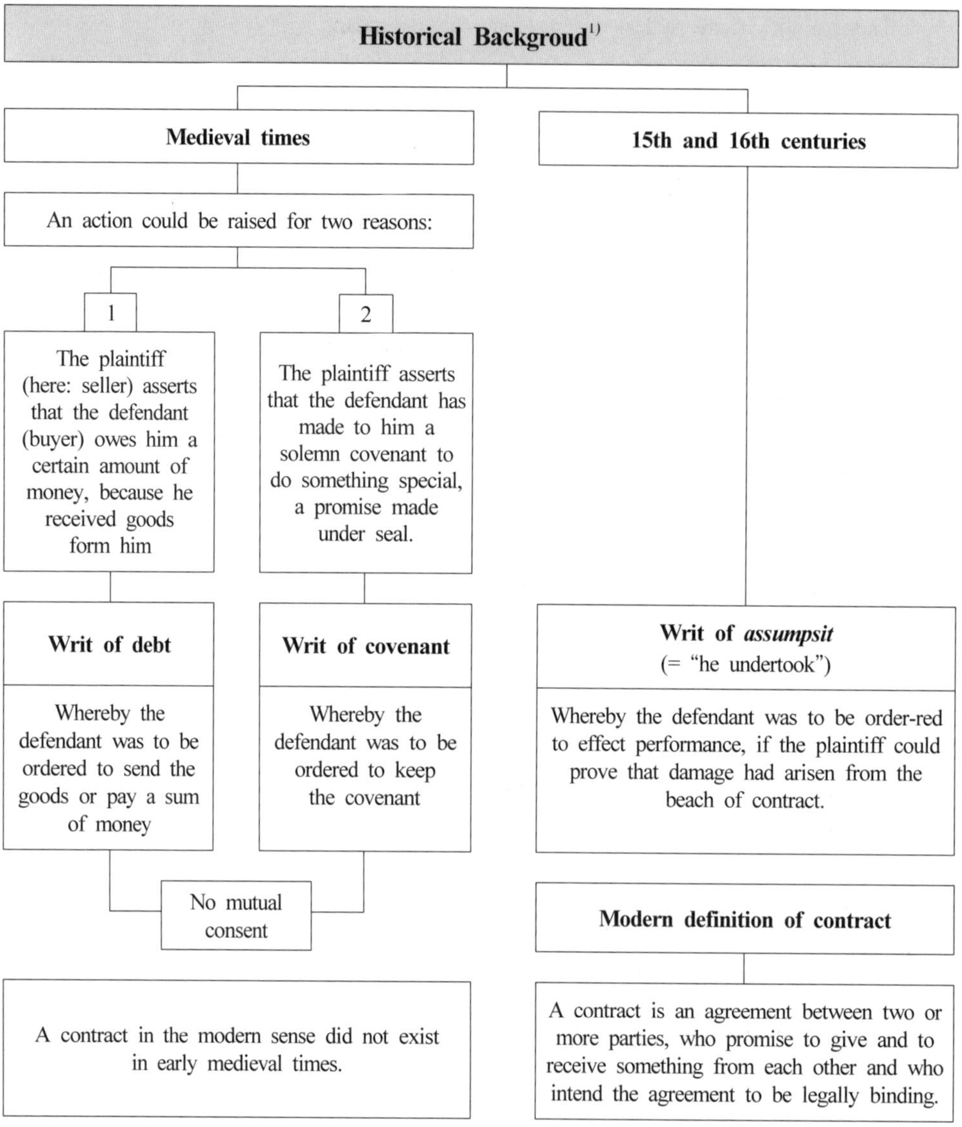

1) A lawyer without history and literature is a mechanic, a mere working mason; if he possesses some knowledge of these, he may venture to call himself an architect.
By *Scott,* Guy Mannering (found in *Williams*, Learning the Law, p.226).

III. Contracts requiring a specific form

1. Contracts which must be in writing

The purpose of formal requirements is to achieve legal certainty and thus avoid disputes.

법적 안정성

Contracts which *must* be in writing are laid down in several Acts of Parliament. For example:

- Bills of exchange, cheques and promissory notes (*Bills of Exchange Act 1882*) — 환어음 / 약속어음
- Contracts of Marine Insurance (*Stamp Act 1891*) — 해상보험
- Hire-purchase contracts (*Hire-Purchase Act 1964*) and other consumer credit agreements (*Consumer Credit Act 1974*) — 할부계약 / 소비자신용계약 / 소비자신용법
- Transfer of shares in a registered company (*Companies Act 1985*) — 판매, (주식) 양도 / 회사법
- Assignments of copyrights (*Copyright, Designs and Patent Act 1988*) — 이전, 양도 / 저작권, 디자인, 특허법

If such a contract does not comply with the written form, it is void.

합치하다 / 서면양식 / 무효의

2. Contracts which must be evidenced in writing

증명하다

There are specific contracts which are valid even without the written form. Thus, they are not to be considered void as such, but without written evidence they are not enforceable in court.

증거 / 제소가능한

In other words this means that, if one of the parties intends to make a claim on such a contract, he need not present the written contract to the court but he must present a written document which proves that the contract was *made*. This written document is called a "*note*" or *memorandum* in writing, which must be signed by the defendant or an agent of his.

계약에 관한 서면 기록 / 대리인

Such *evidence in writing*, is needed not only for those specific contracts mentioned under the *Statute of Frauds 1677*, but also for contracts of sale of land (referring to the preliminary agreement, but not to the conveyance).

서면증거 / 사기 / 부동산 매매계약 / 잠정적인 합의 / 부동산 소유권 이전

Nowadays, according to the *Law of Property (Miscellaneous Provisions) Act 1989*, it is required that such a contract be completely in writing and contain all the terms agreed upon by the parties. In particular the written contract should include:

물권법 / 다양한 조문들

- the parties (names and description)
- the subject-matter of the contract (e.g. land, goods, etc.) 대상
- the consideration (i.e. price)
- any particular or special terms
- the signature of the person to be charged. 부담하다

Without these details in writing this contract is not void but unenforceable.

제소 불가능한, 강제할 수 없는

Thus, contracts which must "only" be *evidenced* in writing are today:

- contracts of guarantee (cf. *Statute of Frauds 1677*) and 보증계약
- contracts of employment (*Employment Protection Consolidation Act 1978*, as amended by the *Employment Act 1982*), which are only mentioned here, but not discussed (as we are not dealing with labour law). 근로계약 / 근로보호법 / 근로법, 노동법

A guarantee is a promise to answer for the debt, default or miscarriage of another person. This definition corresponds to section 4 of the *Statute of Frauds 1677*:

보증, 담보 / 책임지다 / 불이행, 불완전이행

"*No action shall be bought ... whereby to charge the defendant upon any special promise to answer for the debt, default or miscarriage of another person*" unless there is written evidence of the promise.

3. Contracts which must be made by deed

A deed is a sealed document which becomes valid only where its solemn form is observed.

직인을 찍은 문서 / 의식적인, 제식적인

First and foremost, it is important to note that a contract

가장 먼저

under seal which is, as mentioned above, the continuation of the old "covenant" neither becomes effective by means of the congruent agreement of the parties, nor by the performed consideration. It only becomes valid if the official form is observed. This form is the "deed" or the "speciality".

수행하다

A deed becomes binding, valid and enforceable as soon as it is *signed*, *sealed* and *delivered*.

구속력 있는
넘겨주다, 이전하다

In modern common law a deed is only required for the following three transactions:

- conveyances of land, — 부동산 이전
- contracts of lease of land for more than three years, and — (용익)임대차
- articles of partnerships. — 정관

Diagram 22

Contracts Requiring a Specific Form

Contracts which must be in writing	Contracts which must be evidenced in writing	Contracts which must be made by deed
Purpose: legal certainty Without written form the contract is void.	Valid without written form, but not enforceable without written evidence.	A deed is a sealed documents which is binding, valid and enforceable as soon as it is signed, sealed and delivered.
Examples (which are laid down in several Acts of Parliament) • Bills of exchange, cheques and promissory notes • hire-purchase contracts • consumer credit agreements • transfer of shares	Examples: • Contracts of guarantee (Statute of Frauds 1677) • Contracts of employment (Employment Protection Consolidation Act 1978)	A deed is required for: • conveyances of land • contracts of lease of land for more than three years • articles of partnership

Ⅳ. Formation of the contract and consideration

계약성립, 체결

A contract as an enforceable agreement is formed when there is an offer, incorporating ascertainable terms, express or

성립하다, 체결하다
청약 / 확정가능한 / 명시적

implied, which receives unqualified acceptance by the person to whom the offer was made. There must be mutual understanding of the terms and the intention to create legal relations, and – unless the contract is under seal it must be supported by consideration.

묵시적 / 무형식의, 무제한의
상호합의

The essential requirements for the formation of a valid and enforceable contract can be roughly summarised under the following headings:

본질적 요구사항들
대각, 개략적으로
표제, 제목

- There must be an offer and its acceptance.
- There must be an intention to create legal relations.
- The parties must have capacity to contract. 계약능력, 행위능력
- There must be consideration unless the contract is made under seal (by deed).
- There must be consent by the parties to the terms of the contract. 계약조건
- The contract may not conflict with law or public policy. 공공정책
- The contract must observe the form, if there is a requirement of (e.g. written) formalities. 형식을 준수하다

1. Offer

Every contract comes into being after an offer made by one party to another. The party declaring the offer is known as the offeror (also: promissor). The party to whom the offer is made is called the offeree or promisee or acceptor.

성립하다
선언하다
청약자
승낙자

The following rules must be considered when making an offer:

a) Range of offerees

범주, 범위

An offer may be made to a particular party (= person or group of persons) or to a large number of people.

Thus, a legally binding offer can be made to the whole world, it does not have to be made to a specific person. 특정한

Where the offer is made to one person (or group of persons) only, only that person (or group) can be the acceptor.

Where an offer is made to a large number of people, anyone may accept by complying with the terms of this offer.

[이행하다]

For a Korean or German law student who has learnt the principles of the so-called *invitatio ad offerendum* this appears to be strange, but it will be clarified by the following.

[청약으로의 초대, 유인]

Even in the English law of contract there is a general rule that an advertisement is not an offer in the legal sense, unless the advertisement contains elements which show that the advertising person (or firm) intends to create legal relations.

[광고]

> ***Example — Carlill* v *Carbolic Smoke Ball Co. (1893) —:***
>
> The defendants manufactured "carbolic smoke balls" which they advertised as miraculous cures for many ailments and as preventatives against influenza. Moreover, in the advertisement the company promised to pay 100 to anyone who purchased and used the smoke ball remedy for influenza as prescribed, and caught the illness within 14 days. It was further stated that 1,000 had been deposited with a bank to show the sincerity of the company.
>
> [생산하다 / 탄소성분이 포함된 훈제 미트볼 / 광고하다 / 만병통치약 / 병 / 질병예방 / 독감]
> [치료제]
> [~에 걸리다]
> [예탁, 공탁하다]
> [진지성]
>
> The plaintiff, Mrs. Carlill, bought the article, used it as prescribed, but nevertheless caught influenza and claimed the reward of 100.
>
> [보상]
>
> *Held*: that the plaintiff accepted by complying with the conditions of the offer. There was an offer capable of acceptance by all those who used the smoke ball, and communication of acceptance may be implied by the conduct of the acceptor.
>
> [이행, 준행하다]
> [(의사표시의) 통지, 도달]
> [행위]

b) Distinction between offer and invitation to treat

[(청약으로의) 유인, 청약하라는 촉구]

Moreover, under English law an offer must be distinguished from an "invitation to treat". An invitation to treat (*invitatio ad offerendum*) means an invitation to anyone to make an offer.

Typical invitations to treat are made by shopkeepers

[가게주인]

displaying goods in their shops. The price displayed on goods is not the offer, it is only the invitation for the customer to make an offer and the amount shown is an indication of the acceptable price.

전시하다 / 표시된 금액 / 시사, 언급

There is no different result for self-service shops, e.g. supermarkets. The prices on the goods on the shelves are not offers, but invitations to treat. It is the customer who makes the offer when he presents the goods at the cash desk. The acceptance takes place when the cashier accepts the money. The law gives the cashier the right to accept or refuse the customer's offer.

선반 / 계산대 / 발생하다 / 계산원

***Example* — *Fisher* v *Bell (1960)* — :**

This case demonstrates interesting effects of the doctrine of the invitation to treat even in *criminal* law.

이론

The defendant, a shopkeeper, displayed in his shop window a flick knife priced at 4 shillings. He was charged with *offering* for sale a flick knife, contrary to the *Restriction of Offensive Weapons Act 1959*.

(소위) 재크 나이프(날이 튀어 나오는 칼) / 반대로 / 공격 무기 제한을 위한 법률

Held: that according to the law of contract a priced article displayed in a shop window is merely an invitation to treat. "*It is in no sense an offer for sale the acceptance of which constitutes a contract*" as *Parker* L.C.J. stated.

Problems in distinguishing offers from invitation to treat have arisen in the case of auctions, but they are largely resolved to the extent that, when an auctioneer requests bids, potential bidders are invited to make offers. An offer is accepted by the auctioneer with the fall of the hammer.

발생하다 / 경매 / 해결되다 / 정도 / 경매인 / 입찰가 / 입찰자 / 낙찰

Thus, even an advertisement of an auction cannot be regarded as a binding offer.

***Example* — *Harris* v *Nickerson (1873)* — :**

The defendant, an auctioneer (N), advertised that a sale of office furniture would take place at Bury[1]). The plaintiff (H) travelled down from London to Bury to attend the auction, but found the furniture had been withdrawn from the sale. 가구 / 방문하다

H thereupon sued N for his loss of time and expenses. 여기에 대해

Held: that the advertisement was a mere declaration of intention and did not create a binding contract with H when he acted on it. 단지, 단순한

Comment: H would also have had wasted time had he made an unsucessful bid! So what makes this case different from the *Carlill's Case* (see above p. 109)? In the latter case the court held the advertisement to be an offer because the company confirmed its *intention to create legal relations* by depositing 1,000 at the bank. 낭비하다

c) Formulation and communication of an offer 의사표시의 통지(도달)

(aa) *Formulation*

As already mentioned, an offer may be made in writing, orally or by conduct. If you can prove an oral contract (which is supported by consideration) the contract is legal and binding. When distinguishing an offer from an invitation to treat we have learnt that a customer in a supermarket makes an offer to buy when he puts the goods on the cashier's desk. The customer need not make any verbal offer: he makes the offer by conduct and then the cashier may either accept or refuse it.

(bb) *Communication*

It goes without saying that an offer must be communicated before it can be accepted. A person cannot claim to have accepted an offer of which he/she was unaware. 당연하다 / 통지하다 / 주장하다 / 모르는

If, e.g., A by public notice advertises a 100 reward to the 광고하다

1) *Town near Suffolk.*

finder of a lost valuable ring, and B, without having read the advertisement containing the offer, finds the ring and returns it to the loser A, B is not entitled to claim the reward. The offer was not communicated to him; he was unaware of it.

반환하다
분실자 / 요구, 주장하다

Having read this, as a German or Korean student, you may have thought of the "*Auslobung*"? The English language has no suitable word for this notion. "*Auslobung*" is a (public) offer (or promise) of a reward, i.e., a reward offered through public notice for the performance of an act or the bringing about of a particular result.

"현상광고"(한국민법 제675조 이하)
급부, 이행 / (결과를) 가져옴
결과

Whereas in German law the "*Auslobung*" is a legal transaction imposing an obligation on one party only, in English law it is a contract. Also in Korean law the finder (B) of the ring is entitled to claim the reward, and it does not make any difference in law whether B was aware of the offer (advertisement) by A or not.

So once A got what he wanted (his ring), B could get what A promised to any finder.

법률행위
부담시키다 / 일방적 의무
상관이 없다 /
알고 있는

In such a case, under English civil law B is not entitled to claim the reward because he did not return the ring as consideration of a contract. B was not aware of an offer which was communicated to him, and which he had accepted. Thus, where there is no offer there cannot be any acceptance. An offer without acceptance or consideration (see below p. 118) cannot form a contract!

d) *Termination of an offer*

종료

An offer terminates

- on the death of one of the parties before acceptance,
- by non-acceptance within the agreed period, or within a reasonable time,
- when revoked before acceptance, or
- when rejected by the offeree.

효력을 잃다
불승낙 / 합의한 기간
적절한 시간
철회하다
거절하다

Where an offeree dies after acceptance the contract will be valid: If A offers to sell building land to B and B accepts but dies before conveyance, B's heirs may compel A to convey the property to themselves.

건축지
상속인 / 강제하다
양도하다 / 소유권

To answer the question of what could constitute a "reasonable" time in which to accept an offer, the court must consider the circumstances of each individual case. Sometimes an offer has to be accepted immediately, or sometimes within a month or even longer. This is rather a question of acceptance, to which we will return very soon.

각 개별적 사례의 사정

e) *Revocation of an offer*

철회

An offer may be withdrawn before acceptance. Withdrawal or revocation must be communicated to the offeree by the offeror directly or indirectly. Where a notice of revocation does not come directly from the offeror but from a reliable source, it is deemed indirect revocation.

철회하다 / 철회
통지
신뢰할만한 정보원
간주되다

***Example* – *Dickinson* v *Dodds (1876)* – :**

The seller (offeror) of a house (A) sent a letter to the offeree (B) wherein it was stated: "This offer is to be left over until Friday, 9 a.m.". On Thursday B heard from a third person (C) that the house had already been sold to D. Nevertheless, on Friday, 7 a.m., B handed to A his acceptance of the offer.

Held: that there was no contract between A and B because the communication, although by an outside party (C), was good notice of the revocation. Revocation was communicated to the offeree (B) before his purported "acceptance".

유효하다
주장하다

An offer may not be revoked, if consideration (see below, p.118) is given to keep the offer open for a certain time.

Diagram 23

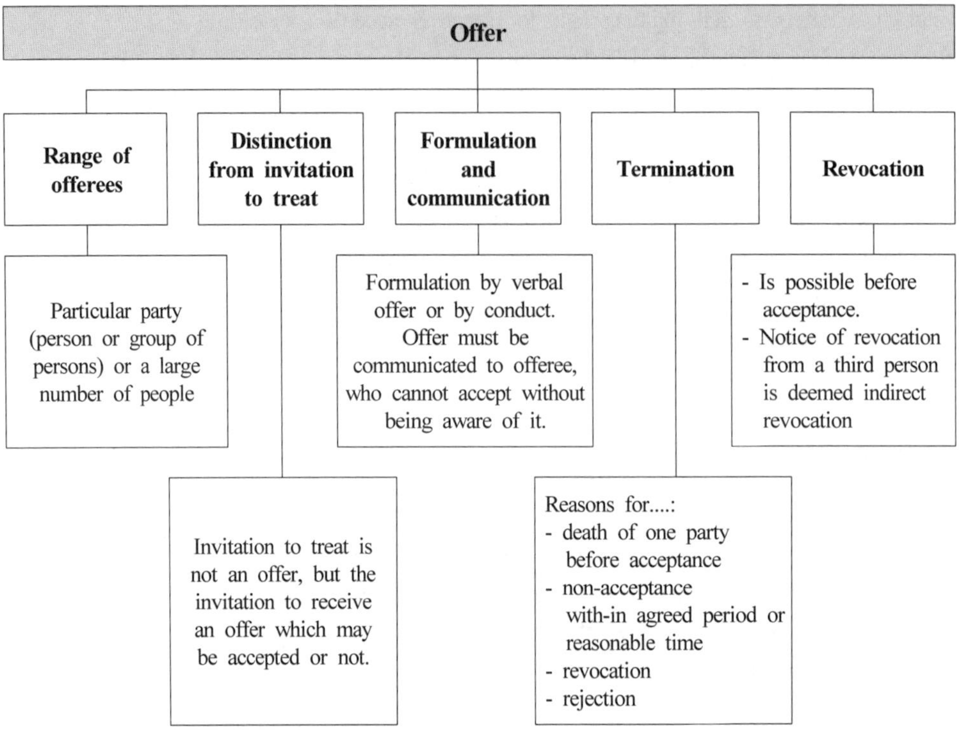

2. Acceptance 승낙

Like an offer, an acceptance can be expressed in writing, orally or by conduct.

Mrs. Carlill (see above, p. 109) did not have to notify the company before using the "smoke ball": she accepted by conduct!

a) Absolute and unqualified acceptance 무제한의, 무조건의

The acceptance of an offer must be absolute and unqualified, which means that the offeree must accept the offer consenting to all its terms. An acceptance under different conditions is a counter-offer which terminates the offer, and the offeror is under no obligation to honour the offer, even if at a later date the acceptor wishes to accept the original terms.

일치하다 / 조건
반대청약, 새로운 청약
인정하다

In fact, when a counter-offer is made, it means that the

acceptor in effect is saying (without expressing it verbally): 실제로는
"I do not accept your offer, will you accept my offer?"

***Example* — *Hyde* v *Wrench (1840)* —:**

The defendant (W) offered to sell land to the plaintiff (H) for £1,000. H said he would pay £950. After W refused this counter-offer H accepted the original offer of £1,000 and when W rejected it, H sued for the land for specific performance. 계약에 따른 이행

Held: that there was no contract. The original offer was terminated by H's counter-offer, which W did not accept.

b) Communication of acceptance

In general, acceptance must be actually communicated to the offeror or an authorised person.

Silence cannot amount to acceptance except where there is a prior consent of the offeror as took place in the *Carlill's Case*. When Mrs. Carlill bought the recommended remedy her acceptance of the company's offer was implied. 표시하다

A person who makes an offer may not stipulate that absence of communication of acceptance within a certain period will be deemed as acceptance. 조건으로 하다 간주되다

***Example* — *Felthouse* v *Bindley (1862)* —:**

The plaintiff (F) negotiated with his nephew John regarding the purchase of John's horse. He wrote to his nephew offering an amount of 30 and added: "If I hear no more, I shall consider the horse to be mine!" 간주하다

The nephew did not reply but told the defendant, the auctioneer B, who was selling farm stock for him, to withdraw the horse from the sale. In error, however, the horse was sold during the auction and F sued B for his loss. 농장의 재고 실수로

Held: that the plaintiff's action failed.

Although the nephew intended to sell the horse to his

uncle, he had not communicated his acceptance of the offer. There was, therefore, no contract between F and his nephew, so that F had no right of action. 소권(訴權)

c) Prescribed method of acceptance 규정하다

Where a particular method of acceptance is not demanded by the offer, any reasonable form of acceptance may be used.

Where, however, an offer states that it can only be accepted in a certain way, the offeror is not, in general, bound unless acceptance is made in that way. Thus, if the offeror asks for the acceptance to be sent to a particular place, an acceptance sent elsewhere will not bind him. 기타의 장소에서

***Example* — *Eliason* v *Henshaw (1819)* —:**

The plaintiff (E) offered to buy flour from H. The offer stated that acceptance must be given to the waggoner who delivered the offer. The acceptance was sent by post and arrived after the waggoner. 밀가루 / 운송업자 / 전달하다

Held: that there was no contract as the prescribed specific method of acceptance was not followed. 따르다

Where the offeror prescribes a method of acceptance, he usually does so with some particular object in view, for instance to secure a speedy acceptance. An acceptance which accomplishes the object just as well as, or maybe even better than the prescribed method, may, by way of exception to the general rule, bind the offeror. 목전(目前)의 특정한 목표 / 확실히 하다 / 빠른 / 예외적으로

If, e.g., the offeror says "reply by letter sent by return of post" this may simply mean "reply quickly". In this case a reply by fax instead of by letter is an acceptance improving upon the prescribed method. The offeror is bound by his offer and the contract is valid.

d) Offer and acceptance by use of post

In the case of contracts made by correspondence, the English courts have laid down the following rule: 편지교신

Where an offer is made by post, it is actually communicated and said to have taken effect only once it reaches the offeree, and not simply when the letter is posted.

***Example* — *Adams* v *Lindsell (1818)* —:**

On 2 September L posted an offer in a letter to sell wool at a certain price, and requested an answer in course of post. The letter was misdirected and reached A on 5 September. The reply of acceptance was sent at once and reached L on 9 September. The wool, however, had been sold on 8 September. 우편으로

Held: that there was a valid contract between A and L, because the offer was accepted at once on being received.

The general rule for acceptance is that acceptance must be received by the offeror.

Where, however, an acceptance is made by post, the contract is made at the precise moment the letter accepting the offer is posted, even if it never arrives.

***Example* — *Household Fire Insurance Co.*v *Grant (1879)* —:**

The defendant (G) applied for shares in the company. The company accepted the offer and posted a letter of allotment of shares to G, but it never reached him. 신청하다 주식의 배당에 관한 통지

Held: that acceptance took place as soon as the letter was posted. The contract was made and G became a shareholder of the company.

A possible reason for this reversal of the general rule is, that it is easier for the offeree to furnish evidence that he 전환 증거를 제시하다

posted a letter than to prove actual receipt by the offeror. 실제의

Diagram 24

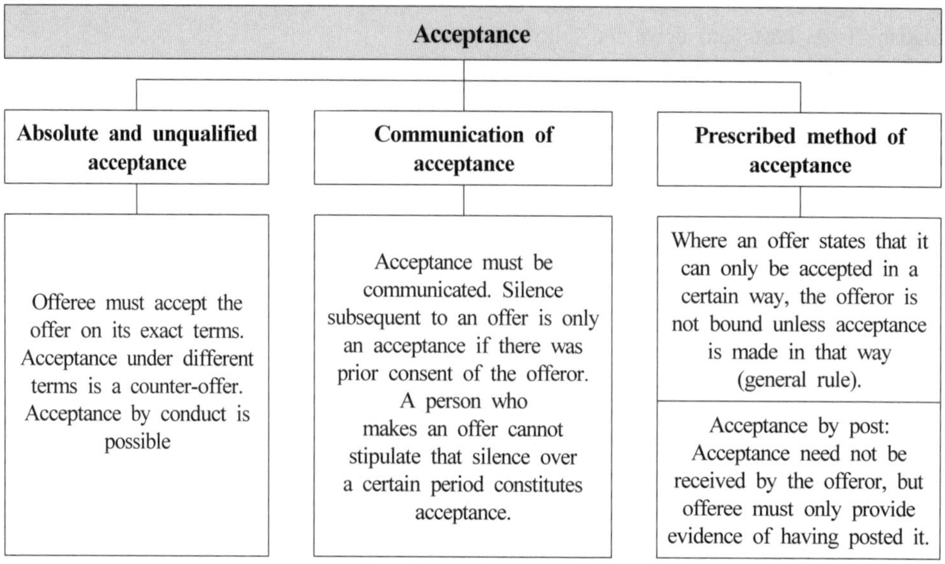

3. Consideration

As has already been stated "*consideration*" under English law is a necessary fundamental element in the formation of a simple valid contract.

This expresses an essential difference from continental law systems. In English law the binding effect of a contract is not derived from the mutual consent of the parties. 유래하다 / 의사의 합치

The requirement of consideration as a precondition for a 요구 simple valid contract becomes understandable if one keeps in mind the historical background to the law of contract.

In previous times an action was only possible if the plaintiff could prove either that he had given something to the defendant who subsequenty became his debtor ("writ of debt"), or that he had suffered damage by breach of promise 위반 ("writ of assumpsit").

Thus, one has to remember this when reading the definitions of *consideration*. A famous and very often cited definition is given in the case *Currie* v *Misa (1875):*

"A valuable consideration, in the sense of law, may consist either in some right, interest, profit or benefit accruing to one party, or some forbearance, detriment, loss or responsibility given, suffered or undertaken by the other". — 적절한 / 이해 / 이익, 수익 / 유익 / 생기다 / 부작위, (권리행사의) 유보 / 손해 / 책임 / 당하다 / 부담하다

Valuable consideration means, therefore, any benefit to the promisor, or detriment to the promisee, which is sufficient in law to support the promise. One can also say, that consideration is the price for which the promise of the other is bought. — 충분한 / 지지하다

It is, as already indicated, the consideration which helped us to understand the difference in meaning between the promise of a reward as understood under English law and that under Korean or German law: The finder of the ring (cf. above, p. 111) who was unaware that a reward was promised to anyone returning it, did not give consideration. — 현상광고

Over the course of time the *doctrine of consideration* has developed, and the courts have established many rules to determine whether or not a promise is sufficient to amount to valuable consideration. — 약인이론(반대급부 이론)

In our "Introduction to English civil law" we can only consider a few of them:

a) Consideration must not be past — 과거의, 지나간

Consideration may be given in two forms: either as *executed consideration* or as *executory consideration*. — 이행된 약인 / 이행할 약인

When executed consideration is wholly performed by one party the contract is immediately entered into. — 완전히 / 계약이 체결된다

For example: A sells his old mountain bike to B for £50 and hands over the bike to B. If A now claims the purchase price, he can say "I've just handed over the bike to B!" This is executed consideration. — 매매가격

If A promised to hand over the bike to B, he can say "We have made a contract, by which I'm obliged to hand — 의무를 진

over the bike to B, when he pays £50". This is executory consideration.

Thus, executory consideration is a promise to confer a benefit or to suffer a detriment at some future time.

이익을 주다
손해를 보다

Variation: A and B made a contract, and B pays £50 for the bike asking A if he can guarantee that the bike has no defect. A answers "yes". There is, however, still no valid contract of guarantee. The reason being that B did not give consideration for the guarantee of faultlessness by A. The paid purchase price is already "past" and therefore there is no valuable consideration. B should have said: "I will pay £10 more for the guarantee of faultlessness". If A had then given the demanded guarantee, B would have given consideration.

무결점, 무과실
과거의

***Example* – *Roscorla* v *Thomas (1842)* –:**

R bought a horse from T for £30. As R was leading the horse away, the previous owner promised that if the horse was vicious, he would return the price. The horse was in fact not free from vice.

흠이 있는
흠결

Held: that R could not recover on the warranty that the horse was not vicious. The promise by the previous owner was not supported by consideration from the plaintiff. The sale had already taken place when the warranty as to the soundness of the horse was given. Thus, the consideration of R was past.

회복하다, 보상받다 / 보증
건강함

b) Consideration must move from the promisee

유래하다, 시작하다

A promisee bringing an action to court must prove that he has performed consideration, or made a promise of consideration.

약속을 받는 자

The relationship between promisor and promisee is known as *privity of contract*. Since the parties to a valid contract must provide consideration, there is a general rule that a third party may not enforce rights under the contract.

약속을 하는 자
계약관계
제공, 이행하다
권리를 주장하다, 관철하다

Thus, in English law, in contrast to German and Korean law, a contract for the benefit of a third party does not exist. A person who did not give or promise to give consideration may not claim on a contract.

반대로
제3자를 위한 계약(한국민법 제539조)

***Example* — *Tweddle* v *Atkinson (1861)* —:**

T was married to William Guy's daughter. To assist the married couple Guy promised to pay T 200 in consideration of T's father paying 100. Guy, however, died before he had paid the 200. T sued A, Guy's executor, and failed.

Held: that no consideration was given by T because he had not promised to do so. Only T's father would have been entitled to sue.

상속집행인 / 실패하다, 잃다

c) Consideration must be real, but need not be adequate

동등한 가치의

Although consideration must be valuable, it need not be adequate, but it must be real (or a promise which can be realised). He who promises something which is impossible or prohibited does not give consideration. But if the consideration is real and has some value, the contract is binding. The parties are free to make any kind of contract they like, for example, by naming the price at which they are prepared to sell their goods. There is an important contractual rule called "*caveat emptor*" which means "let the buyer beware".

금지된
준비된
매수인이여 조심하라

If you buy a picture for ￡100 which turns out to be a real Picasso, you are lucky; the seller is not. The contract is nevertheless good. On the other hand, if you were the seller you cannot seek assistance from a court merely because you have made a bad bargain.

밝혀지다
도움을 구하다
거래

Since consideration need not be adequate, even acts or omissions of very small value can be consideration. In fact this rule can lead to strange results as, e.g., in the *Chappell Case*:

부작위

***Example – Chappell & Co. Ltd.* v *Nestl Ltd. (1960)* –:**

The plaintiff owned the copyright of a dance tune called "Rockin' Shoes", and the defendants were using records of this tune as part of an advertising campaign. A record company made the records for Nestlé who advertised them to the public for 1s.6d. each, but required in addition three wrappers from their 6d. bars of chocolate (which were then thrown away).

소유하다 / 댄스곡(멜로디)
광고 캠페인
포장지 / 초콜릿 파
버려버리다

The plaintiffs sued the defendants for infringement of copyright. According to the *Copyright Act 1956* a person recording musical works for retail need not get the permission of the holder of the copyright, but had merely to serve him with notice and pay 6,25% of the retail selling price as royalty. The plaintiffs asserted that the defendants were not retailing the goods in the sense of the Act and must therefore get permission to use the musical work.

침해
소매
소유자, 권리자
통지하다 / 소매가
실시료, 로열티, 라이센스 피

Since to the plaintiffs "retailing" meant selling entirely for money, whilst the defendants were selling for money plus wrappers, according to the plaintiffs the defendants needed the plaintiffs consent. The defendants argued that the sale was for cash "because the wrappers were not part of the consideration". The House of Lords gave judgment for the plaintiffs.

독점적으로
논증하다
결정하다, 판결하다

Held: that the wrappers were part of the consideration since the offer was to supply a record in return not simply for money, but for the wrappers as well.

It is worthwhile, in relation to the adequacy of consideration, mentioning the statement of *Lord Sommervell*:

동등한 가치

"*It is said, when received, the wrappers are of no value to the respondents, the Nestl Co. Ltd.. This I would have thought irrelevant. A contracting party can stipulate for what consideration he chooses!*

받다
조건을 걸다

A peppercorn does not cease to be good consideration if it is established that the promisee does not like pepper and will throw away the corn."

후추열매 / 멈추다
확실시하다

d) Deficiencies of the doctrine of consideration

하자

The doctrine of consideration has often been criticized.

Its results are not always satisfactory and sometimes seem to be inequitable or even ridiculous, as the *Chappell Case* revealed with its wrappers and peppercorns, although the statement of *Lord Sommervell* is quite logical.

형평에 어긋난 / 우스꽝스러운
공개하다

But it does not seem logical or just and equitable that the party offering a reward should not have to give the reward to the finder who returns the lost ring. The offeror was prepared to pay the reward to the finder and did not require "personal consideration". And it does not seem equitable either to deny a contract for the benefit of a third party for lack of consideration.

정당하고 형평에 맞는
현상공고한 자
청약자
제3자를 위한 계약

Another example is the contract of discharge[1]): If a debtor is unable to pay his debts he can ask his creditor for a discharge of debts by agreement. If the creditor agrees, according to German law, a valid contract of discharge may be formed. Hence, under English law the doctrine of consideration denies a contract: where there is no consideration by the debtor for the promised discharge of debts, there is no contract!

채무면제계약
합의에 의한 채무면제

Suppose, the debtor (D) owes £50 to his creditor (C), but can only pay £25 and C discharges D from the rest of his debt by agreement. The payment of £25 by D is not consideration for the discharge. The rule of the doctrine of consideration is now: agreed variations in contractual obligations are generally unenforceable without consideration.

면제하다
합의된 변경사항 / 계약의무

***Example – Foakes* v *Beer (1884)* –:**

Mrs. Beer (B) had obtained a judgment against Dr. Foakes (F). F agreed to settle the judgment debt by making a cash

지불하다, 해결하다 / 현금으로 첫 할부금(계약금)을 지불하다

1) 한국민법 제506조의 채무면제는 계약이 아닌 채권자의 단독행위이며, 결국 채권의 포기이다. 근대법은 대부분이 채무면제를 계약으로 하고 있으나, 현행 민법은 구민법의 입장을 따라 채무면제를 단독행위로 하고 있다(출처 : Daum백과사전).

down payment of ￡500 and keep on paying ￡150 every six months until the whole amount was paid. B agreed not to take further action on the judgment. F duly paid the amount of the judgment plus costs. Judgment debts, however, carry interest by statute, and while F had been paying off his debt, interest amounting to ￡360 had been accruing on the diminishing balance. B claimed the ￡360.

Held: that B was right in doing so. Her promise not to take further action on the judgment was not supported by any consideration moving from F. That which he had paid by agreement was not consideration for the interest amounting to ￡360.

추가의 소를 제기하다
기한에 맞추어, 합의한 대로
비용 / 판결로 인정받은 채무
법정이자를 지불해야 한다 / 갚아 나가다 / ~에 이른 이자액 / 지불기가 도래한 / 감소한 채무잔고

유래하다

So B could claim for this balance.

The outcome of this case is based on the rules which had already been developed in a previous case, the famous *Pinnel's Case.*

In this case the Court dealt with the question of whether the payment of a lesser sum than the amount due could be consideration. The general rule laid down in *Pinnel's Case* was that payment of a lesser sum is no discharge for a larger:

채무를 진, 지불기가 도래한
확정되다

Example — Pinnel's Case (1602) —:

Pinnel sued Cole for ￡8.10 due on the 11 November 1600. C claimed, that at P's request, he had paid P ￡5.2.s.6d. on 1 October, and that P had agreed to accept this payment in full satisfaction of the original debt.

Held: that a payment of a lesser sum on the due day in satisfaction of a greater sum cannot be consideration for the whole.

청구, 요구
동의하다

Even if the creditor promised to relieve the debtor from the rest of the debt, the creditor is not bound by this settlement. He can sue the debtor the next day for the balance and get the judgment, as *Pinnel* did.

면제하다
화해계약
차액지불, 채무변제

The common law rule of *Pinnel's Case*, that payment of a lesser sum is no discharge for a larger amount because of lacking consideration, as stated in 1602 by *Lord Coke*, was accepted in 1884 by the House of Lords in *Foakes* v *Beer* (see above, p. 123), although this rule was much criticised.

The fact that the doctrine of *Pinnel's Case* was strengthened 강화된
by this decision is one of the disadvantageous effects of the 불리한
common law's system of binding precedents.

Diagram 25

Consideration...

- ... is the necessary element in the formation of a valid simple contract.
- Binding effect of a contract is not derived from the mutual consent of the parties.
- **Valuable consideration**,... ... in the sense of law, may consist either in some rights, profit or benefit accruing to one party or some forbearance, detriment, loss or responsibility given, suffered or undertaken by the other.

The doctrine of consideration

- Two forms:
  - Executed consideration:
    → seller has handed over the object of sale to buyer and claims the purchase price.
  - Executory consideration:
    → is a promise to confer a benefit or to suffer from detriment at some future time
- A person who does not give or promise to give consideration may not claim on a contract.
- In English law a contract for the benefit of a third person does not exist.
- A consideration is valuable if it has a real, economic value
- Example:
  S sells a picture to B for £100, which turns out to be a real Picasso. The contract is valid.

Deficiencies of the doctrine of consideration

- It is not just and equitable that the party offering a reward should not give the reward to the fin-der who returns the lost thing not knowing that a reward was promised.
- It is not equitable to deny a contract for the benefit of a third party for lack of consideration.
- A contract of discharge is not possible: Because there is no consideration by the debtor for the promised discharge of debts, there is no contract

e) Equity: The rule of promissory estoppel[1] 약속의 금반언

The common law doctrine as stated in *Pinnel's Case* was not only criticised, but (as *Lord Denning* describes it in his book "*The Discipline of Law*") has come under heavy fire. It was ridiculed by *Sir George Jessel* ..., it was said to be mistaken by *Lord Blackburn* ..., it was condemned by the Law Revision Committee (1945) ... .

심한 공격 / 우스꽝스럽게 하다 / 틀리다 / 책망하다 / 법률개정위원회

But a remedy has been found. Equity has stretched out a merciful hand to help the debtor. The courts have invoked the broad principle stated by *Lord Cairns* in *Hughes* v *Metropolitan Railway Co.* (1877 = see below).

해결책, 방안 / 뻗치다 / 자비로운 / ~에 호소하다, ~을 근거로 하다 / 폭넓은 원칙

Before dealing with the evolution of this principle, which is applied to cases where a creditor agrees to accept a lesser sum in discharge of a greater, let us remember what exactly the dissatisfaction caused by the common law rule is:

불만

Afterall, if A owes B ￡10 and B agrees to take ￡9 to discharge A's obligation, why should B be allowed afterwards to break his promise to take ￡9 and succeed in action against A? Simply because A gave him no consideration?

면제하다

This situation which led to the doctrine of promissory estoppel was first propounded by *Lord Cairns* in *Hughes* v *Metropolitan Railway Co.* (1877) and later by *Lord Denning* in the "*High Trees Case*" (1947). So we come to our next case.

제출하다, 제안하다

***Example* − *Hughes* v *Metropolitan Railway Co (1877)* −:**

H, landlord, gave MR (lessee) 6 months notice to repair some houses in accordance with the lease. A month later MR negotiated with H to purchase the freehold. Relying on this MR did not repair the houses. Negotiations failed after two months. After 6 months H sued for the ejectment of MR for

부동산 소유자 / 임차인 / 지대, 임차료 / (토지)소유권 / 부동산 점유회복

1) 약속의 금반언이란 약인없이 행한 이전의 약속에 반하는 소를 제기할 경우 권리를 실효하게 하는 금반언이다.

failure to repair. 실패

Held: that equity should override the common law. MR relied on the negotiations as being, in effect, a promise that H would not enforce his demands while negotiations continued. So no repairs were done. H failed in his action.

사실상
강제하다, 소를 제기하다

It is the first principle upon which all courts of equity proceed, that if parties who have entered into definite and distinct terms involving certain legal results ... afterwards, by their own acts ... enter upon a course of negotiations which has the effect of leading one of the parties to suppose that the strict rights arising under the contract will not be enforced, or will be kept in suspense ..., that the person who otherwise might have enforced those rights will not be allowed to enforce them where this would be inequitable, having regard to the dealings which have thus taken place between the parties.

절차를 진행하다
분명한
정지상태에 있다, 미결상태에 있다
형평에 어긋나는, 부당한

This exception from the common law rule that consideration is essential to support a simple valid contract, demonstrates how equitable principles can operate to do justice in a particular case as well as soften the rigid rules of common law.

개별사례 / 유연하게 하다, 부드럽게 하다

Another remedy of equity was developed by *Lord Denning* in the famous *High Trees Case* which forms our following example.

Example — Central London Property Trust Ltd.* v *High Trees House Ltd. (1947) —:

In 1937 the plaintiff granted to the defendants a lease of 99 years of a new block of flats at a rent of ￡2500 per annum. The lease was granted by deed. During the period of the war the flats were by no means fully let owing to the absence of people from the London area.

아파트
절대 ~아니다 / 임대된

The defendant company, which was a subsidiary of the plaintiff company, realised that it could not meet the rent out

자회사, 지사
충분하다, 충당하다 / 임대료

of the profits then being made on the flats, and in 1940 the parties entered into an agreement which reduced the rent to £1250 per annum, this agreement being put into writing but not by deed. The defendants continued to pay the reduced rent from 1941 up to the beginning of 1945, by which time the flats were fully let, and they continued to pay the reduced rent thereafter.

In September 1945, the receiver of the plaintiff company investigated the matter and asked for arrears of £7916 suggesting that the liability created by the lease still existed, and that the agreement of 1940 was not supported by any consideration. The receiver then brought his action to establish the legal position. He claimed £625, that being the difference in rent for the two quarters ending 29 September and 25 December.

Held: that the plaintiffs were entitled to the full rent from 1945, since implied in the 1940 agreement there was a term that the rents should revert to the original rent when the war-time situation ended. It would be inequitable to allow the plaintiffs to go back on their promise as to 1941/45 because, on the strength of it, the defendants had reduced the rents to their tenants, relying on the fact that the agreement prevented the strict legal effects of the first contract from being enforced. It was a case of *equitable estoppel*.

감액하다
(이행) 지체(보통 복수로 쓰임)
복귀하다
~에 기초하여, ~을 믿고
임차인 / ~을 의지하다, 믿다 / 방해하다, 막다
금반언, 권리주장을 하지 못함

Thus, if one party to a contract modifies the liabilities of the other party, then he may be estopped from enforcing the original contract. This may occur if it entails repudiating a promise which was *intended* to be acted upon and was in fact acted upon by the other party, even if there was no consideration for the modification.

변경하다
금반언에 걸리다
결과를 낳다 / 거절하다
~에 따르다

From this we can conclude the following rules:

결론을 내리다

(1) If a promise is given by one party to a contract without consideration, not to insist upon his legal rights, then if that party breaks his promise and sues

(권리를) 주장하다

on the original contract, the promisee has a good defence; 정당한 항변, 방어

(2) provided that it had been intended to create or affect the legal relations between the parties, and that the promisee should act on the promise and that he did so act. ~을 전제로 하고/영향을 주다

This was the decision of *Lord Denning* in the *High Trees Case* in July 1946, when he "had only been a judge in the King's Bench for some six month" (as he wrote himself in "*The Discipline of Law*").

This decision was so important that it created the "*doctrine of promissory estoppel*" which soon was extended by its progenitor, *Lord Denning*, in the following case.

약속의 금반언 원칙
확대하다
창시자

Example — Charles Rickards* v *Oppenhaim (1950) —:

Mr. Oppenhaim wanted a body built on a chassis of a Rolls Royce "Silver Wraith". In July 1947 the coachbuilders promised to deliver it "within six or at the most seven months". They did not deliver within that time. Mr. Oppenhaim still pressed them to deliver, but on 29 June 1948 he wrote to the coachbuilders saying that he would not accept delivery after 25 July 1948. The body was not ready by then and O bought another car. The body was completed in October 1948, but O (the defendant) refused to accept the delivery and counterclaimed for the value of the chassis which he had purchased.

차체/차대
유령/차체 제작자
압력을 행사하다
완성하다
반소를 제기하다

Held: that the time was the essence of the original contract, though the defendant had waived the question of time by continuing to press for delivery after the due date.

납품시기, 납기/원계약의 핵심적 내용/포기하다

However, *by his letter of 29 June he had again stressed the importance of time and gave reasonable notice.*

강조하다
합리적인 통지(기간)

Judgment was given for the defendant on the claim and counterclaim!

Comment: Should Oppenhaim not have written his letter on 29 June 1948, according to the equity rule of promissory estoppel he should have failed. His previous waiver of the date of delivery (by pressing the coachbuilder) without consideration would have been binding.

포기

According to the old common law rule that there will be no valid contract without consideration, Mr. Oppenhaim could have refused the delivery if it had been tendered by the plaintiffs in accordance with his pressing request, although he waived the question of time.

제안하다, 제공하다
~에 따라서 / 압력적 요구

This would not have been just and equitable. *Lord Denning* pointed out this difficulty and gave the solution (in "*The Discipline of Law*"):

~을 언급하다

In the old (common law) cases... "... *it would have been said that there was no consideration..., but... those difficulties are swept away now. If the defendant, as he did, led the plaintiffs to believe that he would not insist on the stipulations as to time, and that, if they carried out the work, he would accept it, and they did it, he could not afterwards set up the stipulation as to the time against them.*

쓸어버리다 / ~하게 하다, 유인하다
(납품)시간에 관한 약정 / 급부를 이행하다
수립하다, 확정하다

Whether it will be called waiver or forbearance on his part, or an agreed variation or substituted performance, does not matter. It is a kind of estoppel. By his conduct he evinced an intention to affect their legal relations. He made, in effect, a promise not to insist on his strict legal rights. That promise was intended to be acted upon, and was in fact acted upon. He cannot afterwards go back on it...."

포기 / 지불유예
합의 변경 / 대체급부
명시하다
(약속을) 어기다, 철회하다

This would have been a particular application of the principle of promissory estoppel which *Lord Denning* established in the *High Trees Case*.

적용

Referring to this principle, a defendant (or a plaintiff) can only use it as "a shield not a sword", which means it gives him no right of action, but only of objection.

칼이 아닌 방패로
항변

The *Oppenhaim* case, however, is an example of the

doctrine of promissory estoppel being used by a plaintiff as "*a sword not a shield*" because a seller, usually, may tender delivery after the date agreed originally relying on the buyer's promise to accept such delivery by reason of his waiver. If the buyer then refuses to accept such delivery the seller can claim damages and is in essence suing upon the waiver which is unsupported by consideration.

제공하다
~을 의지하다, 믿다
핵심에 있어서
(약인이) 없는 (약인의 지지를 받지 않는)

Diagram 26

The Rule of Promissory Estoppel

If a promise is given by one party to a contract, not to insist upon his legal rights without consideration, then if that party breaks his promise and sues on the original contract, the promisee has a good defence,....

....provided that it had been intended to create or affect the legal relations between the parties, and that the promisee should act on the promise and that he did so act

Example: If a defendant leads the plaintiff to believe that he would not insist on the stipulation as to time, and that, if they carried out the work, he would accept it, and they did it, he cannot afterwards rely upon the stipulation as to the time against them

4. Intention to create legal relations

법률관계

The principle of the *High Trees Case* revealed that a promise which intended to create legal relations, and which, to the knowledge of the promisor, is to be acted upon by the promisee, and which *is* in fact *acted upon* (e.g. by retaining the lease as in that case), must be honoured.

보여주다
~을 준수하다, ~에 따라 행위하다 / 유보함
이행하다

Above all, the promise was binding because the intention to create legal relations was obvious.

명백한

As was shown previously when dealing with offer and acceptance, it is essential to a contract that the parties intend to create legal relations.

The law will not necessarily recognise the existence of a

contract enforceable in a court simply because of the presence of mutual promises.

For an agreement to be enforceable in court, the parties must intend it to be legally binding. 제소가 가능한

If for example a wife promises her husband "I'll wash up, if you fix my car" and he answers "ok", obviously in this case, neither person intends to take the other to court on failure. There is no intention to create legal relations. 수리하다 / 잘못된 행위 때문에

a) Family or "domestic" agreements 가사의, 가족에 관한

As a general rule we can state that agreements of a purely social domestic nature are not contracts. Such agreements are mostly not intended to be binding at law but instead rely upon bonds of mutual trust and affection. 전적으로 사회적인 / 관계에 의존하다 / 신뢰 / 친밀함

***Example* — *Balfour* v *Balfour (1919)* —:**

A husband who was a civil servant in Ceylon (now Sri Lanka) came to England on leave with his wife. 휴가를 떠난

When his leave was nearing its end and he had to return to Ceylon, he promised his wife who, on the doctor's advice had to remain in England, a household allowance of £30 a month until she joined him in Ceylon. Later the parties separated and the wife sued for the allowance. 가계지출비

Held (by the Court of Appeal): that there was no enforceable contract because in this sort of situation it must be assumed that the parties did not intend to create legal relations. 짐작하다, 전제하다

The provisions for a payment of £30 per month for an indefinite period with no attempt to take into account changes in the circumstances of the parties did not suggest a binding agreement. 시도 / 고려하다 / 제안하다

In addition the court seems to have based its decision on the fact that the wife had not given any consideration.

Example — Jones* v *Padavatton (1969) —:

A mother who lived in Trinidad wanted her daughter to study English law and after completion of her studies to practise as a lawyer in Trinidad. 완성

At a time when mother and daughter were very close, the mother bought a house in London to enable the daughter to reside there during her studies. Later, differences arose and the mother claimed possession of the house. 살다 / 분쟁, 차이점 점유(회복)를 청구하다

Held: that the arrangements in relation to the house were made without contractual intent and that the mother was entitled to possession of the house.

On the other hand, however, there are some "domestic" agreements which *do* create legal obligations.

If the parties are in a domestic or social relationship, but intend their agreement to have legal consequences, an enforceable contract is concluded. 닫다, 종결하다

Example — Merritt* v *Merritt (1970) —:

A husband had formed an attachment with another woman and the spouses intended to separate. They negotiated in the husband's car about certain arrangements for the future. 관계를 맺다 부부

Before the wife left the car she insisted that the husband gave her a written statement in which he agreed to transfer the ownership of the house to the wife when she had completed paying all the mortgage repayments on the house (which was in the name of her husband). The wife paid the mortgage and sued for the transfer of the house. 양도하다 모기지 할부금

Held (by the Court of Appeal)*:* that this case is distinguishable from *Balfour* v *Balfour*, because there the parties lived in amity, whereas the *Merritts* had decided to separate and for this purpose made an agreement which reasonable persons would regard as intending to be binding in law. The agreement of the parties, having been made when they were 친선, 우호 관계

no longer living together in amity, was intending to create legal relations and the wife had given consideration by paying the mortgage. Thus, she was entitled to the house.

A contractual intention was also included in the following family agreement other than those between husband and wife.

***Example* – *Simkins* v *Pays (1955)* –:**

The defendant (P) and his granddaughter made an agreement with the plaintiff (S) who was a paying boarder, that they should submit in the defendant's name a weekly coupon, containing a forecast by each of them, to a newspaper fashion competition. 손녀 / 유료 숙박객 / 제출하다 / 예측 / 패션 경연

A forecast by the granddaughter proved correct and the defendant received a prize of £750. The plaintiff sued for her share of £250 of that sum. The defence was that there was no intention to create legal relations, and that the transaction was a friendly arrangement binding in honour only.

Held: that there was an intention to create legal relations. This was not a mere domestic arrangement, but the evidence showed that there was a joint enterprise and that the parties expected to share any prize that was won. 공동기업

b) Advertisement

It was previously mentioned above that advertisements are mere statements of opinion with no intention to create legal relations. Usually advertisements include only an invitation to treat which cannot be legally binding.

Mrs. Carlill's Case formed an exception because the court considered that the advertisement was intended to be an offer to several people as the company had stressed the sincerity of its intention to create legal relations by depositing £100 with the bank. 공탁하다

c) Commercial and business agreements

In a commercial agreement, the parties will normally intend to create legal relations. In commercial and business agreements, the law and the courts will presume that the parties entering into such an agreement intend that the other party shall have the right to enforce the agreement in court.

This presumption, however, may be rebutted by express terms of the parties excluding the formation of legal relations.

반론을 펴다, 반증을 들다
배제하다

Example — Rose & Frank Co.* v *Compton Bros. Ltd.(1925) —:

R. & F. made an agreement with C whereby they were appointed agents for sale of paper supplied by C. The agreement included the following clause: "This arrangement is not, nor is this memorandum written as a formal legal agreement and shall not be subject to legal jurisdiction in the law courts".

Held: that there was no legally binding contract between the parties because the clause excluded an intention to create legal relations.

수권 대리인
조항

Even where there are commercial agreements without such a clause excluding an intention to create legal relations, the strong presumption that legal relations are intended in commercial transactions is not irrebuttable.

This was decided by the House of Lords in the following famous case.

반증, 반론할 수 없는

Example — Esso Petroleum Ltd.* v *Commissioners of Custom and Excise (1976) —:

관세 및 소비세청

At a time when the English national football team was winning the World Cup, Esso petrol station proprietors displayed posters supplied by Esso stating:

"The World Cup coins — one coin given with every four gallons of petrol".

동전
1 영국 갤런=4,5459 리터

Millions of coins were distributed. The Commissioners claimed that the coins were chargeable to purchase tax under section 2 (1) of the *Purchase Tax Act 1963* on the ground that they had been "produced in quantity for general sale". Esso argued that the coins were the subject of a gift not a sale.

납세의무를 지는 / 매입세
~을 이유로
증여, 선물

Held (at first instance): that the transaction constituted a sale. The poster was primarily an invitation to treat but subsequently became a contract (the offer to buy is made by the customer and it is accepted by the seller's conduct in putting petrol into the tank): Thus, according to this decision the coins were included in the sale.

구성하다

The Court of Appeal allowed Esso's appeal, holding ("as a matter of common sense", per *Lord Denning*, M.R.) that the coins were not *sold* but distributed as free gifts. Thus, there was *no* binding contract to supply a World Cup coin to the customer in return for him agreeing to buy four gallons of petrol.

(건강한) 상식

The Commissioners' appeal to the House of Lords was dismissed. By majority of four to one (*Lord Fraser* dissenting) the House of Lords *held*: that there was no "sale" of the coins. Nevertheless, the majority of the Lords was equally divided on the question whether there was any contract at all with regard to the coins.

기각하다 / 동의하지 않다
균등하게 (의견이) 나뉜
~에 관하여

Lord Simon and *Lord Wilberforce* held that there was a contract to supply the coins, but it was not a contract of sale. The poster was an offer to supply a coin which the customer accepted by offering to buy four gallons of petrol. The *consideration* for the promise to supply a coin was *not money* (and therefore it was not a sale!), but the offer to buy petrol.

Moreover, *Viscount*[1] *Dilhorne* and *Lord Russel* held that Esso did not enter into legal relations; it was aquivalent to

자작(<영국의> 백작 marquis과 남작 baron 사이의 귀족)

1) Duke(듀크, 공작), Marquis(마키스, 후작), Earl 또는 Count(얼, 백작) Viscount(바이카운트, 자작), Baron(배런, 남작)의 순서

an advertisement offering "free air", and the coins were free gifts (which was also the persuasive opinion of *Lord Denning* before ... "common sense") but, if there had been a contract, they agree that it was no contract of sale.

On the other hand, *Lord Fraser* agreed with the first instance decision that the customer *contracted* to buy four gallons of petrol and a coin: it was like the case of a baker offering an extra bun "free of charge" to anyone who bought a dozen buns.

공짜 공기

달고 작은 빵 / 공짜로

Diagram 27

Intention to Create Legal Relations

For an agreement to be enforceable in court, the parties must intend it to be legally binding.

Family / Domestic Agreements	**Advertisements**	**Commercial / Business Agreements**
Rule: Agreements of a purely social or domestic nature are not contracts.	*Rule*: Advertisements do not contain offers, but only an invitation to treat.	*Rule*: There is a presumption of law that the parties entering into a commercial or business agreement intend to create legal relations.
Exception: Agreements in the case of separation of spouses. (e.g. *Merritt v Merritt, 1970*)	Exception: A particular statement or action by the advertiser shows the intention to create legal relations. (e.g. *Mrs. Carlill's Case, 1893*)	Exception: Express terms excluding any legal relations. (e.g. *Rose & Frank Co.* v *Compton Bros. Ltd., 1925*)

V. Capacity to contract

(법률)행위능력, 계약을 체결할 (법적) 능력

Under English law, capacity to contract or contractual capacity (which is the same) is also a fundamental precondition for a valid contract. Generally, adult citizens have full

유효한

capacity to enter into any kind of contract, but for certain groups of persons in law the contractual capacity is limited or denied entirely.

체결하다
제한된
부정하다, 거절하다

The consequences of missing or limited capacity to contract are, however, often different in English law than those which follow in German or Korean law. Above all, where a person is denied full contractual capacity, the aim of English civil law is to protect this person and not to prohibit any contract. In the following paragraphs, natural and legal persons who have less than full capacity to contract shall be dealt with.

빠진
목적, 목표 / 보호하다
막다

1. Infants/Minors

A minor, according to s. 12 of the *Family Law Reform Act 1969*, is a person who has not yet reached the age of majority. As you may have already learnt by now, this age was reduced from 21 to 18 years by s.1 of this 1969 Act. A person attains majority at the commencement of his eighteenth birthday [s.9 (1) of the 1969 Act].

Under English law, as a general rule, a minor is not bound by any contract made during his minority. There are, however, three main exceptions to this rule: contracts for necessaries, contracts of an educational nature or of employment for the minor's benefit, and certain contracts which are voidable. As a result of the *Minors Contract Act 1987*, minors' contracts can be divided into the following categories:

생필품 / 교육에 관한 / 노동관계 / 유익, 이익
취소가능한 / 미성년자 계약법

- binding contracts,
- voidable contracts and
- void contracts.

a) Binding contracts

For binding contracts the minor has full contractual capacity. These contracts are enforceable by the minor as well as by the other party.

Binding contracts can be:

- contracts for necessaries and
- contracts for the minor's benefit, particularly educational and employment contracts.

(aa) *Contracts for necessaries*

The term "necessaries" is not only restricted to those things which are required to maintain a bare existence such as bread and clothes, but includes all "goods suitable to the condition in life of the minor or other person concerned and to his actual requirements at the time of the sale and delivery" [as defined by the *Sale of Goods Act 1979*, s.3 (3)].

제한된
유지하다 / 벌거벗은 (최소한의) 생존 / ~에 어울리는
생활여건
실제 필요들

In this definition is included that contracts for necessaries must be executed ("at the time of the sale and delivery") in order to bind the parties. If the goods correspond to this definition they are necessaries and the minor may be compelled to pay a reasonable price.

강제하다

This will usually, but not necessarily, be the contract price. The minor is, however, not liable if one of the four preconditions of s.3 (3) of the *Sale of Goods Act* 1979 is not satisfied.

Thus, a shopkeeper or another person with whom the minor enters into a contract or a court (in the case of litigation) has to prove that the goods are

(1) suitable to the minor's condition in life,
(2) necessary to his requirements at the time of sale,
(3) necessary to his requirements at the time of delivery, and
(4) such goods with which he was not sufficiently supplied at the time of sale and delivery.

충분하게 / 공급하다

Example – Nash* v *Inman (1908) –:

The plaintiff was a Savile Row tailor and the defendant was a minor undergraduate at Trinity College, Cambridge. The defendant ordered clothes (including 11 fancy waistcoats) which together amounted to £145.

양복쟁이, 테일러
대학생(학부생)
화려한 조끼
값이 ~이다

The plaintiff sued the defendant for this sum. The defendant's father, an architect, proved that his son was already supplied with adequate clothes suitable to his condition in life when the clothes made by the plaintiff were delivered.

Held: that the plaintiff's action failed, because the clothes supplied were not "necessaries".

(bb) *Contracts for the minor's benefit*

Two points should be stressed under this heading:

(1) Not every contract for the benefit of a minor is binding upon him, and

(2) the question of what is "for the minor's benefit" is one for the court to decide from the particular facts of each case. 개별 사건의 특수한 정황

As a general rule, we may say that contracts for education, service or apprenticeship, or similar contracts to enable the minor to earn his living (except trading contracts) are binding unless they are detrimental to the interests of the minor. To reach a just and equitable decision the court has to look at the contract as a whole. Let us leaf through the case books for some examples.

교육
서비스 / 직업훈련
상사계약들, 상업계약들
불리한, 해로운
(책장을) 넘기다

One of the most common cases found in nearly all textbooks is the following

***Example* — *Doyle* v *White City Stadium (1935)* —:**

D, a minor professional boxer, made a contract with the British Boxing Board of Control. Under the terms of the contract it was provided that if D were disqualified, his prize money would be withheld. D fought a match and lost being disqualified, and the Board withheld the money. D sued the Board to recover the money.

Held: that there was a contract of employment which was on the whole for D's benefit, although the particular clause appeared onerous. Thus, D's action failed.

영국복싱감독위원회(감독청)
(지급을) 보류하다
되찾다, 반환받다
귀찮은, 의무를 지우는

In contrast to this case is the next

Example — De Francesco* v *Barnum (1890) —:

A minor was apprenticed for stage dancing by deed, which provided that she should be entirely at the disposal of the master; that he should not pay her unless he actually employed her, which he was not bound to do; that he could send her abroad; that he could put an end to the contract if, after fair trial, he found her unsuitable; and that she should not accept any professional engagement without his consent. The minor accepted a professional engagement with the defendant without the master's consent. The action of the master failed.

Held: that the master could not sue the defendant for inducing a breach of the apprenticeship contract as it was unreasonably harsh and thus invalid.

(직업)교육하다 / 무대댄스
처분에 따르는
공정한 절차
~하게 하다, 유도하다, 설득하다 / 가혹한

In other words, because the apprenticeship deed was not for the minor's benefit, it was not enforceable.

b) Voidable contracts

무효화할 수 있는, 취소할 수 있는

Contracts which are not binding are voidable at the minor's discretion: when a minor acquires an interest in an object of permanent nature, e.g. leases of property, partnership agreements, or the taking of shares in a company, the contract cannot be enforced against him during minority, but the minor can force an adult to perform the contract.

If, however, a minor repudiates a contract which has been partly performed by the other party, the minor has to pay for the benefit received.

재량, 선택 / 얻다
계속적 성격의 목적물 / 부동산 임대차 계약
이행하다
거부하다, 인정하지 않다

Example — Steinberg* v *Scala (Leeds) Ltd. (1923) —:

The plaintiff, a minor, applied for and was allotted shares in the defendant company. She paid sums on allotment and on the first call on the shares. When she was unable to pay further calls she repudiated the contract. She requested, since still being a minor, that her name should be removed from

할당하다
피고회사 / 할당
주금납입요구
요구하다

the register of shareholders and also requested the return of all money she had paid. — 주주명부

Held: that the infant was entitled to the removal of her name from the register to avoid future calls on her shares, but she could not recover the money paid because there had not been a *total* failure of consideration. Although no dividends had been paid on the shares, the shares nevertheless had some value.

삭제, 제거 / 되찾다, 반환받다 / 완전 불이행 / 배당금

When a minor refuses to perform a voidable contract, the *Minor's Contract Act 1987*, gives power to the courts, when it is "just and equitable", to allow the other party to recover from the minor any property acquired under the contract. When, for example, a minor receives goods under a contract and then refuses to pay for the goods, the court may order the minor to return the goods to the plaintiff. Similarly, if a minor has taken the benefit of a *void* contract for the sale of goods other than necessaries, he cannot retain the goods and recover the money he has paid for them. In the case of *Nash* v *Inman*, (cf. page 138), the minor would have had to return the waistcoats to the supplier or else pay for them.

권능을 부여하다 / 정당하고 형평에 맞는 / 거부하다 / 유사한 방식으로 / 보유하다, 계속 가지다 / 반환하다 / 그렇지 않은 경우

If a minor delivers goods under a contract which is not binding on him, he cannot recover them unless there is a total failure of consideration.

Example — Pearce v Brain (1929) —:

Pearce, a minor, exchanged his motor cycle for a car belonging to Brain. Pearce had little use of the car, and had in fact driven it only 70 miles when it broke down because of serious defects in the back axle. Pearce then sued Brain to recover his motor cycle, claiming total failure of consideration.

Held: that a contract for the exchange of goods, whilst not a sale of goods, is a contract for the supply of goods, and because the car was not a necessary good the contract was void. However, since a minor can only recover money paid under a void contract if the consideration had failed, entirely

뒷축 / ~는 아니라 하더라도 / 공급

Pearce could not recover the motor cycle. The court considered that the minor had received a benefit. Thus, there was not a total failure of consideration but only inadequacy of consideration.

불균형함, 비례하지 않음, 상응하지 않음

On the other hand, if the minor had bought a sports bag on credit and then sold it, using all the proceeds of the sale to attend a *Michael Jackson* concert in London, the seller could not recover anything from the minor, because all the money had gone. But, if the minor had used the proceeds of the sale to buy a CD, instead of attending the concert, the plaintiff could recover the CD.

수입

~에 가다, 참석하다

A voidable contract, not repudiated by the minor during his minority, becomes binding on the attainment of full age unless he repudiates it within a reasonable time after having reached 18. What constitutes a "reasonable time" is a matter for decision by the court and varies with each type of contract.

성년에 이름

적절한 시간

c) Void (unenforceable) contracts

무효의 / 강제할 수 없는, 소권이 없는

Under the *Infants Relief Act 1874*, three types of contract were declared to be absolutely void, namely, contracts of loan, contracts for goods other than necessaries and all accounts stated with minors.

미성년자 구제법

대출계약

당좌계정

However, although such contracts were declared to be void, they were not completely without effect, as we have seen in the example *Pearce* v *Brain*, unless there had been a total failure of consideration.

2. Persons of unsound mind and drunks

Persons of unsound mind as well as drunks are liable for contracts of necessaries and, similar to minors, must pay a reasonable price.

만취한 자

Other contracts are voidable at their option if a person of unsound mind or an alcoholic can prove that at the time of entering the contract

- they were so ill or so intoxicated that they did not know what they were doing, and — 술(=독)에 취한
- the other party knew of their condition. — 상태

This was the view taken by the court in the following case.

***Example — Imperial Loan Co.* v *Stone (1892)* —:**

This was an action on a promissory note. The defendant pleaded that at the time of making the note he was insane, and that the plaintiff knew that he was. The jury found that he was in fact insane but could not agree on the question of whether the plaintiff knew it. The judge of the lower court entered judgment for the defendant.

Held: that he was wrong. The defendant in order to succeed must convince the court on both issues.

약속어음 / 하급심 법원 / 확신시키다 / 쟁점

This means that the person who is mentally disordered not only has to prove his illness, but has also the burden of proving the other party's knowledge of the illness.

정신장애가 있는 / 부담

This was confirmed by the Privy Council in the New Zealand case of *Hart* v *O'Connor* (1985): The Privy Council refused to set aside an agreement to sell farmland because although the seller was of unsound mind, his affliction was not apparent. If it *had* been, the Privy Council said that the contract could have been set aside for "equitable fraud".

실효(失效)시키다 / 정신박약상태 / 명백한 / 사기

In this context the expression means unfair or unconscionable conduct, such as victimization or taking unfair advantage.

미풍양속에 반하는 / 착취 / 과도한 이익

This rule would presumably also apply to the case of a drunken person.

짐작컨대 / 적용하다

Persons of unsound mind, moreover, will be liable on contracts made during a lucid interval, notwithstanding the fact that their disability was known to the other party.

(정신이 잠깐) 밝은 순간 / ~에도 불구하고 / 행위무능력

Where the property of an insane person is by order under the control of the court under Part Ⅶ of the *Mental Health Act 1983*, the insane person has no capacity to contract as regards that property. ～에 관련하다

3. Corporations

a) Introduction

The legal position and capacity of corporations had already been discussed in Chapter Five.

The contractual capacity of corporations depends upon the manner in which they are created.

It goes without saying that corporations are incapable of making certain contracts of a personal nature, e.g. a contract to marry. 분명하다 / 결혼하다

b) Kinds of corporation

(aa) *Chartered corporations* 국가공인법인

Chartered corporations are, as you should know by now, created by a Royal Charter. There are no legal limits to the contractual capacity of these corporations. The charter may be, however, withdrawn if contracts are persistently made outside of the limits of the corporation's powers as defined in the particular charter. 문서(공인서) / 취소하다, 철회하다 / 계속하여

(bb) *Statutory corporations* 법정(法定) 법인

These corporations derive their contractual capacity from the statutes (Acts of Parliament) which created them. Contracts may only be made within the limits of the creating statute, and contracts formed beyond the powers contained in the statutes are "*ultra vires*" and void. ～에서 유래하다 / 권한 바깥의 / "권한을 넘어선", 무권대리

(cc) *Registered (limited) companies* 등록회사

These companies are governed by the *Companies Act 1985* and have their powers specified in the objects clause of the *memorandium of association*. A contract made in excess of these powers is also "*ultra vires*" and void, i.e. of no effect. 규정하다 / 회사목적조항 / ～을 넘어선, 위반한

c) The doctrine of *ultra vires*

(영미의) 무권대리 이론

According to the *doctrine of ultra vires*, the contractual capacity of statutory corporations and registered companies is limited by statute or the memorandum of association, which determines the objects of the corporation or the company.

규정하다, 정하다 / 회사목적

The most important consequences of acting "beyond the powers" have already been indicated: Contracts made *ultra vires* are void or voidable, the state may delete automatically the corporation or company, and it is possible that the directors of the administration become liable to the corporation or company.

직권으로 삭제하다
이사회 회원(이사) / 책임지다

In practice these consequences are often prevented by a wide formulation of the objects. Moreover, the doctrine of *ultra vires* has been restricted by the *European Communities Act 1972*, which provides that if a person deals with a company in good faith any contract is valid, whether or not it is beyond the powers of the object clause. A person acts in good faith if he he is not aware of the powers of the object clause.

막다
넓게 규정함
조항을 두다
선의
~을 알고 있다

Example – Ashbury Railway Carriage and Iron Co. Ltd. v Riche (1875) –:

In this leading case the objects set out in the company's memorandum were "to make and sell, or lend or hire, railway carriages and waggons, and all kinds of railway plant, fittings, machinery and rolling stock; to carry on the business of mechanical engineers and general contractors; to purchase, lease, work and sell mines, minerals, land and buildings; to purchase and sell as merchants, timber, coal, metals, or other materials on commission or as agents."

리딩케이스, 모범사례
임대 / 임차
객차 / 화물차 / 공장
핏팅류 / 차량보유상태 / (사업을) 유지하다, 수행하다 / 포괄 계약인 / 임대 / 가공 / 광업
목재
수수료를 받고

The directors of the company purchased a concession for the construction of a railway system in Belgium and purported to contract with Riche that he should construct the railway line. Riche commenced the work and the company paid over certain sums of money in connection with the contract. The

허가, 인가
의도하다
개시하다 / 지불하다

Ashbury company later ran into difficulties, and the shareholders wished the directors to take over the contract in a personal capacity and to indemnify the shareholders. The directors thereupon repudiated the contract on behalf of the company and Riche sued for breach of contract.

Held (by the House of Lords): that the directors were able to repudiate because the contract to construct a railway system, as distinct from rolling stock, was *ultra vires* and that therefore the contract was void.

Lord Chancellor *Lord Cairns* stated:

"... the question is as to the competancy and power of the company to make the contract. Now I am clearly of the opinion that this contract was entirely, as I have said, beyond the objects of the memorandum of the association. If so, it was thereby placed beyond the powers of the company to make the contract. If so, it is not a question whether the contract was ever ratified. It was a contract void at its beginning, it was void because the company could not make the contract."

면책하다

~에 뒤이어 / (인정을) 거부하다, 인정하지 않다

~와는 다르게

추인하다, 인정하다

Diagram 28

Capacity to Contract (Contractual Capacity)

Infants/Minors

Binding contracts

- contracts of necessaries
- contracts for the minor's benefit (particularly educational and employment contracts

Voidable contracts

Contracts which are not binding are voidable at the minor's discretion: the contract cannot be unforced against him, but the minor can force an adult to perform the contract.

Void (unenforceable) contracts

- contracts of loan
- contracts for goods other than necessaries
- all accounts stated with minors

Persons of unsound mind and drunks

liable for contracts of necessaries

Voidable contracts

At their option, if they can prove that at the time of entering the contact

- they were so ill or so intoxicated that they did not know what they were doing and
- the other party knew their condition

Corporations

The contractual capacity of corporations depends upon the manner in which they are created.

Chartered corporation

There are no legal limits to the contractual capacity.

Statutory corporation

Derive contractual capacity from the statutes.

Registered (limited) corporations

Their powers (and contractual capacity) follow from the memorandum of association

A contract made in excess of the powers is *ultra vires* and void

Ⅵ. The contents of contracts

1. Introduction

This paragraph is concerned with the situation where the parties have fulfilled all the requirements for making a valid contract, as described in the previous paragraphs. It may then become necessary to determine exactly what the obligations under the contract are. Problems can arise in a number of ways.

단락
의무(책임)

There may, perhaps, have been a long period of pre-contractual negotiations, and it may not be clear which, if any, of the statements made by the parties were intended to form a part of the contract.

계약 前의 협상
계약의 일부분

The contract may be in writing, and yet one party may allege that it does not correctly represent their intentions, or the contract may be merely verbal, in which case there may be a dispute as to what was said or promised, and by whom. Some of these problems may be resolved by the rules which the English courts have developed to enable terms to be implied into a contract. Moreover, in certain situations, terms will be implied by statutes, irrespective of the wishes and intentions of the parties.

그럼에도 (불구하고)
주장하다
단지(~에 불과한)
해결하다
가능하게 하다 / 조건 / 계약 내용으로 (해석하여) 넣다
~에 상관없이

2. Terms and representations

표현, 진술, 주장

The undertakings and promises contained in a contract are known as *the terms of a contract*.

보증, 약속
계약 조건, 계약의 내용

In its simplest form the term “I will drive your car to London” might be answered by the term “Then, I will pay you ￡100”.

The terms of contract have to be distinguished from representations which are made during pre-contractual negotiations and are not intended to form an integral part of the contract (liability for misrepresentation will be considered below in paragraph Ⅶ).

필수항목
허위진술, 허위표시, 거짓주장

3. The kinds of terms

The terms of a contract which define the rights and duties of the parties can be simply divided into two kinds: *express terms* and *implied terms*.

정의를 내리다(밝히다), 정하다
명시적인
묵시적인

a) Express terms

The parties will usually state expressly in their contract the terms which they consider material, and little difficulty exists in ascertaining these *express terms*.

중요한, 본질적인
확인하다

Where a contract has been put into writing the parties are not allowed adducing evidence "to add to, vary or contradict" the term of the written agreement. Therefore, oral evidence will not be admitted in order to prove that some other terms have been omitted from the written document.

제시하는 / 증거 / 더하다 / 변경하다 / 부정하다
삭제하다

If, however, the written contract is not complete and does not, in fact, represent the whole transaction, oral evidence will be admitted by the court to prove a *collateral agreement*, i.e. an agreement which is subsidiary to the main purpose of the contract.

거래
부수적인(2차적인) 합의

The question the courts often have had to decide, in this context, is: "Is there a real *contractual term or mere representation*?"

***Example – Couchman* v *Hill (1947)* –:**

The plaintiff purchased a heifer at an auction. The heifer was described in the catalogue as "unserved", but the catalogue and the printed conditions of sale made it clear that the accuracy of any description was not guaranteed and the lots were to be sold with all errors of description. The plaintiff required an unserved heifer for service by his own bull. Before the sale, when the heifers were in the ring, he asked both the defendant (the owner) and the auctioneer if they could confirm that the heifer was unserved.

(젊은) 암소
교배하지 아니한
정확성
(상품의) 각 항목들
울타리 친 장소

They both answered "Yes". After he had bought the heifer it was found to be in calf and died from carrying a calf at too young age. — 새끼를 밴 상태

Held (by the Court of Appeal): that the answers of the defendant and the auctioneer amounted to an offer of a warranty, overriding the conditions of sale, that the offer was accepted by the plaintiff's bid and that the misdescription amounted to a breach of condition, which the plaintiff was entitled to treat as a breach of warranty and he could recover damages.

값을 매기다
보증 / 변경하다
입찰 / 허위기재사항
보증의무위반 / 손해배상을 받다

This case differs from the next example.

Example — Routledge* v *McKay (1954) —:

The plaintiff and the defendant were discussing the possible purchase of the defendant's motorcycle. Both parties were private persons. On 23 October the defendant taking the information from the registration book, said that the cycle was a 1942 model. On 30 October a written contract of sale was made. — 차량등록증

However the actual construction date of the cycle was later found to be 1930. The buyer's claim for damages for breach of warranty failed.

Held (by the Court of Appeal): that in this case the interval between the negotiations and the conclusion of the contract was well marked and that the statement was not a term, but an inducement only.

계약체결
권유, 유인

Similar to this case is the following.

Example — Oscar Chess Ltd.* v *Williams (1957) —:

In May 1955, the defendant acquired a new car from the plaintiffs who were motor car dealers and who took the defendant's Morris[1] in part exchange. The defendant said it

자동차 판매업자
헌물건을 새물건 값의 일부로 치다

1) 영국의 차종명

was a 1948 model, as per the registration document, and the plaintiffs gave him an allowance of ￡290. The registration book had been altered by an unknown third party and the car was, in reality, a 1939 model worth ￡175. The County Court judge held that it was a *condition (term)* of the contract that the car was a 1948 model.

차량등록증
할인
변경하다

Held (by the Court of Appeal): that the defendant's statement as to the age of the car was a *mere representation,* not a term of the contract. The defendant had no special knowledge as to its age and the plaintiffs knew that he was relying on the date in the registration book. Therefore the defendant was not liable.

신뢰하다

Let us examine some arguments of *Lord Denning* in stating the reasons for the decision:

"I entirely agree with the judge [of the County Court] that both parties assumed that the Morris was a 1948 model and that this assumption was fundamental to the contract. But this does *not* prove that the representation was a term of the contract.

~라고 생각하다, 전제하다
전제

The assumption was based by both of them on the date given in the registration book as the date of first registration .... They both were mistaken and their mistake was of fundamental importance. The effect of such a mistake is this: It does not make the contract a nullity from the beginning, but it does in some circumstances enable the contract to be set aside in equity.

처음부터 무효, 원천무효
무효화하다

If the buyer had come promptly (here he came eight months later!), he might have succeeded in getting the whole transaction set aside in equity on the grounds of this mistake; but he did not do so and it is too late for him to do it.

즉시
~라는 이유로(구실로)

His only remedy is in damages, and to recover these he must prove warranty.

변상(구제책) / 되찾다, 얻다

In saying that ... I use the word 'warranty' in its *ordinary* English meaning to denote a binding promise. Everyone knows what a man means when he says 'I guarantee it' or 'I

표시하다

warrant it' or 'I give you my word on it'. He means that he binds himself to it ... . During the last fifty years, however, some lawyers have come to use the word 'warranty' in another sense. They use it to denote a *subsidiary* term in contract as distinct from a *vital* term which they call a 'condition'. In so doing they depart from the ordinary meaning, not only of the word 'warranty' but also of the word 'condition'.

필수불가결한
벗어나다

There is no harm in their doing this, so long as they confine this technical use in its proper sphere, namely, to distinguish between a vital term, the breach of which gives the right to treat the contract as at an end, and a subsidiary term which does not. But the trouble comes when one person uses the word 'warranty' in its ordinary meaning and another uses it in its technical meaning.

손해
제한하다 / 고유 분야(범위)

... Turning now to the present case, much depends on the precise words that were used. If the seller says 'I believe it is a 1948 Morris. Here is the registration book to prove it', there is clearly no warranty. It is a statement of belief, not a contractual promise. But if the seller says 'I guarantee that it is a 1948 Morris. This is borne out of the registration book, but you should not rely solely on that. I give you my own guarantee that it is', there is clearly a warranty. The seller is making himself contractually responsible even so the registration book is wrong.

생겨나다, ~에 근거를 두다
오직 ~에만

In this case much reliance was placed by the judge on the fact that the buyer ... paid ￡290 on the footing that it was a 1948 model: but that fact seems to me to be neutral. *Both* sides believed the car to have been made in 1948 and in *that* belief the buyer paid ￡290.

신뢰
~을 근거로

That belief can be just as firmly based on the buyer's own inspection of the log-book as on a contractual warranty by the seller ...

~와 마찬가지로 / 확고하게
차계부, 차량일지

One final word: It seems to me clear that the motor-dealers who bought the car relied on the year stated in the log-book. If they had wished to make sure of it, they could have checked it there and then, by taking the engine number and chassis number and writing to the makers. They did not

거기서 그리고 그 때
제작자

do so, but only eight months later. They are *experts*, and, not having made that check at the time, I do not think they should now be allowed to recover against the <u>innocent</u> seller who produced to them all the evidence he had, namely, the registration book. 결백한

I agree that it is hard on the dealers to have paid more than the car is worth: but it would be equally hard on the seller to make him pay the difference ...

<u>The right course</u> is to let the buyer set aside the transaction *if* he finds out the mistake *quickly* and comes *promptly* before other interests have <u>irretrievably</u> intervened; other wise the loss must lie where it falls: and that is, I think, the course prescribed by law. I would allow this appeal accordingly." 올바른 (진행)과정 / 회복할 수 없게

In my opinion this judgment of *Lord Denning* not only reflects brilliant and logical arguments, but it also <u>reveals</u> that equity can protect innocent lay men even against professional experts. 나타내다(밝히다)

b) Implied terms

One of the basic rules of the law of contract is, as we have seen, the fact that the parties are free to determine their own terms. Similary to German civil law, under English law the <u>*freedom of contract*</u> not only <u>comprises</u> the freedom to enter a contract as well as the freedom to choose the person with whom the contract is to be entered, but also the freedom of the parties to create a legal relationship by <u>mutual</u> declarations. 계약의 자유 / 내포하다(의미하다), 포함하다 / 상호의(서로의), 상호합의하여

It is not the function of the courts to make the parties' contract for them. However, in some <u>exceptional</u> cases the law may <u>imply</u> terms into the contract. 예외적인 / 포함하다(뜻하다), 암시하다

In other words: sometimes, even though the parties have not expressly mentioned something as being a term of contract, it may be implied into contract. If, e.g., you buy a new pair of shoes, which then <u>fall apart</u>, such case in point constitutes a breach of contractual condition by the seller. 찢어지다, 서로 떨어지다

The seller may not have stated that the shoes are in good condition, but the term is implied into the contract by the *Sale of Goods Act 1979.* Sections 12-15 of this Act imply certain terms into contracts for the sale of goods which are for the protection of the buyer. Section 13, e.g., makes it an implied condition that goods shall correspond with their description. Section 14 provides that goods shall be of merchantable quality (unlike the shoes which were not!). Section 15 lays down that in a sale by sample, the bulk shall correspond with the sample.

(상거래상) 통상적인 품질
견본매매
견본

***Example — Harlingdon & Leinster Enterprises Ltd.* v *Christopher Hull Fine Art Ltd. (1990)* —:**

In 1984, Mr. Hull, the owner of the defendant company, was asked to dispose of two oil paintings which, in a 1980 auction catalogue, had been described as being the work of Gabriele Münter (1877-1962), an artist of the German impressionist school. Hull contacted the plaintiff art dealers and, after he had made it clear that he did not know much about the paintings and that he was not an expert in them, the plaintiffs bought one of them for £6,000. Hull made out the following invoice:

유화
작성하다
송장, 인보이스

"3 December 1984
Gabriele Mnter (1877-1962)
Dorfstrae in Oberbayern
oil on board, 39×48cm, £6,000"

액자를 한

In February 1985 the customer (who bought the painting from the plaintiffs) discovered that the painting was not by Münter but was only a forgery. The plaintiffs took it back and refunded the price. The defendant, however, refused to take it back. The plaintiffs sued, alleging a breach of contract on four points: (1) for the sale of goods by description [*Sale of Goods Act 1979*, s. 13 (1)], (2) that the painting was not of merchantable quality, (3) that the painting would be not reasonably fit, and (4) that it was a misrepresentation according to the *Misrepresentation Act 1967*.

위조
환불하다
주장하다
적합하다

The judge held in favour of the defendant on all four points. The plaintiffs appealed.

Held: that the appeal would be dismissed. The buyers had not relied on the description of a forged painting to be one of Gabriele Münter, bringing the sale under s.13 (1) of the *Sale of Goods Act 1979*, and they had failed to establish the painting was not of merchantable quality under s. 14 (2) and (6) of the Act.

~를 위하여(승소를 의미)
항소하다
기각하다
위조된
입증하다

This example manifests one of the sources of implied terms:

(aa) *Terms implied by statute*

As has already been indicated, it is the *Sale of Goods Act 1979* which implies certain terms into the contract for the sale of goods.

Beside those mentioned above s. 12 provides that the goods must belong to the person selling them and moreover in s. 14 (3), it is required that the goods be fit for the purpose for which they are sold. If the seller breaks any of the terms implied by the *Sale of Goods Act* the contract is void and the buyer can reclaim the purchase money.

반환청구하다 / 매매대금

One other statute, which implies terms into a contract is the *Supply of Goods and Services Act 1982*. This Act applies to anyone giving a service, such as a bank, a builder or a plumber. According to this Act it is implied into the contract that the service will be carried out within a reasonable time [s.14 (1)] and that, if no price is mentioned, a reasonable price will be paid [s.15 (1)].

공급 / 서비스, 용역
건축업자
배관공
수행하다

(bb) *Terms implied by common law*

The courts will imply terms into a contract if they are obvious and necessary. This is the case, if you can state that such a consideration “goes without saying”: If, e.g., you rent a flat at the top of the house, it goes without saying that you can walk through the house to reach it.

명백한(분명한)
말할 필요가 없는

Generally, a term is said to be implied if it is necessary to carry out the presumed intention of the parties and it is so obvious that the parties must have intended it to apply to the contract and therefore thought it was unnecessary to express it. The term's implication must be necessary to give the business efficacy to the contract which the parties intended.

실행하다 / 추정하다
함축(내포)
사업 / 효과

Example — The Moorcock (1889) —:

The owner of the *Moorcock* agreed with the defendant wharfingers that his vessel should be discharged and loaded at their wharf and for that purpose should be moored at a jetty which belonged to the wharfingers and extended into the river Thames. When the tide ebbed and the vessel took the ground, it struck a ridge of a rock and suffered damage. *Held*: that the contract contained an implied obligation on the part of the wharfingers that it was reasonably safe for the vessel to be berthed at the jetty: "What the law desires to effect by the implication is to give such a business efficacy to the transaction as have been intended at all events by both parties who are businessmen" (Lord Justice *Bowen*).

선창주인(관리인) / 배 / 짐을(승객을) 내리다 / (짐을) 선창에 풀다 / 선창, 부두 / (배가) 정박하다 / 부두 / 펼치다, 뻗치다 / 조수가 썰물일 때
충돌했다 / 모퉁이에
정박하다

(cc) *Terms implied by custom*

Terms may be implied by custom if they are certain, reasonable and well-known to all affected by them, and they must not offend any statute.

영향 받는
(죄를) 범하다, (법을) 어기다

Example — Hutton* v *Warren (1836) —:

The defendant was the landlord, and the plaintiff the tenant of a certain farm. At Michaelmas 1833 the defendant gave the plaintiff notice to quit on the Lady Day following. In October 1833 the defendant insisted that the plaintiff was bound to continue to cultivate the farm in due course of husbandry according to the custom of the country, and gave him formal notice to that effect. The plaintiff quitted in accordance with the notice and then alleged that he was

(대천사)미가엘 축일(9월 29일)
그만두다(떠나다) / 성모영보대축일 (천사가 마리아의 수태를 알림)
통상적인 경영의 방식대로

entitled to a fair allowance for seeds and labour on the arable land. It was proved that by the custom of the country a tenant was bound to farm according to a certain course of husbandry for the whole of this tenancy, and, on quitting, was entitled to a fair allowance for seeds and labour on the arable land.

보상 / 씨
경작할 수 있는
과정
전체 임대계약기간

Held: that the plaintiff succeeded. The judgment of the court was delivered by *Parke* J.

"We are of the opinion that this custom was, by implication, imported into the lease. It has long been settled, that, in commercial transactions, extrinsic evidence of custom and usage is admissible to annex incidents to written contracts, in matters with respect to which they are silent. The same rule has also been applied to contracts in other transactions of life, in which known usages have been established and prevailed; and this has been done upon the principle of presumption that, in such transactions, the parties did not mean to express in writing the whole of the contract by which they intended to be bound, but to contract with reference to those known usages ..."

(용익)임대차
외부의
사용(취급) / 허용가능한 / 부가하다 / 부대조건 / 그들이 침묵하는 것에 관한 사안들
지배적이다 / 추정의 원칙
의미하다
계약을 맺다

c) Conditions, warranties and innominate terms

조건, 보증 그리고 익명의(미언급된)

If a particular statement is a term of a contract it can be either a condition or a warranty.

(aa) *Conditions*

A condition is a term of major importance and forms the main basis of the contract. It is so essential to the very nature of the contract that if it is broken, the innocent party can treat the contract as discharged. He will not, therefore, be bound to do anything further under that contract.

위반하다
해지하다

***Example — Poussard* v *Spears and Pond (1876)* —:**

Madame Poussard had entered into an agreement to play a part in an opera. One day before the first performance she was taken ill and was unable to appear for eleven days. The defendants had hired a substitute, and discovered that the only way in which they could secure a substitute to take Mme. Poussard's place was to offer that person the complete engagement. This they had done, and they refused the services of Mme. Poussard when she presented herself after the end of her illness.

아픈
고용하다 / 대체인력
보장하다

The plaintiff (Mme. Poussard) then sued for a breach of contract.

Held: that the failure of Mme. Poussard to perform the contract as from the first night was a breach of *condition*, and that the defendants were within their rights in regarding the contract as discharged.

실패, 해태

(bb) *Warranties*

A warranty is a term of minor importance, which means that it is collateral or subsidiary to the main purpose of the contract. It is not therefore so fundamental as to effect a discharge of the contract. A breach of warranty only gives an action to damages. So the importance of the differentiation between conditions and warranties lies in the remedy in the event of breach.

부차적인 / 보완적인
해지, (계약의무의) 해소
구제책 / ~한 경우

***Example — Bettini* v *Gye (1876)* —:**

The plaintiff was an opera singer. The defendant was the director of the Royal Italian Opera in London. The plaintiff had agreed to sing in Great Britain in theatres, halls and drawing rooms for a period of time beginning on 30 March 1875, and to be in London for rehearsals six days before the engagement started. The plaintiff was taken ill and arrived on 28 March 1875, but the defendant did not accept the plaintiff's

객실
리허설(예행연습)

services, treating the contract as discharged.

Held: that the rehearsal clause was subsidiary to the main purpose of the contract, and its breach constituted a breach of *warranty* only. The defendant had no right to treat the contract as discharged and therefore had to compensate the plaintiff, but he had a counterclaim for any damage he had suffered by the plaintiff's late arrival.

조항
보상하다
반대청구권, 반소청구권

(cc) *Innominate terms*

Innominate (also: intermediate) terms combine the nature of condition and warranty in so far as the breach of such a term may either entitle the innocent party to rescind the contract or otherwise entitle him only to claim damages, depending upon the circumstances.

중간
해지하다, 해제하다

Example — Hong Kong Fir Shipping Co. Ltd.* v *Kawasaki Kisen Kaisha Ltd. (1962) —:

The defendants chartered the vessel "Hong Kong Fir" from the plaintiffs for 24 months. The charter-party provided "she being fitted in every way for ordinary cargo service". It happened that the engine room stuff was incomplete and the vessel spent not less than nine weeks of the first seven months of the charter at sea because of breakdowns and subsequent repairs required to make her seaworthy. The defendants repudiated the charter party and claimed that the term as to seaworthiness was a *condition* of the contract, and breach of which entitled them so to do.

Held (by the Court of Appeal): that *the term was neither a condition nor a warranty*, and in determining whether the defendants could terminate the contract, it was necessary to look at the consequences of the breach to see if they deprived the innocent party substantially of the whole benefit he should have received under the contract. On the facts, this was not the case, because the charter party still had a substantial time (17 months) to run. So the charterers were not entitled to repudiate the contract because the unseaworthi-

전나무
용선계약(서)
화물서비스
재료
용선계약 / 고장
항해에 적합한
부인했다
내항능력
빼앗다 / 매우 중요한 정도로
상당한(많은) / 용선계약자
항해 부적합성

ness of the ship was of such trivial consequence that the charterers had to abide by the contract and could only claim damages if they had suffered a loss.

평범한, 사소한
계약을 준수하다
손해를 입다

The principle embodied in the *Hong Kong-Fir-Shipping-Case* applies to contracts for the sale of goods just as all other contracts. Consequently, the term in a contract of sale that "shipment is to be made in good condition" can be interpreted as neither referring to a "condition" nor to a "warranty" within the meaning of these expressions used in the *Sale of Goods Act 1979*.

구체화된
선적

It may, however, be indicative of one of those *innominate* stipulations which gives the buyer no right to reject the goods unless the breach goes to the root of the contract.

표시하는
약정(조항), 합의
근본, 기초

Where an innominate term is broken "while in many instances breach of it can adequately be sanctioned by damages, cases may exist in which, in fairness to the buyer, it would be proper to treat the cancellation as not having effect. On the other hand, always so to treat it may often be unfair to the seller, and unnecessarily rigid" *(Lord Wilberforce* in *Bremer Handelsgesellschaft mbH* v *Vanden Avenne-Izegem P.V.B.A. [1978]).*

보기(사례), 경우
적당한 / 취소, 해지
엄격한

Diagram 29

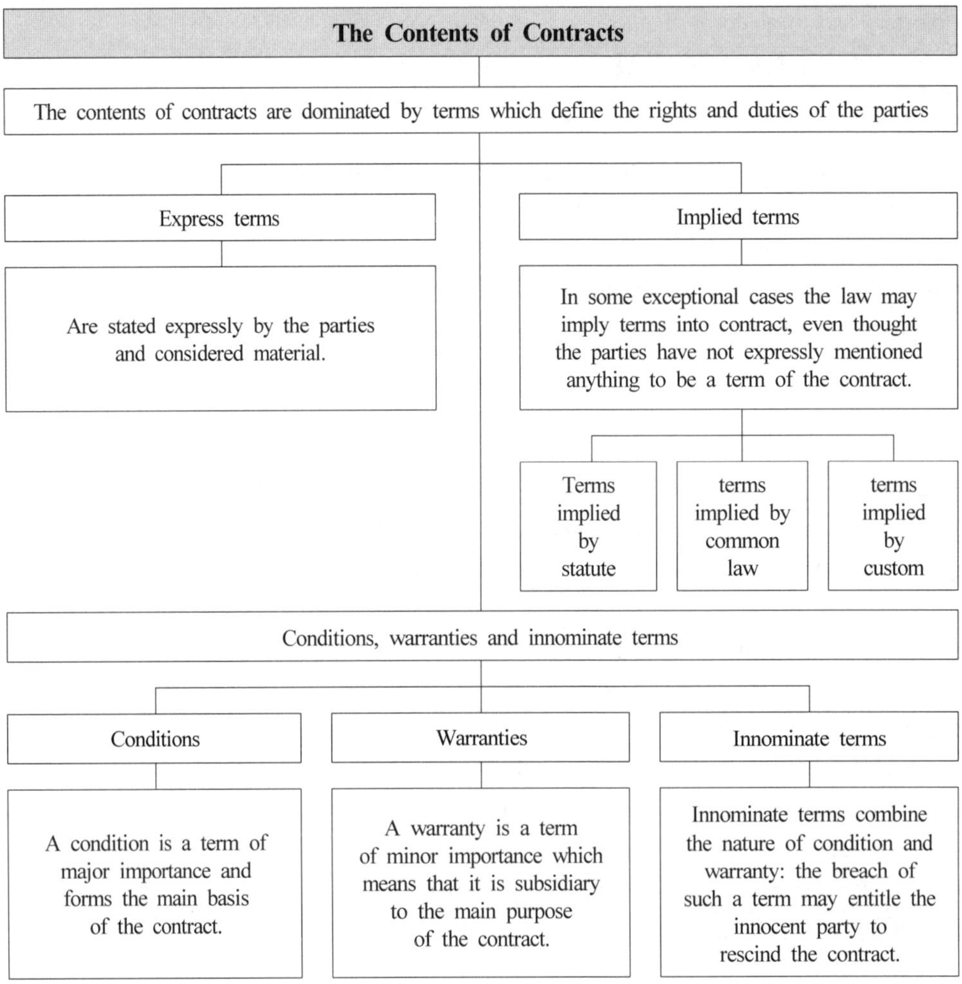

4. Exemption (or exclusion) clauses

Sometimes, one party may try to limit his liability by putting an exemption clause in the contract. Exemption clauses may be fair or unfair and therefore they have to be controlled. There are different ways to control such clauses: firstly the position at common law and secondly the position under statute, especially under the *Unfair Contract Terms Act* 불공정 계약 조항
1977.

a) Exemption clauses at common law

Contractual exemption clauses often discriminate against the consumer. Particularly buyers and sellers are by no means always on equal terms. Selling is often done on a "take it or leave it" basis, and the customer is often at the mercy of the seller.

결코 ~이 아니다
~마음대로

For the purpose of controlling exemption clauses the common law courts have set up numerous rules which may be summarized as follows

요약되다

(1) To be effective, an exemption clause must be written into the contract. The offeror must do all that is reasonably necessary to bring the clauses to the notice of the offeree. This is a question of fact in all cases.

Example — Thornton* v *Shoe Lane Parking Ltd. (1971) —:

The plaintiff drove into the entrance of the defendants' car park where a notice displayed stated "All cars parked at owners risk". The plaintiff took a ticket from an automatic machine and entered the garage. The ticket stated that it was "issued subject to the conditions of issue as displayed on the premises".

~조건에 따라서
토지, 공간

These conditions, displayed inside the car park, purported to exempt the defendants from liability for damage to cars, or any injury to the customer howsoever caused. When the plaintiff went to collect his car, he was injured in an accident, partly caused by the defendants' negligence.

~라고 말하다
손해 / 아무리 ~해도
부상당하다
원인이 되다 / 부주의

The judge of the lower court held that the defendants were liable and they appealed.

Held (by the Court of Appeal): that the exemption clause was not a term of the contract and it did not, therefore, enable the defendants to escape liability. *Lord Denning* put it thus: "The offer is made when the proprietor of the machine holds it out as being ready to receive the money. The acceptance takes place when the customer puts his money into the slot. The terms of the offer are contained in the

그러므로 / 소유주
~의 외양을 제공하다, ~라는 인상을 주다
(동전 넣는) 구멍

notice placed near the machine, stating what is offered for the money. The customer is bound by those terms as long as they are sufficiently brought to his notice beforehand, but not otherwise. He is not bound by the terms printed on the ticket if they differ from the notice, because the ticket comes too late. The contract had already been made ..."

충분히 / 사전에

(2) The clause must be brought to the notice of the offeree either before or contemporaneously with the making of the contract.

동시에

Example — Olley* v *Marlborough Court Ltd. (1949) —:

O booked a hotel, having paid in advance. O went to the room allotted, and on one of the walls was a notice: "The proprietors will not hold themselves responsible for articles lost or stolen unless handed to the manageress for safe custody".

이전에, 사전에
배당하다
여자 지배인
보관, 관리

O closed the self-locking door of the bedroom and handed the key to the reception clerk downstairs. A third person took the key and stole a certain number of O's furs from her room. O sued for the loss.

모피

Held: that the contract was completed at the reception desk, and no *subsequent* notice (e.g. in the bedroom) could affect O's rights.

후속의
영향을 미치다

(3) An exemption clause printed on a receipt after the contract is formed is not valid.

Example — Chapelton* v *Barry U.D.C. (1940) —:

C wished to hire deckchairs on a beach. He went to a stack near to which was a notice "Hire of chairs 2d. per session of three hours". He took two chairs, later he paid 4d. to the attendant and received two tickets which he put into his pocket without reading what was on them. Printed on the back of the tickets were the words: "The Council will not be

휴대용 의자, (누울 수 있는) 접의자
쌓여있음, 더미
승무원
시의회, 평의회

liable for any accident or damage arising from hire of chairs". When C sat on the chair it collapsed and he was injured. C sued the local council who had provided the chair. — 주저앉다

Held: that the ticket was a mere voucher or receipt, and that the term printed on it could not form a part of the contract. The only terms of the contract were those contained in the notice displayed near the pile of chairs. C was entitled to succeed in damages. — 표, 영수증 / 쌓아올린 더미

(4) Where a party seeks to rely on an exemption clause misrepresenting the extent of the clause, it will not be binding. This happened in the following case where the plaintiff gave a wedding dress to be dry cleaned, and was asked to sign a form with an exemption clause. — 잘못 전하다, 허위표시하다 / 범위 / 웨딩드레스 / 드라이클리닝하다

Example — Curtis v Chemical Cleaning and Dyeing Co. (1951) —: — 염색하다

Curtis (C), the plaintiff, took a dress with beads and sequins to the defendants for cleaning. C was asked to sign a paper headed "Receipt". When C asked about the terms of the document the defendant's assistant informed her that it exempted the company from liability for certain types of damage such as damage to beads and sequins. C signed. — 비즈(여성복 등에 쓰이는 장식용 구슬) / (장식용) 금속조각 / 제목, 표제를 붙이다

In fact, the paper contained a clause excluding *all* liability for damage to the garment. The dress came back stained, and C sued. — 옷 / 더러워진, 얼룩진

Held: that the defendants could not rely upon the signed document because the assistant had misrepresented its terms so that C ran the risk of damage merely to beads and sequins. — 모험하다

(5) Where the terms are signed, the parties are as a general rule bound.

Example — L'Estrange v Graucob (1934) —:

L, a shopkeeper bought a slot machine from G. L signed a — 슬롯머신

sales agreement containing the following clause: "Any express or implied condition, statement or warranty, statutory or otherwise, is hereby excluded". L did not read the relevant clause, which was in small print. The machine did not work and L sued for damages. 작은 활자

Held: that the clause was binding on L because she had signed the document and there had been no misrepresentation.

b) Exemption clauses and fundamental breach of contract

Where there has been a fundamental breach of contract it is a question of construction whether the clauses of the contract give exemption from the consequences of the breach. 해석

The courts held that, in common law, an exemption clause had to be construed as not protecting a party if that party committed a breach which went to the foundation of the contract, unless the clause was sufficiently clear to indicate an intention of the parties that it should operate even in this event. According to this "*doctrine of fundamental breach (of contract)*" theoretically no exemption clause could excuse a fundamental breach. This principle is not a rule of law when the injured party carries on with or affirms the broken contract. 해석하다 기초 작용하다, 작동하다 계속해서 하다 / 확인하다

In such a case, rules of construction must be used and the exemption clause might have to be applied. However, if the injured party elected to repudiate the contract for fundamental breach thus voiding the contract, the exemption clause goes with it and can never apply to prevent the injured party from suing for the breach. The same was stated by *Lord Denning (in Harbutt's Plasticine Ltd. v Wayne Tank & Pump Ltd.* [1970]) where the consequences of the breach in the case were so disastrous that one could *assume* that the injured party had elected to repudiate. 선출하다 / 거부하다 무효화하다 적용하다 / 방지하다 재난과도 같은 / 생각하다, 전제하다

This *Harbutt*-decision, however, was overruled by the House of Lords in the following case, in which the doctrine of fundamental breach was "forcibly evicted" from the common law. 강제적으로 내쫓긴

***Example — Photo Production Ltd.* v *Securicor Transport Ltd. (1980)* —:**

The plaintiff company had contracted with the defendant security company for the defendant to provide security services at the plaintiff's factory. A person employed by the defendant <u>lit a fire</u> in the plaintiff's premises while he was carrying out a night patrol. The fire got out of control and burned down the factory. The <u>trial judge</u> was unable to establish from the evidence precisely what the motive was for lighting the fire it may have been <u>deliberate</u> or merely <u>careless</u>. The defendant relied on an exclusion clause in the contract which read:

방화하다
1심 판사
고의로
부주의한, 과실의

"Under no circumstances shall the company (Securicor) be responsible for any <u>injurious act</u> or <u>default</u> by any in employee of the company unless such act or default could have been foreseen and avoided by the exercise of due diligence on the part of the company as his employer ...".

침해행위 / 과실

It was accepted that Securicor were not negligent in employing the person who lit the fire. He came to them with good references and there was no reason for them to suppose that he would act as he did.

Held (by the House of Lords): that the exclusion clause applied so that Securicor were not liable. The judges in the House of Lords were <u>unanimous</u> in the view that there was no rule of law by which exclusion clauses became inapplicable to fundamental breach of contract, which this <u>admittedly</u> was. Although the *Unfair Contract Terms Act 1977* was not in force at the time this action was brought and therefore could not be applied to the facts of this case, the existence of the Act and its relevance was referred to by Lord Wilberforce who said that the doctrine of fundamental breach had been useful in its time as a <u>device</u> for avoiding injustice. He then went on to say:

만장일치의
명백한, 인정받는
장치

"But ... Parliament has <u>taken a hand</u>; it has <u>passed</u> the *Unfair Contract Terms Act 1977*. This Act applies to consumer contracts and those based on standard terms and

직접 챙기다 / 통과시키다

enables exception clauses to be applied with regard to what is just and reasonable. It is significant that Parliament refrained from legislating over the whole field of contract. After this Act, in commercial matters generally, when the parties are not of unequal bargaining power, and when risks are normally borne by insurance ... there is everything to be said. ... for leaving the parties free to apportion the risks as they think fit ...".

refrained from: ~을 하지 않다
commercial matters: 상사 문제, 상사 사건
bargaining power: 교섭력, 협상력
to apportion: 배분하다
fit: 적당한

c) Exemption clauses under the Unfair Contract Terms Act 1977

Over the years judges had tried to prevent the operation of exemption clauses, which often deprived a consumer of nearly all his rights, by strict interpretation of terms and by propounding the doctrine of fundamental breach. Over the years Parliament had come to intervene more and more extensively in this area. The most important result which eminated from of these interventions was the *Unfair Contract Terms Act 1977* (hereafter "UCTA").

deprived: 빼앗다
propounding: 적용하다
area: 분야
hereafter: 앞으로(차후에), 이하

The title of the Act is misleading, because it does not deal with all unfair contractual terms but only with unfair exemption clauses.

The UCTA 1977 has in practice replaced the common law in many areas, though it does not apply to all contracts.

(aa) *Scope of the UCTA*

Scope: 범위

The UCTA applies to the following types of contract:

(1) contracts for the sale of goods [s.6(2)(a) of the UCTA and s.55(1) of the *Sale of Goods Act 1979*];
(2) contracts of hire-purchase [s.6(2)(b) of the UCTA];
(3) other contracts under which the possession or ownership of goods passes [s.7 of the UCTA]; and
(4) contracts for the supply of goods or services to which the *Supply of Goods and Services Act 1982* applies, e.g. the leasing or repair of goods (1982 Act, ss.11 and 16).

possession / ownership: 점유 / 소유권

Those contracts which are outside the scope of the Act are itemized in schedule 1, e.g. insurance contracts or contracts concerning land. 항목별로 나누다 / 테이블, 도표 / 보험

The strongest protection given by the Act is to persons who deal as consumers. To be a consumer, one must be dealing as *a private buyer* with a person in *business*. Thus, a contract between a private buyer and a private seller is not a consumer transaction. 행위하다 거래

The most important provisions protecting the consumer are sections 2 to 7. They apply to "business liability". Business liability is defined as "liability" for breach of obligations or duties arising 정의하다

- from things done or to be done by a person in the course of a business, or
- from the occupation of premises used for business purposes by the occupier. 사업용 부동산의 소유 / 소유자

(bb) *Clauses rendered ineffective by UCTA* 결정하다

1) Exclusion of liability for negligence 배제 / 부주의, 과실

Generally, a business cannot exclude by contract or by notice, liability for negligence resulting in a consumer's death or personal injury [s.2(1)]. Other losses caused by negligence can be excluded if the clause is "reasonable" under s.11 배제하다

2) Exclusion of liability arising from contractual obligations

According to s.3 which applies "as between contracting parties where one of them deals as consumer or on the other's written standard terms of business", all attempts to exclude or restrict liability or to re-define obligations so as to avoid liability will be subject to the requirement of reasonableness in s.11. 재정의하다 합리성의 요구

The requirement of reasonableness means:

the clause must be a "fair and reasonable one to be included" in the contract, at the time it was made. The burden of proof is on the defendant [s.11(5)]. 입증책임

3) Guaranties of consumer goods

S.5 is concerned with the relationship between manufacturer or distributor of goods and the customer. 제조업자 배급업자

A manufacturer's or distributor's guarantee may not exclude or restrict liability for any loss or damage suffered by a consumer due to negligence.

4) Unreasonable indemnity clauses 면책

By s.4 a consumer may not be required by contract to indemnify any other person against a liability incurred by that other for negligence or breach of contract, unless it is shown that the requirement of reasonableness is satisfied. 면책하다

d) Exemption clauses and reasonableness

In his last judgment in the Court of Appeal *Lord Denning* gave a review of the law relating to exemption clauses. He gave it in his usual clear and concise way, making it admirable and worth reading. Therefore his statement will follow the next case below. 간결한 훌륭한

Example — George Mitchell (Chesterhall) Ltd.* v *Finney Lock Seeds Ltd.(1983) —:

In December 1973, the appellants, seed merchants, agreed to supply the respondents, farmers, with 30 *lbs* of Dutch winter cabbage seed for £192. The seed was delivered with an invoice containing a clause *purporting to limit the liability of the seller, in the event of the seed not complying with the express terms of the contract to replacing defective seed or repaying the price*. The seed supplied was of a different and inferior variety with the result that the crop failed and had to be ploughed in. Parker, J. awarded the respondents £61,513.78 damages and £30,756 interest. The Court of Appeal dismissed the appeal, *Oliver* and *Kerr,* L.JJ, *Lord Denning* dissenting, on the ground (1) that the clause, on its true construction, did not apply to the breach which had occurred; and, (2), *Lord Denning* concurring, that it would not be fair

종자 / (양)배추 / 의도하다, 표현하다 / 일치하다, 충족하다 / 작물 / (땅을) 파뒤집다 / (판결로) 부여하다 / 일어나다 / (의견을) 같이 하다

and reasonable to permit reliance on the clause. 신뢰(의지)

Held (by the House of Lords): that the appeal is dismissed on ground (2), agreeing with *Lord Denning* that the clause on its true construction did not apply to the breach.

Lord Denning M.R.,stated:

"*The effect of the changes*

What is the result of all this? To my mind it heralds a revolution in our approach to exemption clauses; not only where they exclude liability altogether and also where they limit liability; not only in the specific categories in the *Unfair Contract Terms Act 1977*, but in other contracts too. Just as in other fields of law we have done away with the multitude of cases on 'common employment', 'last opportunity', 'invitees' and 'licensees' and so forth, so also in this field we should do away with the multitude of cases on exemption clauses. We should no longer have to go through all kinds of gymnastic contortions to get round them. We should no longer have to harass our students with the study of them. We should set about meeting a new challenge. It is presented by the test of reasonableness ... .

heralds: 예고하다
approach: 접근
done away with: 폐지하다
multitude / common employment / last opportunity: 다수의 / 일반적 고용 / 마지막 기회
invitees / licensees / and so forth: 초청 받은 사람들 / 면허소지자 / 등등
gymnastic contortions / to get round: 관절을 비트는 동작 / 회피하다
harass: 괴롭히다
set about: (~할 일을) 하다

Fair and reasonable

There is only one case in the books so far on this point. It is *R.W. Green Ltd. v Cade Bros. Farm* (1978). There *Griffiths,* J. held that it was fair and reasonable for seed potato merchants to rely on a limitation clause which limited their liability to the contract price of the potatoes. That case was very different from the present. The terms had been evolved over 20 years. The judge said: 'They are therefore not conditions imposed by the strong upon the weak; but are rather a set of trading terms upon which both sides are apparently content to do business.' The judge added: 'No moral blame attaches to either party; neither of them knew, nor could be expected to know, that the potatoes were infected.' In that case the judge held that the clause was fair and reasonable and that the seed merchants were entitled to rely on it.

the strong / the weak: 강자(에 의해) / 약자(에게)

Our present case is very much on the borderline. There is this to be said in favour of the seed merchants. The price of this cabbage seed was small: ￡192. The damages claimed are high: ￡61,000. But there is this to be said on the other side. The clause was not negotiated between persons of equal bargaining power. It was inserted by the seed merchants in their invoices without any negotiation with the farmers. — 경계선에 놓인 / 협상력 / 삽입하다

To this I would add that the seed merchants rarely, if ever, invoked the clause. Their very frank director said: 'The trade does not stand on the strict letter of the clause .... Almost invariably when a customer justifiably complains, the trade pays something more than a refund.' The papers contain many illustrations where the clause was not invoked and a settlement was reached. — 의지하다, 근거로 삼아 주장하다 / 솔직한 / 항상 / 정당하게 / 환불 / 합의하다

Next, I would point out that the buyers had no opportunity at all of knowing or discovering that the seed was not cabbage seed, whereas the sellers could and should have known that it was the wrong seed altogether. The buyers were not covered by insurance against the risk. Nor could they insure. But, as to the seed merchants, the judge said: — 보험으로 커버하다

'I am entirely satisfied that it is possible for seedsmen to insure against this risk. I am entirely satisfied that the cost of so doing would not materially raise the price of seeds on the market. I am entirely satisfied that the protection of this clause for the purposes of protecting against the very rare case indeed, such as the present, is not reasonably required. If and in so far as it may be necessary to consider the matter, I am also satisfied that it is possible for seedsmen to test seeds before putting them on the market.' — 만족하다 / 씨앗장수 / 요구하다

To that I would add this further point. Such a mistake as this could not have happened without serious negligence on the part of the seed merchants themselves or their Dutch suppliers. So serious, that it would not be fair to enable them to escape responsibility for it. — 중과실, 심각한 과실(부주의) / 공급자 / 책임을 피하다

In all circumstances I am of the opinion that it would not be fair or reasonable to allow the seed merchants to rely on the clause to limit their liability. — 의지하다 / 제한하다 / 책임

I would dismiss the appeal accordingly." — 그에 따라서

e) The unfair terms in consumer contract regulations 1995 소비자 계약 규정들

The European Community Directive on unfair terms in consumer contracts became part of English law on July 1, 1995. Under these rules a consumer, acting outside of his business or trade, may challenge any contract made between himself and a seller of goods or a supplier of services, which is considered unfair and causes a significant imbalance to the detriment of the consumer. An action may be started in the courts or through the Office of Fair Trading.

Consumer contracts must be written in plain, intelligent English. Contracts produced in small, unreadable type or in legal "gobbledygook" would be regarded as unfair, whether or not the actual content of the contract was fair.

The consumer should be given an opportunity to examine all the terms and, if in any doubt, the interpretation most favourable to the consumer should be used. Any contract which is considered to be unfairly weighted against a consumer could be judged as invalid.

An example of how the regulations may be interpreted could be where a holiday insurance policy required any loss or theft to be reported to the police immediately, and one was camping in a remote area of a foreign country without a police station within a reasonable distance. If the insurance company refused compensation, because of failure to comply with this clause, it could be considered unreasonable and therefore unfair, and consequently invalid.

Directive: 규정, 지침
imbalance: 불균형
detriment: 손해
Office of Fair Trading: 공정거래국, 소비자보호국
legal "gobbledygook": 법적으로 까다로운 표현
weighted: 가중된
insurance policy: 보험증권
remote: 멀리 떨어진
compensation / comply with: 보상 / 따르다

Diagram 30

Exemption (or: Exclusion) Clauses

Sometimes, one party may try to limit his liability by putting an exemption clause in the contract. Exemption clauses can be fair or unfair, and therefore they have to be controlled.

Exemption clauses at common law	**Exemption clauses and fundamental brach of contract**	**Exemtion clauses under the UCTA**	**Exemption clauses and reasonableness**
• To be effective, clause must be written into the contract. • Clauses must be known to the offeree before or contemporaneously with the making of the contract. • A signed clause is binding.	Where there had been a fundamental breach of contract it is a question of construction whether the clauses of the contract give exemption from the consequences of the breach.	The *UCTA 1977* has replaced the common law in many areas, though it does not apply to all contracts.	The matter of reasonableness must be decided with regard to the circumstances as they were when the contract was made.

VII. Simple (formless) contracts with mistakes and misrepresentations 착오, 과오

1. Miscellaneous

Simple contracts are not made under seal. They *may* either be made in writing, orally or implied by conduct. A simple contract is only valid if it is supported by valuable consideration. In the absence of consideration the contract will be, as we have already learnt, void.

묵시적인, 행동에 의해 암시되는
적절한 대가, 반대급부

2. Void and voidable contracts

A void contract has no binding effect at all, whereas a voidable contract is valid, but one party has the right to set it aside under certain conditions. Two factors to be considered

무효로 하다, 제거하다

in this context are mistake and *misrepresentation*. 부실표시, 허위설명

a) Mistake

The general rule of common law is that a mistake does not affect the validity of a contract.

Example (which we have already treated above): If B buys a painting for £100 from S, and after the sale discovers that the painting is a Picasso worth £100.000, B is fortunate, S is not.

S merely sold a painting, not knowing that it was a real Picasso. He mistook its real value, and the law will do nothing to assist him. The mistake of S did not affect the validity of the contract. In other words, the mistake was not operative because S made an error of judgment as to its value.

오해하다

효력, 유효성 / 효력이 없는, 고려되지 않는 / S가 이것의 가치에 대한 판단의 착오를 했기에

To be operative the mistake has to be one of fact. Mistakes of law are also inoperative. If one makes a mistake about a rule of law, one cannot plead in court that one was unaware of its existence. Thus, the maxim "ignorance of the law is no excuse" applies.

사실

법의 착오 / 효력이 없는, 고려되지 않는

격언 / 법을 몰랐다고 해서 죄를 면할 수는 없다, 법에 대한 무지는 변명이 되지 않는다

A mistake as to private rights (which could be considered a mistake of law) is, however, treated as a mistake of fact and not of law.

Example — Cooper* v *Phibbs (1867) —:

C agrees to lease some land belonging to P and it subsequently transpires that, unknown to both parties, C had been the true owner of the land.

Held: that there was a mistake of fact and not of law. The contract was void.

알려지다

The courts have rendered void contracts due to the following mistakes:

무효판결을 내리다

(aa) *Mistakes as to the subject-matter* ~에 관해 / 본건

This normally occurs when one party sells specific goods to another party who is under the mistaken belief that he is buying different goods. 일어나다

Example — Raffles* v *Wichelhaus (1864) —:

R offered cotton from the ship "*Purless*", sailing in December from Bombay. On the other hand W agreed to buy cotton which was meant "to arrive on the *Purless* sailing in October". 목면

Held: that there was no binding contract between the parties as the plaintiff meant one ship and the defendant another.

(bb) *Mistakes as to the existence of the subject-matter*

This kind of mistake occurs in cases where both parties make a contract under the mistaken belief that a particular thing is in existence when, in fact, it has ceased to exist, rendering the contract void. 신념, 믿음 / 멈추다 / 판결내리다

Example — Couturier* v *Hastie (1856) —:

A contract was made between C and H for the sale of Indian corn which was being shipped. Unknown to both parties the cargo had become overheated during the voyage and had to be sold at port. 배로 운송하다 / 화물 / 항해

Held: that there was no contract, since the corn was not really in existence. 왜냐하면

(cc) *Mistakes as to the nature of the contractual document*

Thirdly, the contract is rendered void in cases where the party who had signed a document thought the document to be of a completely different nature and was not negligent in signing the document ("it is not my deed" = *non est factum*). 부주의한, 과실있는

Example — Foster* v *Mackinnon (1869) —:

M, an old man of feeble sight was induced to endorse a bill of exchange for ￡3000 on the assurance that it was a guarantee. The bill was endorsed for value to F who sued M for the bill.

시력이 약한, 근시의 / 유인하다 / 환어음에 배서하였다
~을 수익자로 하여

Held: that M's plea of *non est factum* was good, and he was not liable to pay the money.

Example — Saunders* v *Anglia Building Society (1970) —:

An old lady handed over to her nephew a signed deed of gift of her house. She had not read the deed, and a defrauder had substituted his own name for that of the nephew, and later had mortgaged the house to the building society.

조카 / 증여증서
사기꾼
대체하다
저당잡다

Held: that there was a valid contract. The plea *of "non est factum"* failed because the lady had signed the kind of document she intended to sign: it was the contents which were different.

내용

(dd) *Mistake as to the identity of the other party*

Finally, where there are mistakes as to the personal identity of the other party the contract will be void if it is proved.

(1) that the identity of the party contracted with is material to the contract, and

계약당사자 / 중요한, 본질적인

(2) that the party contracted with knows that he is not the person with whom the other party intended to make a contract.

In ordinary contracts for the sale of goods in a shop, where the parties are in a face-to-face position, the identity of the customer is not material to the seller.

고객

To decide if there was a mistake in personal identity which could as a result affect the validity of a contract, the court must answer the question: Did the party intend to contract with a particular person only, and none other than him?

영향을 미치다

Example – Phillips* v *Brooks (1919) –:

A rogue entered a jeweller's shop to purchase jewellery and paid by cheque. The jeweller said delivery would be delayed until the cheque was cleared by the bank.

사기꾼, 부랑자 / 보석 가게 / 보석
배송이 지연될 것이다
결제하다

When the rogue claimed to be "Sir George Bullogh" and gave an address in St. James Square the jeweller allowed him to take some of the jewels with him. The rogue then pawned them for a sum of money to Brooks Ltd.

주장하다
성 제임스 스퀘어(광장)
저당잡다

When the cheque later proved worthless the jeweller sued the pawnbroker for the jewel.

무가치한 것으로 판명났다 /
고소하다
전당포업자

Held: that there was no void contract because the jeweller's mistake was not as to the customer's identity, but his financial position. The identity of the party (the customer) was immaterial, when the jeweller made the contract in his shop. The contract, therefore, was not void for mistake, but voidable for fraud. Brooks had good title.

재정상태
중요치 않은
사기 / 권리, 청구권

There are a lot of distinctions to be made to decide whether a mistake is operative, i.e. with effect upon the contract, or inoperative. The given example should illustrate two points:

효력, 영향력
보여주다, 설명하다, 알려주다

Firstly, in order to be operative a mistake must affect the substance of the thing which is the subject-matter of the contract. If a party makes a mistake as to some minor matter the law will not heed his complaint. If you buy my tomcat, for example, under the mistaken impression that he answers to the name of "Tom" and it turns out that his name is "Carlo" you cannot force me to take him back! Your mistake was not a mistake as to the identity of the cat but only as to its name.

부수적인, 사소한
주목하다 / 수고양이
강요하다

Secondly, people who plead to a contractual mistake must necessarily be judged by their action rather than by their *innermost thoughts*. This is well illustrated by *Blackburn* J. in *Smith* v *Hughes* (1871). "If whatever a man's real intention may be, he so conducts himself that a reasonable man would

가장 깊은 생각, 내심의 의사

believe that he was assenting to the terms proposed by the other party, and that the other party upon that belief enters into the contract with him, the man thus conducting himself would be equally bound as if he had intended to agree to the other party's terms."

Diagram 31

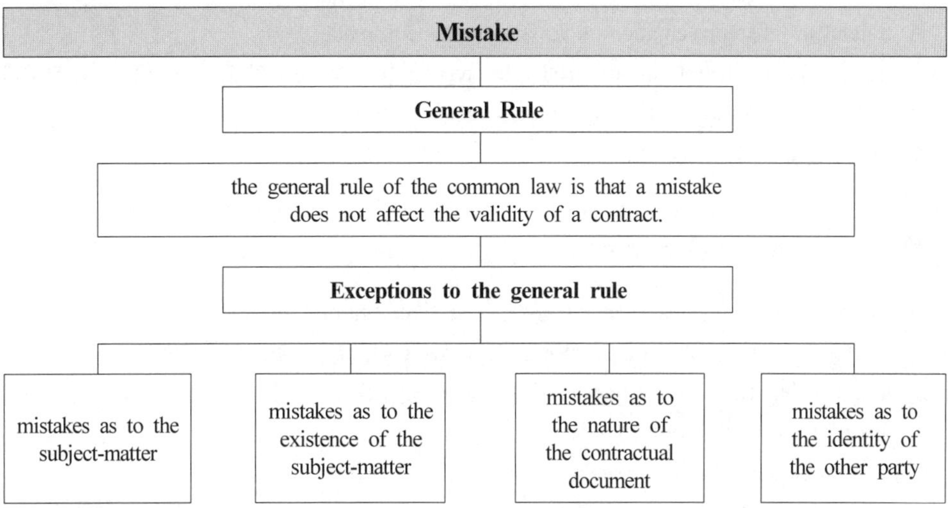

b) Misrepresentation

A representation is a statement made by one party to the other, before or at the time of the contract, with regard to some existing fact or some past event, which is essential to the contract. Consequently a *misrepresentation* is a statement of fact, which induces the other party to enter into a contract and as a result suffer damage. The statement may be in writing, by conduct, or communicated orally, but generally, silence will not be considered as a misrepresentation.

- representation: 진술
- event / essential: 사건 / 필수적인, 본질적인
- induces: 유도하다, ~하게 하다
- suffer damage: 손해를 입다
- silence: 침묵

Misrepresentation must be a statement of fact, not law, not even opinion. If a seller, for instance, offers a car as being "accident-free" it would be a misrepresentation if, in fact, the car had had an accident. If the car, however, was offered by the seller who "thought it accident-free", there is no misrepresentation. It would be the buyer's responsibility to check whether it may have been involved in any accidents.

- not even: 심지어 ~도 아니다
- accident-free: 무사고의
- involved: 연관된(연루된)

The effect of misrepresentation of a contract is less serious than that of a mistake, because the contract is not void, but becomes voidable. We have to distinguish between three types of actionable misrepresentation: fraudulent, negligent and innocent misrepresentation.

덜 심각한, 덜 엄격한
소송을 제기할 수 있는 / 사기의 / 부주의한 / 결백한, 책임이 없는

(aa) *Fraudulent misrepresentation*

A fraudulent misrepresentation is a false statement made knowingly, without belief in its truth, or recklessly, not caring whether it is true or false (as *Lord Herschell* decided in the following case).

고의로 / 무모하게, 부주의하게

***Example* – *Derry* v *Peek (1889)* –:**

A tramway's company was entitled under a special Act of Parliament to run trams by animal power, and with official consent by mechanical or steam power. D and other appellants were directors of the company and issued a prospectus inviting subscriptions from the public for shares. The prospectus stated that the company had permission to run trams by steam power, and assumed that the official consent would be granted as a matter of course. But this permission was officially refused and the company was wound up.

P, a share subscriber, sued the directors for fraud.

Held: that D and the other directors were not fraudulent because they honestly believed the statement in the prospectus to be true.

시내 전철
관(官)의 승인
증기
안내서
간주하다
당연한 일
청산하다
지분권자 / 사기
정직하게

(bb) *Negligent misrepresentation*

A negligent misrepresentation is a false statement which the maker had no reasonable grounds for believing to be true.

As a result of the *Misrepresentation Act 1967* a new and serious liability was imposed on anyone making a representation of fact in the course of negotiations. If that representation turns out to be mistaken then, however, innocent he may be, he is equally liable as if he had made it fraudulently.

협상 과정에서
오류로 판명나다

***Example* — *Hedley Byrne & Co.Ltd.* v *Heller & Partners Ltd. (1964)* —:**

The appellants were advertising agents and had a client (X) who was a customer of the respondents, merchant bankers. 항소인 / 광고회사 / 항소피고 / 상업은행

The appellants, who intended to give X credit asked the bank for a reference as to the credit worthiness of X. The bank gave a positive reference, but they gave it "in confidence and without responsibility on our part". When X went into liquidation the appellants suffered a loss of ￡7,000. They sued the respondents for the loss, alleging that the respondents had given a misleading reference, had not informed themselves sufficiently about X, and were therefore liable in negligence. 신용도 / 신뢰하며 / 책임없는 / 겪다 / 주장하다 / 오도하는(오해시키는)

Held: that the appellants failed because the respondents had given the reference "without responsibility" on their part.

Without this exemption clause the reference would have been negligent. 부주의한

(cc) *Innocent misrepresentation*

An innocent misrepresentation is a false statement which the maker believed to be true.

Before the *Misrepresentation Act 1967* any misrepresentation which was not fraudulent was "innocent", whether made negligently or not. In the case of innocent misrepresentation in common law it was not possible to either obtain rescission of the contract once it was executed, nor to obtain damages for loss arising from the misrepresentation. Equity, however, allowed a limited right to compensation. 해제 / 이행되다(시행되다) / 손해 / 보상, 배상

The *Misrepresentation Act 1967* altered this position and distinguished between negligent and entirely innocent misrepresentation: 전적으로

Section 1 of this Act provides that neither the fact that the misrepresentation has been incorporated into the contract and become a term of it, nor the fact that the contract has been performed, will preclude an action for rescission. 포함된 / 시행하다 / 배제하다

Section 2 of the Act provides that where one party (e.g. A) has entered into a contract as the result of innocent misrepresentation by another party (e.g. B), and A suffers loss therefrom, then B would be liable for damages as if the misrepresentation had been made fraudulently. But B as the respondent will escape liability if he "proves that he had reasonable ground to believe and did believe up to the time the contract was made that the facts represented were true".

~인 것처럼
면하다(벗어나다)

You may feel or presume that this is a field of contract law which could give rise to some borderline cases or cases of doubt. When this arises, the court must consider the circumstances of the individual case and take into account all of the facts to assess liability. The result could be the award of damages or rescission.

일으키다(초래하다) / 경계선 사례 (이도 저도 아닌 경우) / 의심의 여지가 있는 사례 / 개별사례 / 고려하다 / 평가하다 / 판결액

(dd) *Silence as misrepresentation*

In the law of contract, silence of a party does not in general amount to misrepresentation. Usually, there must be a statement for there to be a misrepresentation. In some situations, however, silence can amount to misrepresentation. This may happen, e.g., if there is a *change of circumstances*.

~이 되다

Example – With* v *O'Flanagan (1936) –:

A doctor represented in January that the takings of his medical practice were £2,000. Five months later, when the contract was signed, the takings had fallen considerably due to the doctor's own illness. The doctor failed to disclose the reduction.

Held: that the contract could be rescinded owing to the doctor's failure to disclose the fall in the takings.

매출액
상당히
실패하다 / 공개하다
해제하다
불이행, 하지 않음

Silence can also be a misrepresentation if a party says something to the other which amounts to a half-truth. If a vendor of land, e.g., states that all farms are let he must not omit the further fact that the tenants have given notice to

판매자 / 임대하다
빠트리다(생략하다)

quit (cf. *Dimmock v Hallett* [1866]). By stating only half the facts, the vendor had given a misleading picture, and this was held to be a misrepresentation.

떠나다
오해시키는

Silence as a misrepresentation is also possible with contracts of *uberrimae fidei* ("the utmost good faith"). These are contracts in which disclosure of material facts must be made. Failure to disclose material facts, whether they are asked for or not, renders the contract voidable at the option of the party prejudiced, i.e. the party to whom disclosure ought to have been made. A typical example of a contract *uberrimae fidei* is an insurance contract: In contracts of marine, fire, and life insurance the insured should disclose all facts which might influence the judgment of the insurer in deciding whether or not he is to take the risk of insuring or rather increase the premium.

최고의 선의
공개
편파적인(불공평한)
해상 / 보험가입자
보험회사
보험료를 인상하다

Diagram 32

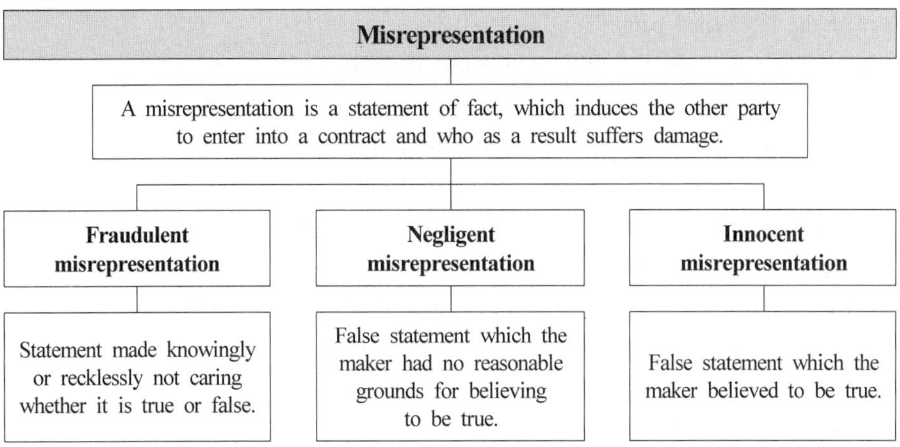

3. Unenforceable contracts

제소 불가능한, 강제 실현할 수 없는

These are contracts which, as already indicated, are valid in all respects, except that they cannot be enforced in a court by one of the parties should the other refuse to carry out his obligations under it. As an example of an unenforceable contract already mentioned is the contract of guarantee.

수행하다
의무

VIII. Duress and undue influence 강요 / 부당압력

1. Duress

Duress at common law means actual violence or threatened violence to the contracting party or those near and dear to him. 폭력 / 위협하다

Although it is possible that a person could be physically forced to sign a contract, e.g. by someone holding his arm and moving it, a contract will seldom be procured by actual violence. The most obvious form of duress is the threat of violence. However, examples of duress include not only threats of physical harm to the contracting party and his close family or friends, but also threats of dishonour and unlawful imprisonment. 유도하다 협박(위협) 손상, 상해 모욕 불법감금

A contract entered into under duress is voidable at the option of the threatened party. This, at least, is the view in *Cheshire/ Fifoot & Furmston's Law of Contract* (one of the leading textbooks on contract law) and the dominant opinion, though other writers have argued that the effect of duress renders a contract void. The question whether the contract is rendered void or voidable becomes important if questions of affirmation or third party rights are involved. For example: if B procures goods from A by duress and then sells the goods to C, who has knowledge of the duress, A will be able to recover the goods from C if the contract is void, but will not be able to do so if it is voidable. 지배적 의견 확인 구하다(획득하다)

The courts have often decided that a contract under duress is void.

Examples:

– Cummings* v *Ince (1847) –:

An agreement to give up deeds made under threat of confinement in an asylum was held not to be binding on the plaintiff. 계약증서 감금, 구속 / 보호시설

— ***Welch* v *Cheeseman (1973)* —:**

In fear of violence from the man with whom she lived, W transferred her home to him. It was held that the transfer would be set aside for duress.

— ***Barton* v *Armstrong (1975)* —:**

A deed executed under threats to kill was held to be void (by the Privy Council). 발행하다

In recent years the principle of duress has been extended to economic duress where strong commercial pressure is applied.

***Example — Atlas Express Ltd.* v *Kafco Ltd. (1984)* —:**

The plaintiffs, a national road carrier, contracted with the defendants, a small company, to deliver cartons of basketware to branches of Woolworths throughout the United Kingdom. Before entering into the contract, the plaintiffs' manager had inspected the cartons and estimated that each load would contain a minimum of 400 and possibly as many as 600 cartons:

나무 바구니

점검하다(면밀히 살피다) / 추측하다 / 짐

on that basis he agreed a charge of £1.10 per carton. In fact, the first load contained only 200 cartons, so the manager said they would not take any more unless the defendants agreed to pay a minimum of £440 per load. As they were heavily dependent on their Woolworths contract and could not at that time find an alternative carrier, the defendants agreed to the new terms but later refused to pay at the new rate.

운송인

Held: that (1) economic duress may make a contract voidable if the coercion applied affects the consent, and therefore the defendants need not pay at the new rates because their agreement to do so was due to the economic duress exerted by the plaintiffs; and (2) there had been no consideration for the promise to pay the new rate, and therefore the plaintiffs were merely performing an existing contractual duty.

강압, 강요 / 작용하다

가하다

2. Undue influence — 부당압력

Whereas duress is forcing someone to make a contract, undue influence involves pressurising or influencing someone in such a way, that he does not have a free choice.

(involves / pressurising: 의미하다 / 압력)

Relationships in which undue influence is normally presumed are those between solicitor and client, doctor and patient, parents and child or teacher and pupil.

The presumption of undue influence is rebuttable, so it is up to the stronger party to prove that he did not unfairly influence the weaker party.

(rebuttable: 반론할 수 있는(반박이 가능한))

Example — Lloyds Bank* v *Bundy (1975) —:

The defendant and his son's company both banked with the plaintiffs, the defendant having been a customer for many years. The company's affairs deteriorated over a period of years and at the son's suggestion the bank's assistant manager visited the defendant and said that the bank could not continue to support an overdraft for the company unless the defendant entered into a guarantee of the account. The defendant received no independent advice, nor did the bank's assistant-manager suggest that he should do so.

(banked: 은행계좌를 가지다; deteriorated: 나빠지다; to support / overdraft: 지지하다 / 마이너스 인출; entered into a guarantee: 담보를 제공하다; independent advice: 중립적 조언)

The defendant charged his house as security for the overdraft, and shortly afterwards the company went into receivership. The bank obtained possession of the house from the defendant in the county court, where the assistant branch manager in evidence said, that he thought that the defendant had relied upon him implicitly for advice about the charge.

(security: 담보; went into receivership: 파산절차가 개시되다; in evidence: 증거조사시에; implicitly / charge: 묵시적으로 / 담보를 세우는 일, 입보)

The defendant appealed to the Court of Appeal in an attempt to set aside the guarantee and the security.

(to set aside: 무효화하다)

Held (allowing the defendant's appeal): that in the particular circumstances a special relationship existed between the defendant and the bank's assistant manager, as agent for the bank. The bank was in breach of its duty of fiduciary care in procuring the charge, which would be set aside for undue influence. The defendant, without any benefit to himself, had

(fiduciary care: 수탁자의 관리(의무); procuring: 입수하다, (담보를) 받다)

signed away his sole remaining asset without taking independent advice.

서명으로 양도하다 / 자산

For a claim of undue influence to be successful, the contract must clearly be to the weaker party's disadvantage. If undue influence is proved, the contract is voidable, and the party may apply, within a reasonable time, to the court to have it set aside.

(법원에) 신청하다, 요구하다

***Example — Allcard* v *Skinner (1887)* —:**

The plaintiff joined a Protestant sisterhood, taking vows of poverty and obedience. She gave property to the value of £7,000 to the sisterhood in accordance with her vows. Some nine years later she left the Order to become a Roman Catholic. Only £1671 of her property remained with the sisterhood, the balance having been spent. The plaintiff claimed the return of the £1671 from the Mother Superior (Miss Skinner) and alleged undue influence.

Held: that undue influence existed in this case, since the plaintiff was bound not to seek independent advice whilst in the Order. However, the plaintiff's claim was barred by her delay of five years, after leaving the sisterhood, in claiming the money.

수녀회, 자매회 / 맹세하다
가난 / 순종
수녀회, 수도회
수녀원장
배제하다
지연(지체)

Diagram 33

Duress and Undue Influence

- **Duress**: is actual violence or threatened violence towards the contracting party or those near and dear to him.
- **Undue Influence**: ... involves pressurizing or influencing someone in such a way that he cannot make a free choice.

IX. Illegality and public policy 위법(불법) / 공서(公序)

This paragraph, like the previous one, is concerned with situations where the courts will intervene to prevent the enforcement which on its face has all the characteristics of a binding contract, but in fact the contract is illegal. 위법의, 불법의

A contract is said to be illegal either when it is forbidden by statute or else contravenes the common law. 위반하다

Above all, contracts containing a criminal element are illegal. This is easy to understand: if A made a contract with B to steal C's car for £100, the court would not award A a remedy if B later refuses to carry out the contract. It goes without saying that contracts which involve the commission of a tort are also illegal. Contracts may also be illegal for reasons quite different from crimes or torts. Such contracts are declared illegal because they offend against certain fundamental rules of the common law laid down by the judges and generally described as matters of "public policy".

주다, (판결로) 인정하다 / 행하다(저지르다) / 불법행위 / 위반하다 / 공서, 공익

The general rule is that an illegal contract will not be enforced by the courts and is considered to be void. 강제집행하다

This principle is called *"ex turpi causa non oritur actio"* which means "no action arises from a base or wrongful cause". 저열한 / 부당한 사유

In other words: an agreement to do an act that is illegal or immoral or contrary to public policy is unlawful and therefore void. 부도덕한 / 비합법적인

1. Contracts forbidden by statute

Certain statutes declare that some kinds of contracts are illegal and void. Thus, the *Gaming Act 1845* declares certain gaming and wagering contracts illegal.

도박 / 내기(노름)

Example — Lipkin Gorman* v *Karpnal Ltd. (1991) —:

A partner in the plaintiff's firm stole money from the firm which was exchanged for gambling chips and used to make bets with the defendants.

Held: that the transaction was void as a gambling contract under s.18 of the Gaming Act 1845, and therefore did not constitute valuable consideration.

걸다(내기를 걸다)
구성하다, ~이 되다

The *Consumer Credit Act 1974*, renders certain money lending contracts void, e.g. those of extortionate or unconscionable kind.

소비자 신용법 / 금전 소비대차 계약(대출) / 폭리의 / 비양심적인(부당한)

The *Race Relations Act 1976*, makes it unlawful to discriminate against a person on the ground of colour, race or ethnic or national origins in a number of specified situations.

인종관계법

The *Sex Discrimination Act 1975*, renders unlawful certain kinds of sex discrimination and discrimination on the grounds of marriage.

성차별법

According to this act (and also according to common law: see next paragraph) contracts which encourage sexual immoralty are illegal.

부도덕

The *Trade Description Act 1968*, provides criminal sanctions in the case of false trade descriptions and, that a contract for the supply of goods shall not be void or unenforceable by reason only of a contravention described in this Act. If such a contravention constitutes a misrepresentation, the normal civil remedies for misrepresentation are available.

거래표시법
위반

2. Contracts illegal at common law

According to common law a contract is illegal, as mentioned above, when it is contrary to public policy, i.e. when it is in the public interest that it should not be enforced.

~에 반하는
공익

Examples of contracts considered to be against public policy are the following:

a) Contracts to commit a crime or tort

Example — Alexander* v *Rayson (1986) —:

A lease of a flat made provision for a rent of ￡450 p.a. and the rendering of certain services to the tenant: a separate agreement provided for the rendering of substantially the same services on payment by the tenant of ￡750 p.a. The landlord, it was alleged, adopted this dual approach with a view to defrauding the rating authority by leading them to believe that his only income in respect of the flat was ￡450 p.a. The landlord sued for rent under the lease and payment under the agreement.

Held: that his action could not succeed, unless he could disprove the charge of fraud.

조항을 가지다
제공하다 / 세입자
기본적으로, 본질에 있어
지주 / 주장하다 / 채택하다 / 이중합의 / ~할 목적으로 / 사기를 치다, 속이다 / 국세청
사기 혐의를 벗다

Example — Dann* v *Curzon (1911) —:

An agreement was made for advertising a play, by means of collusive criminal proceedings, brought as a result of a prearranged disturbance at the theatre. The plaintiffs, who agreed to create the disturbance and did in fact do so, sued for the remuneration due to them under the agreement.

Held: that the action failed because it was an agreement to commit a criminal offence and was therefore contrary to public policy.

공모의(결탁한)
소란(소동)
보상
범죄행위

Example — Foster* v *Driscoll (1929) —:

A partnership agreement was entered into, in England, for the purpose of smuggling whisky into the United States at a time when the American prohibition laws were in force. An action on the agreement was begun in England.

Held: that the agreement was illegal and void.

금주법

b) Contracts to corrupt public life

부패하다, 뇌물을 주다

It is considered illegal for a person to make a contract to purchase a public honour.

공적 직함

Example — Parkinson* v *The College of Ambulance Ltd. and Harrison (1925) —:

The first defendant was a charitable institution and the second defendant was the secretary, who fraudulently represented to the plaintiff, Colonel Parkinson, that the charity was in a position to obtain some honour (probably a knighthood) for him if he would make a suitable donation to the funds of the charity. The plaintiff paid over the sum of £3,000 and said he would pay more if the honour was granted. No honour of any kind was received by the plaintiff and he brought this action to recover the money he had donated to the College.

Held: that the agreement was contrary to public policy and illegal. No relief could be granted to the plaintiff.

자선협회
명예, 직함, 작위
기사의 작위 / 적당한 기부
되찾다
구제수단

c) Immoral contracts

부도덕한

Contracts which offend public morality or are contrary to the sanctity of marriage are considered illegal.

위반하다
신성함(고결)

Example — Pearce v Brooks (1866) —:

A prostitute bought a brougham (carriage) on hire-purchase terms from a firm of coachbuilders. It was known that she intended to use the carriage for attracting male customers. The woman failed to keep up her contractual repayments for the carriage and the coachbuilders sued for the arrears.

Held: that as the plaintiff knew the purpose for which the carriage was to be used the contract was void.

말이 끄는 4륜 마차 / 탈 것 / 할부
자동차 차체 제조공
끌다
연체금

To the category of immoral contracts other contracts claiming damages for the birth of a healthy child were added.

It had previously been considered that, as a matter of public policy, damages should not be awarded, when as a result of a breach of contract (e.g. sterilisation) a healthy baby is born, but in the following case the Court of Appeal decided differently.

awarded: 수여하다, 주다

***Example* – *Thake* v *Maurice* (1986) –:**

In that case, a vasectomy operation was performed, but the operation was ineffective and a healthy child was born to the parents. The surgeon did not warn the parents that there was a chance that a pregnancy could occur. The parents sued for damages.

Held: that the defendant committed a breach of contract by not warning the plaintiffs of the risk, and awarded damages for the cost of the birth, the upkeep of the child and for the discomfort of the normal pregnancy.

vasectomy: 정관절제
surgeon: 외과의
pregnancy / occur: 임신 / 일어나다, 발생하다
committed: 범하다
upkeep: 부양
discomfort: 불편함

d) Contracts tending to impede the administration of justice

tending / impede / administration of justice: ~하는 경향이 있는 / 방해하다 / 사법

An agreement to stifle a prosecution for a criminal offence is void, because the public has an interest in the proper administration of justice. In this context, a contract to defeat bankruptcy law is also void.

stifle / prosecution / criminal offence: 늦추다, 막다 / 처벌, 형사소추 / 범죄행위
defeat: 무효시키다, 막다, 회피하다

***Example* – *John* v *Mendoza* (1939) –:**

The defendant owed the plaintiff some £852. The defendant was made bankrupt and the plaintiff was intending to prove for his debt in the bankruptcy. The defendant asked him not to do so, but to say that the £852 was a gift whereupon the defendant would pay the plaintiff in full regardless of the sum received by other creditors.

owed: 빚지다
made bankrupt: 파산하다
to prove for his debt in the bankruptcy: 파산채권을 신고하다
whereupon: 그래서, 그에 뒤이어서
regardless: ~와 관계없이, ~을 고려하지 않고

In view of the defendant's promise, the plaintiff withdrew his application, but in the event all the other creditors were paid in full and the bankruptcy was annulled. The plaintiff then sued for the debt.

~을 고려하여 / 철회하다(취소하다) / (파산채권) 신청

Held: that there was no claim, as the plaintiff abandoned all rights to recover on failure to claim in the bankruptcy, and the defendant's promise to pay in full was unenforceable, being an agreement designed to defeat the bankruptcy laws.

청구권

회피하다

e) Contracts of trade with the enemy

적성국가, 적국, 적

These contracts are illegal at common law, and also by virtue of the *Trade with the Enemy Act 1939*. All contracts made with a person voluntarily residing in enemy territory in time of war are void unless made with the licence of the Crown.

~에 의하여

자발적으로 / 거주하다

f) Contracts in restraint of trade

억제, 제한

Contracts which stop someone from carrying on a trade or profession are prima facie illegal and void as they are against public policy.

한눈에 보기에도, 일응(一應)의

(aa) *Contracts of employment*

고용계약

Employers may try to protect their business by putting a clause in the contract, forbidding the employee to compete within a certain area, or to give away trade secrets. These restraints are permitted if they are reasonable. They may be reasonable, e.g., to protect business connections, when an employee leaves the business and may take customers away.

고용주들

피고용인 / 경쟁하다

기업(영업)비밀

If the restraint is allowed, however it must be for a reasonable time, and within a reasonable area. What is reasonable will depend on the type of contract and the circumstances of the case.

***Example* — *Mason* v *Provident Clothing and Supply Co Ltd. (1913)* —:** 의류 / 공급

The plaintiffs were a clothing and supply company with branches all over England. The defendant was employed by them as a canvasser. In his contract of employment the defendant agreed to a restraint of trade clause which stated: 외판원

"... that the (defendant) would not within three years after termination of employment be in the employ of any person, firm or company carrying on or engaged in a business the same as or similar to that of the (plaintiff) company, or assist any person employed in any such business within 25 miles of London." 고용(관계)

Held (by the House of Lords): that the clause was wider than was reasonably required for the plaintiffs' protection, because the area, 25 square miles of London, was many times bigger than the area he worked in for the company previously. The restraint clause would therefore not be enforced. 더 포괄적인

(bb) *Contracts for the sale of a business*

A business may be sold on condition that the seller will not carry on a similar business within a fixed time and/or area.

***Example* — *Nordenfeldt* v *Maxim Nordenfeldt Guns & Ammunition Co.(1894)* —:** 탄약(무기)

Nordenfeldt, known throughout the world as an inventor and manufacturer of guns and ammunition, sold his business to a company, and promised that for 25 years, he would not engage in similar work in any part of the world. After some years Nordenfeldt entered into business with a rival company dealing with guns and ammunition and the respondents served an injunction to restrain him from doing so. 발명자 / 경쟁회사 / 신청하다 / 가처분(명령)

Held (by the House of Lords): that the injunction would be granted as the agreement was reasonable and valid: The fact that Nordenfelt (with over £200,000) was liberally compensated rendered the contract reasonable in itself.

후하게 / 보상하다

(cc) *Solus agreements*

독점계약

Traders often agree to be supplied by only one company. The courts consider such restraints as illegal unless reasonable.

상인들 / 공급받다

Example — Esso Petroleum Co. Ltd.* v *Harper's Garage (Stourport) Ltd. (1967) —:

The defendant company owned two garages with attached filling stations, the Mustow Green Garage, Mustow Green, near Kidderminster, and the Corner Garage at Stourport-on-Severn. Each garage was tied to the plaintiff oil company: the one at Mustow Green by a solus supply agreement only with a tie clause binding the dealer to take the products of the plaintiff company at its schedule prices from time to time. There was also a price-maintenance clause which was no longer enforceable and a "continuity clause" under which the defendants, if they sold the garage, had to persuade the buyer to enter into another solus agreement with Esso. The defendants also agreed to keep the garage open at all reasonable hours and to give preference to the plaintiff company's oils. The agreement was to remain in force for four years and five months from 1 July 1963, being the unexpired residue of ten-years tie of a previous owner. At the Corner Garage there was a similar solus agreement for 21 years and a mortgage under which the plaintiffs lent Harpers £7000 to assist them in buying the garage and improving it. The mortgage contained a tie covenant and forbade redemption for 21 years. In August 1964, Harpers offered to pay off the loan but Esso refused to accept it. Harpers then turned over all four pumps at the Corner Garage to VIP, and later sold VIP at Mustow Green. The plaintiff company now asked for an injunction to restrain the defendants from buying or selling fuels other than Esso at

첨부된
주유소
~과 묶인, 연결된
독점공급계약
의무(구속) 조항
가격유지조항
지속성조항
만료되지 않은 / 잔여(기간) / 10
간의 의무(구속)
부동산저당
향상시키다 / 구속합의
되물림, 변제
대출액 전액을 반환하다
가처분명령 / 막다
연료

the two garages during the subsistence of the agreements.

Held (by the House of Lords): that the rule of public policy against unreasonable restraints of trade applied to the solus agreements and the mortgage. 제한, 구속

The shorter period of four years and five months was reasonable so that the tie was valid but the other tie for 21 years in the solus agreement and the mortgage was invalid, so that the injunction asked for by the plaintiffs could not be granted.

Diagram 34

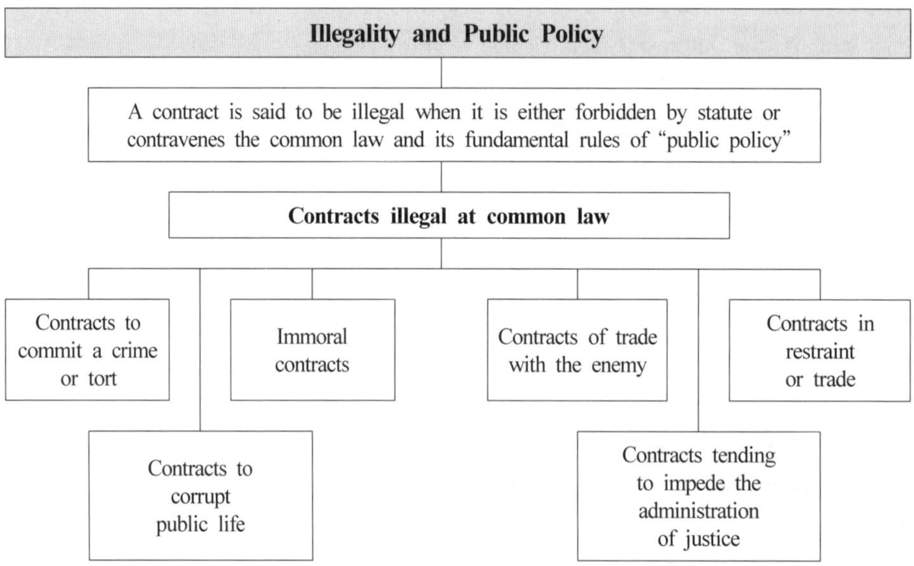

X. Discharge of a contract

계약관계의 종료

In English civil law there are four ways in which a contract can be discharged, i.e. by performance, agreement, breach and frustration (or impossibility).

종료하다 / 이행 / 계약위반 / 계약달성불능 / 불가능, 불능

1. Performance

The usual rule is that a contract is discharged when it is performed according exactly to its terms, i.e., when the parties have carried out their promises. Anything less will not do! If A agrees to paint B's house for 500, the contract is performed when the house is painted and payment made. 페인트 칠하다

***Example* — *Cutter* v *Powell (1795)* — :**

The defendant contracted to pay a seaman on a ship from Jamaica to England 30 guineas "provided he proceeds, continues, and does his duty as second mate in the ship from hence (Kingston, Jamaica) to the port of Liverpool". The seaman died in course of the voyage and his administratrix sued for work and labour done.

기니, 옛날 영국의 금화
2등 항해사
여기에서
(여성) 상속관재인

Held: that the action could not succeed, because the contract was for the whole journey and it was never completed.

***Example* — *Moore & Co. Ltd.* v *Landauer & Co.'s Arbitration (1921)* —:**

The plaintiffs entered into a contract to sell the defendants a certain quantity of Australian canned fruit, the goods to be packed in cases containing 30 tins each. The goods were to be shipped "per S.S. Toromeo". The ship was delayed by strikes in Melbourne and in South Africa, and was very late in arriving at London. When the goods were discharged about one-half of the consignment was packed in cases containing 24 tins only, instead of 30, and the buyers refused to accept them.

과일통조림
깡통
배송된 물품

Held: that although the method of packing made no difference to the market value of the goods, the sale was by description under s.13 of the *Sale of Goods Act 1893*, and the description had not been complied with. Consequently the buyers were entitled to reject the whole consignment.

Generally a party must do everything promised in the contract, and part-performance is no performance, unless it is a divisible contract. If it is not a divisible contract, the

부분이행
분할가능한 계약

plaintiff cannot claim on a *quantum meruit* basis. *Quantum meruit* means "as much as he has earned". For example, if someone completes one third of the work under a contract, they may be able to claim one third of payment owing, on a *quantum meruit* basis.

부분이행에 대한 적절한 반대급부 / 그가 벌어올 것 만큼

***Example* — *Bolton* v *Mahadeva (1972)* —:**

Bolton installed a central heating system in the defendant's house. The price agreed was a lump sum of £560. The work was not done properly and it was estimated that it would cost £179 to put the system right.

정액

Held (by the Court of Appeal): that the lump sum payment suggested that the contract was entire and since Bolton had not performed his part of it properly and in full he could not recover anything for what he had done.

Exeptions to the rule that performance must be complete are not only admitted in divisible contracts, but also because of faults of the other party. If one party makes it impossible for the other party, to finish the contract, for example, the other party can claim on a quantum meruit basis, or sue for a breach of contract. If one party carried out substantial performance, i.e., if there are just a few minor defects, the performing party can claim the contract price, but not the costs of putting it right. However, if it costs any more than ¼ of the contract price to put right the defects, this would probably not count as substantial performance.

상당한(대단한)
작은 결점들, 흠결
정정하다, 보수하다

***Example* — *Hoenig* v *Isaacs (1952)* —:**

The defendant employed the plaintiff who was an interior decorator and furniture designer to decorate a one-room flat owned by the defendant. The plaintiff was also to provide furniture, including a fitted bookcase, a wardrobe and a bedstead, for the total sum of £750. The terms of the contract regarding payment were as follows: "Net cash as the

장식업자
공급, 제공하다
꼭 맞게 만들어진 / 책장 / 옷장
침대틀

work proceeds and the balance on completion". The defendant made two payments to the plaintiff of £150 each, one payment on 12 April and the other on 19 April. The plaintiff claimed that he had completed the work on 28 August, and asked for the balance, i.e. £450. The defendant asserted that the work done was bad and faulty, but sent the plaintiff a sum of £100 and moved into the flat and used the furniture. The plaintiff now sued for the balance of £350, the defence being that the plaintiff had not performed his contract, or in the alternative that he had done so negligently, unskilfully and in an unworkmanlike manner.

준공 잔액
장인답지 않은(솜씨가 서툰)

The Official Referee assessed the work that had been done, and found that generally it was properly done except that the wardrobe required replacing and that a bookshelf was too short and this meant that the bookcase would have to be remade.

중재심판, 중재판사 / 평가하다
책꽂이
다시 만들다

The defendant claimed that the contract was entire and that it must be completely performed before the plaintiff could recover. The Official Referee was of the opinion that there had been substantial performance, and that the defendant was liable for £750 less the cost of putting right the above mentioned defects, the cost of this being assessed at £55 18s 2d.

온전한

Held: in accordance with the opinion of the Official Referee the defendant has to pay the sum of £294 1s 10d.

~에 따라서

The Official Referee is a judge designated to consider cases referred to him by a court because they involve consideration of documents and accounts in order to assess exactly what damages should be payable.

판단, 심리하다
배정된 / 고려하다

2. Agreement

Since the parties to a contract enter the relationship by agreement, it goes without saying, that they can also end the contract by mutual agreement.

끝내다

The mutual release of both parties from their obligations

면제, (의무의) 해소

under the agreement provides the consideration for the agreement to discharge the contract. There are three possibilities leading to discharge of a contract by agreement. black

a) Discharge by deed and accord and satisfaction

재판 외 화해

When one party has performed the contract, the other party may be released from the promise to perform, either 약속에서 면제되다

- by deed, where no consideration for the release is given, or 증서
- by accord and satisfaction, where the parties agree to fresh consideration, by giving and accepting something outside the original contract. 새롭게 하다

However, if one party has already performed his part of a simple (formless) contract (without deed), the other party cannot be released from his obligation without any consideration (e.g. payment of a cancellation fee). This is due to the rule found in *Pinnel's Case* which we have already mentioned above (p. 123). 취소비용

b) Discharge where neither side has performed

양쪽 다 아닌

Where neither side has performed, the parties may agree to waive the contract and release each other from their obligations. In this case both sides give consideration by the promise not to enforce the contract. 포기하다

c) Discharge on occurrence of specific events

사건 / 특정한 계기

The parties may include terms in their original contract beforehand mentioning expressly that the occurrence of some specific event may discharge the contract. A charter party contract for the hire of a ship, e.g., may contain a term that a dock strike will discharge the contract. 포함하다 사전에 용선계약(계약서) 항구파업

3. Breach

A breach of contract may occur in several forms:

Firstly we have to distinguish between an actual breach and an *anticipatory breach*. 선행(先行)의 계약위반

The breach may be an actual breach when, e.g., a seller fails to deliver the goods in due time, or when one party fails to carry out the contract properly, because the goods delivered are not up to standard as to quality or quantity.

기일 안에, 적기에
적절히, 정상적으로
표준에 부합하지 않다

Anticipatory breaches can be:
either express repudiation which arises when one party states that he will not perform his part of the contract, or some other action by a party which makes performance impossible.

명시적인 거절표명
이행 불가능하게 하다

***Example* — *Hochster* v *De La Tour (1853)* —:**

In April 1853, D agreed to engage H as a courier for a European tour to commence on 1 June. On 11 May D informed H that he no longer required his services. The plaintiff (H) sued for breach of contract on 22 May, and the defence was that there was no cause of action until the date due for performance.

Held: that D had broken his contract by express repudiation, and H could, because of this anticipatory breach of contract, bring an action immediately.

여행가이드
시작하다

4. Frustration (or impossibility)

If something happens without the fault of either party, to make performance impossible, illegal or radically different, both parties are released from the contract.

극단적으로
계약(의 의무)에서 면제되는

***Example* — *Taylor* v *Caldwell (1843)* —:**

C let a music-hall to T for a series of concerts on certain days. The hall was accidentally burnt down before the concert opened.

Held: that the contract was discharged. Destruction of the subject-matter means that the contract is frustrated.

임대하다
우연히 / 전소되다
파괴
계약목적물

Where the contract depends on the happening of a certain event and this event does not occur, the contract is also frustrated and regarded as discharged.

Example – Krell* v *Henry (1903) –:

The defendant agreed to hire the plaintiff's flat to watch the coronation procession of Edward VII. The King was taken ill and the procession was cancelled.

Held: that the contract was discharged because of frustration and no rent was payable by the defendant, who only rented the flat to watch the coronation procession.

아파트
대관 행렬

The postponed coronation of Edward VII provided another interesting case, where frustration of contract was denied.

연기하다 / 제공하다
거절하다

Example – Herne Bay Steamboat Co.* v *Hutton (1903) –:

The plaintiffs agreed to hire a steamboat to the defendant for two days, in order that the defendant might take paying passengers to see the naval review at Spithead on the occasion of Edward VII's coronation. An official announcement was made cancelling the review, but the fleet was assembled and the boat might have been used for the intended cruise.

The defendant did not use the boat, and the plaintiffs employed her on ordinary business. The action was brought to recover the fee of £200 which the defendant had promised to pay for the hire of the boat.

Held: that the contract was not discharged, as the review of the fleet by the Sovereign was not the foundation of the contract. The plaintiffs were awarded the difference between £200 and the profits derived from the use of the boat for ordinary business on the two days in question.

기선
함선 퍼레이드
함대
선상여행
통상적인 사업, 사용
근거, 기초, 전제
(판결로) 인정받다

If a contract is frustrated and therefore discharged, problems may arise, where money or property has been

소유권

transferred beforehand, or when a party has worked on the contract before the frustrating event.

In these cases *the Law Reform (Frustrated Contracts) Act 1943*, applies. However, one should note here that this Act does not apply to charter-parties, carriage of goods by sea and insurance contracts. Nevertheless, as a general rule, from such an Act one may conclude that any money paid or any property transferred is recoverable, and any money payable ceases to be payable.

양도하다
계약급부이행장애에 관한 개정법
선편 운송
반환청구가 가능한
중단하다, 멈추다

Diagram 35

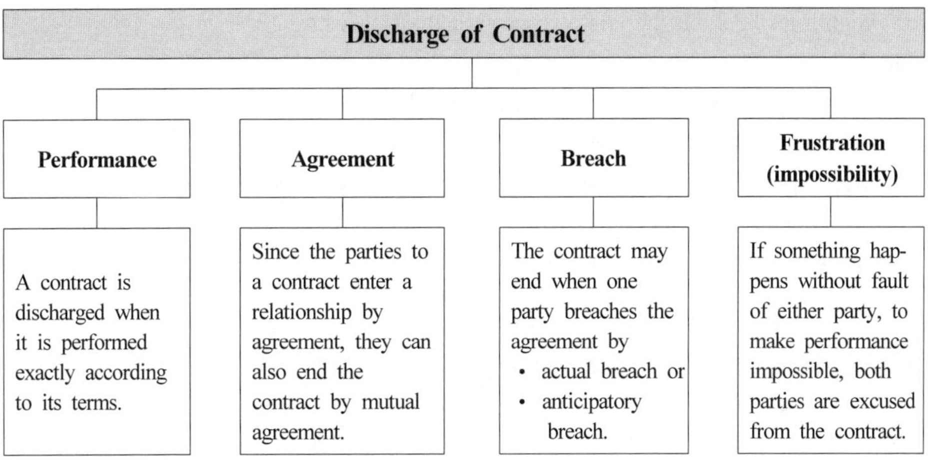

XI. Remedies for breaches of contract

When there has been a breach of contract, various remedies are available. Some of them have already been mentioned in the paragraphs above. The most common remedies are: damages, injunction, specific performance and rescission.

손해배상 / 가처분명령 / 계약급부의 정확한 이행 / 폐지, 철회

1. Damages

The aim of damages at common law is to put the injured party in the same financial position he would have been in, had the contract been properly completed.

If, e.g., a contract was made for the sale of a car for

£2,000 and the seller refuses to transfer the car (or he is not able to do so, since the car was destroyed owing to his negligence), and another similar car was purchased at the market price of £2,200, the purchaser would claim £200 damages. If the sum is deducted from the £2,200 paid for the second car, the purchaser would have paid £2,000, the price agreed upon in the original contract. However, not all losses will be recoverable to the injured party.

파괴하다
공제하다
반환청구 가능한

A line has to been drawn somewhere and the common law does this by applying the following principles established in the leading case *Hadley* v *Baxendale* (which you will find in every English textbook on the law of contract and which will follow below).

어딘가에는 선이 그어져야 한다

The injured party will be entitled to damages where

- they arise naturally from the contract, or
- they were reasonably in the contemplation of both parties at the time they entered into the contract, as
- the probable result of the breach.

예상, 의견

Example — Hadley v Baxendale (1854) —:

A miller sent a broken crankshaft by a carrier (Baxendale) to deliver to an engineer for copying in order to make a new one. The miller informed the carrier that the matter was urgent and that there should be no delay. The carrier accepted the consignment on those terms. The miller did not inform the carrier that the mill would be idle and unable to work.

크랭크샤프트(크랭크축) / 운송업자
화물
사용되지 않는

The carrier had no reason to believe that the crankshaft was an essential mechanism of the mill.

The carrier delayed delivery of the crankshaft to the engineer, and, as a consequence, the mill was idle for longer than it need have been. Hadley sued for loss of profits for the period during which the crankshaft was not working.

배송을 지체하다

Held: that the carrier was not liable for the loss of profits during the period of the delay.

The court considered that the defendant (Baxendale) in this case had no idea that the mill would be out of action during his delay.

Another case showing how these two principles mentioned above are followed by the courts forms the next case.

Example — Victoria Laundry v Newman Industrie Ltd. (1949) —: 세탁소

V, launderers and dyers, required another boiler to expand their lucrative dyeing contracts. N agreed to sell to V a second-hand boiler and to deliver on 5 June. The boiler was damaged whilst being dismantled, and was not delivered until 8 November. V claimed for the loss of profits on his laundry business which would have been earned had the boiler been delivered on time, and loss of profits on a certain remunerative dyeing contract from the Ministry of Supply.

세탁소 및 염색소 / 분해되다 / 세탁업 / 이익이 되는 / 가사부

Held: that laundry profits were recoverable as N must have foreseen their loss if there was delay, but that the loss of the dyeing contracts, which could not have been contemplated, was not recoverable.

예상, 고려하다

The amount of damages may be liquidated or unliquidated, when an action is brought before the court. If it is unliquidated it is left to the court to determine.

양 / 확정 정산된 / 정산되지 아니한 / 결정하다

If the amount of liquidated damages is much higher than the actual loss suffered, it may be considered as a penalty clause, which can be struck out by the courts, and a fairer (lower) amount substituted.

위약금조항 / 삭제하다 / 대신하다, 대체하다

On the other hand, where an agreed sum is in the nature of liquidated damages no greater sum will be awarded by the court even if it is proved that the consequences of the breach of contract have been more serious than the parties have foreseen.

합의금액 / (판결로) 인정하다 / 진지한 / 예측하다

Example — Dunlop v New Garage Co. (1915) —:

Dunlop sold tyres at reduced rates to wholesale traders on the terms that no private customer should be supplied with tyres at a lower rate than the retail prices laid down. New

타이어 / 소매업

Garage Co. agreed to this clause and to pay the sum of ￡5 as "liquidated damages" for each tyre sold in breach of the term. New Garage Co. sold a tyre at less than the agreed current list price and was sued by Dunlop. New Garage pleaded that the ￡5 per tyre was an inadmissable penalty.

Held (by the House of Lords): that it was liquidated damages. The sum of ￡5 was really and genuinely a pre-estimate of the interest of Dunlop in the due performance of the contract.

사전에 그 액수를 정한 손해
허용되지 않는
진정으로 / 미리 어림짐작하다
이익

Similar to the German law of damages even under English civil law the party suffering damage must do all in his power to mitigate his losses. If, e.g., an employee is dismissed from his job he should try to find other suitable work, not merely sit down and do nothing. In the same way a hotel owner is obliged to re-let the room if possible to other guests if the booking of a room is cancelled.

당하다, 받다
완화하다
다시 임대하다

If a buyer refuses to accept the ordered goods the seller must try to sell them to another person, and if he succeeds in getting the same price, he has suffered no loss. If, however, he obtains a lower price, he can claim the difference in damages.

성공하다

2. Injunction

An injunction is an equitable remedy, a court order stopping a person from doing something which breaches a term of a contract.

형평법에 따른 구제책 / 법원 명령, 결정

Example — Warner Brothers Pictures Incorporated* v *Nelson (1937) —:

The defendant, the film actress Bette Davis, had entered into a contract in which she agreed to act exclusively for the plaintiffs for twelve months. She was anxious to obtain more money and so she left America, and entered into a contract with a person in England.

근심하는, 몹시 바라는

The plaintiffs now asked for an injunction restraining the defendant from carrying out the English contract.

Held: that an injunction would be granted. The contract contained a negative stipulation not to work for anyone else, and this could be enforced. However, since the contract was an American one, the court limited the operation of the injunction to the area of the court's jurisdiction, and although the contract stipulated that the defendant would not work in any other occupation, the injunction was confined to work on stage or screen.

금지하다
이행하다
조항
영화스크린

3. Specific performance

특정이행, 합의한 계약급부의 이행

Specific performance is also an equitable remedy. It is a court order which makes the defendant carry out his promise under the contract.

The courts will give an order of specific performance when damages are not enough to compensate.

Example — Beswick* v *Beswick (1967) —:

A owned a small coal stocks, and his nephew, B, helped him to run it. A, being in poor health and wishing to retire from the business, drew up an agreement under which A, the uncle, transferred his business to the nephew, B. A would be retained as adviser and consultant at £6 10s. per week, and on his death his widow, C, would receive an annuity of £5 per week. A retired and was paid the £6 10s. per week. A subsequently died but B made no payment to the widow, C. Accordingly C sued the nephew: (1) as administratrix of her husband's estate, and (2) in her personal capacity for the arrears of the annuity and for specific performance of the agreement.

Held: that as administratrix, the widow could obtain an order of specific performance which would enforce the provision in the contract for the benefit of herself; but that in her personal capacity she could derive no action from the statute.

석탄창고
작성하다
유보하다
연금
(여자) 상속관재인
사인(私人)의 자격으로
연체금
미망인
얻다, 도출하다 / 법령

Specific performance, however, will not be granted by the courts to enforce a contract for personal services such as teaching, or an agreement to work for someone.

Moreover, specific performance is never granted in the following cases:

- Where damages are an adequate remedy.
- Where one party is a minor.
- In moneylending contracts. 대출, 현금소비대차
- In contracts for the sale of goods, unless the goods are unique. 독특한

4. Rescission

Rescission is an equitable remedy which was already mentioned when dealing with misrepresentation (cf. p. 176).

Rescission means that the parties are no longer bound by the contract, and endeavours to place them in the precontractual position by returning goods or money to the original owners. 위임하다

Diagram 36

Remedies for Breaches of Contract

Damages	Injunction	Specific performance	Rescission
Aim: to put the injured party in the same financial position he would have been in, if the contract was properly completed.	A court order, stopping a person from doing something which breaches a term of a contract.	A court order which makes the defendant carry out his promise under the contract.	The parties are no longer bound by the contract. Parties are placed in the precontractual position.

XII. Privity of contract

직접적 계약관계
(프리비티=공동의 법률관계)

1. General rule

The principle of *privity of contract* is a typical characteristic of English civil law. It means that in general third persons cannot sue for the carrying out of promises made by the parties to a contract. So under English civil law, as already mentioned above (p. 120), a contract for the benefit of a third party, is not recognised.

특징
약속을 이행하다
제3자를 위한 계약
인정하다

Thus, if a contract between A and B requires B to benefit C, the privity rule prevents C from suing B. However A may sue B if B breaks the contract, and the court may award A damages or may grant a decree of specific performance, under which B must perform the contract for the benefit of C.

내리다, 발하다 / 판결, 결정, 명령

If A and C were, in fact, both parties to the contract with B, then C cannot sue B unless he has provided some consideration. In this context you have to remember the doctrine of consideration, which has as one of it maximes: "consideration must move from the promisee." The situation is different to that example if A, B and C were parties to a contract by deed. As deeds do not require consideration, C could now sue B for damages if B fails to carry out his promises in the deed. The leading case which illustrates the doctrine of privity of contract is the next example, which has already been presented in short (p. 120) when dealing with the doctrine of consideration.

Example — Tweddle* v *Atkinson (1861) —:

William Tweddle, the plaintiff, was married to the daughter of William Guy. In order to provide for the couple Guy promised the plaintiff's father to pay the plaintiff £200 if the plaintiff's father would pay the plaintiff £100. On 11 July, an agreement was made in the following terms:

제공하다

"Memorandum of an agreement made this day between William Guy of the one part it is agreed that John Tweddle of the other part.

Whereas of the one part it is mutually agreed that the said William Guy shall and will pay the sum of ￡200 to William Tweddle, his son-in-law, and the said John Tweddle, father to the aforesaid William Tweddle, shall and will pay the sum of ￡100 to William Tweddle, each and severally the sums on or before the 21st day of August 1855. And, it is hereby further agreed by the aforesaid William Guy and John Tweddle that William Tweddle has full power to sue the parties in any court of law or equity for the aforesaid sums hereby promised and specified." 앞서 말한

The plaintiff was the son of John Tweddle and, before the making of the agreement, had married the daughter of William Guy. Before the marriage, William Guy, in consideration of the proposed marriage, had promised a marriage portion (which had not been performed at the time of the making of the agreement). By 21 August 1865, the plaintiff had not been paid the ￡200 by William Guy, who had subsequently died, or by Guy's executor. The plaintiff sued Guy's executor for the ￡200. 결혼 지참금 유언 집행자, 상속집행인

Held: that the plaintiff's action failed because he had not given any consideration to Guy in return for the promise to pay ￡200. The provision in the agreement allowing William Tweddle to sue was of no effect without consideration. 조항

Wightman J. stated: "... But there is no modern case in which the proposition has been supported. On the contrary, it is now *established that no stranger to the consideration can take advantage of a contract, although made for his benefit.*" 제안

The doctrine of the privity of contract was expressly confirmed by the House of Lords: 명시적으로

Example — Dunlop Pneumatic Tyre Co. Ltd.* v *Selfridge & Co. Ltd. (1915) —:

The appellants were motor tyre manufacturers and sold tyres to Messrs Dew & Co. who were motor accessory dealers. 자동차부품

Under the terms of the contract, Dew & Co. agreed not to sell the tyres below Dunlop's list price, i.e. £4.05 per tyre, and as Dunlop's agents, to obtain from other traders a similar undertaking. In return for this undertaking Dew & Co. were to receive special discounts, some of which they could, if they wished, pass on to retailers who bought tyres. Selfridge & Co. accepted two orders from customers for Dunlop covers at a lower price. They obtained the covers through Dew & Co. and signed an agreement not to sell or offer the tyres below the list price. For giving this undertaking Dew & Co. gave them part of the discount received by Dew & Co. from Dunlop. It was further agreed that £5 per tyre sold should be paid to Dunlop by way of liquidated damages.

Selfridge supplied one of the two tyres ordered below list prices, i.e. at £3.65 per tyre. They did not actually supply the other, but informed the customer that they could only supply it at list price. The appellants claimed an injunction and damages against the respondents for breach of the agreement made with Dew & Co., claiming that Dew & Co. were their agents in the matter.

Held: that there was no contract between the parties. Dunlop could not enforce the contract made between the respondents and Dew & Co., because they had not supplied consideration. Even if Dunlop were undisclosed principals,[1] there was no consideration moving between them and the respondents. The discount received by Selfridge was part of that given by Dunlop to Dew & Co. Since Dew & Co. were not bound to give any part of their discount to retailers the discount received by Selfridge operated only as consideration between themselves and Dew & Co. and could not be claimed by Dunlop as consideration to support a promise not to sell below list price. (See now *Resale Prices Act 1976*, s.26)

Lord Haldane explained: "... In the law of England certain principles are fundamental. One is, that only a person who is

undertaking: 의무를 지는 의사표시

retailers: 소매상인

covers: 타이어 덮개

gave them part: 나누도록 하다

undisclosed principals / moving: 감추어진 채 대리되는 사업주(비현명 사업주) / 옮기다, 교환하다

Resale Prices Act: 재판매 가격법(가격고정법)

---

1) 대리인의 대리권이 외부에 드러나지 아니하였더라도, 대리권의 범위 내에서 행한 계약은 피대리인을 구속한다는 개념

a party to a contract can sue on it. Our law knows nothing of a *ius quaestium tertio* arising by way of contract."

The rule stated in this case is fairly distinct from the rule that "consideration must move from the promisee". Here, the basis of the decision is, that Dunlop was not a party to the agreement made between *Dew & Co. and Selfridges*. 꽤 다른

The doctrine of privity of contract has existed for more than a century and has been reaffirmed in cases ranging from *Tweddle* v *Atkinson* (1861) to *Scruttons Ltd.* v *Midland Silicones Ltd.* (1962), which is another leading case and forms our next example. 재확인하다

***Example* — *Scrutton Ltd.* v *Midland Silicons Ltd. (1962)* —:**

A (shipper) and B (carrier) contracted for the carriage of a cargo owned by B. A further contract existed between A and C (stevedore) regarding the unloading of the goods from B's ship. The goods were damaged through C's negligence during the unloading, and B claimed damages from C. An exemption clause existed in the contract between A and B, and on that clause C relied. 해운업자 / 운송업자 화물 하역인부

Held (by the House of Lords): that C was a stranger to the contract between A and B, and as a result could not rely on the exemption clause. His defence therefore failed because he had not been asked for, and had not given, any consideration to the shipper. The appeal of C was dismissed. 기각하다

Even *Lord Denning*[1], who dissented, agreed that the 의견을 달리하다

1) If you have read this book and particularly the illustrative cases attentively you should have noticed that in 1947 *Lord Denning* decided in the *High Trees Case* (above p. 127) as a "Justice" (J.) of "Kings Bench Division" only; then in *Combe* v *Combe* (1951) he decided as a "Lord Justice" (L.J.) and member of the Court of Appeal. Later he advanced into the House of Lords, the highest court, where he dissented in this case of 1962, and in *George Mitchell Ltd.* v *Finney Lock Seeds Ltd.* (1983), he gave his last judgment as "Master of the Rolls" (M.R.). 그림을 그려 설명하는 듯한
Knowing that the M.R. is the president of the Court of Appeal, you might have presumed that *Lord Denning* was "downgraded" from the House of Lords. To the contrary: it was his own desire to 짐작하다 / 등급을 낮춘 욕구, 바램

stevedore (C) could not rely on the contract between A and B. But in *Lord Denning's* opinion C's appeal should be allowed because C could rely on his contract with A. The carrier (B) is a bailee of the shipper's (A) goods and, according to *Lord Denning*, it is a special feature of the law of bailment that the bailor (A) is bound by any contract which he has authorised the bailee (B) to make in relation to the goods.

수탁자
특징 / 공탁법
공탁자
권한을 부여하다, 허락하다

The shipper (A) of goods must know that the carrier(B) will have to make contracts with stevedores (as C) for loading and unloading the goods, so he is bound by any exemption clause in such a contract.

선적 / 하역

Lord Denning, with his brilliant dissenting speech, could not get the majority of the House of Lords to support his opinion.

2. Exceptions

There are some exceptions to the general rule of privity of contract, which means that there are cases in which a person is allowed to sue upon a contract to which he is not a party. Some exceptions are listed below:

a) Action by a beneficiary under a trust[1)]

수익자 / 신탁(관계)

If the facts show that the entitled is a beneficiary he may sue under the trust itself though not being a party to the contract.

신탁문제로 인해 고소하다 / 계약 당사자가 아닐지라도

b) Certain insurance contracts

보험계약

Section 11 of the *Married Women's Property Act 1882*, for instance, provides that if a man insures his life for the

이익을 위해

go back to the Court of Appeal because there his influence was more effective: whereas in the House of Lords a minimum of five judges (with a majority of three) decide, there are only three judges in the Court of Appeal (with a majority of two). It is naturally easier to convince one judge to adhere to his opinion than two judges ...

효과적인
설득하다 / 따르다

1) See Vol. Ⅱ, Chapter Nine.

benefit of his wife and/or children, or a woman insures her life for the benefit of her husband and for children, a trust is created in favour of the objects of the policy. The wife or the husband or the children, although they are not parties to the contract with the insurance company, can sue upon it. It is worth mentioning that the policy moneys are not liable for the deceased's debts.

수익자(cf. policy = 보험증권)
언급할 가치가 있다 / 보험금
고인의

c) Negotiable instruments

유통 가능한 유가증권

These are, e.g. cheques and bills of exchange.

수표 / 환어음

Bills of exchange provide an exception. Suppose A buys goods from B but does not wish to pay immediately; then, if B agrees, a period of credit can be achieved by using a bill of exchange.

예외를 두다
취득하다, 이루다

A takes the goods and B draws up a bill of exchange on a standard form, under which A (the drawee) agrees to pay the bill at some time in the future, say three months from the date on the bill. B (the drawer) can make himself or another person the payee. Let us suppose he makes himself the payee. B has now a choice: he can wait three months and get the money from A; or he can discount the bill with a bank, so that the bank will present the bill for payment by A after three months; or B can sign it (indorse it) over to someone else. Suppose he indorses it to his daughter C as a birthday present. Can C sue A if she presents him with the bill for payment on the due date and he does not pay it? The answer is "yes" because, although C gave no consideration to A or B, s.27 of the Bills of Exchange Act 1882 gives C a statutory right to sue. C could not sue B on the bill because, as between immediate parties, consideration is required.

지급인
발행인
수취인
할인하다
배서하다
밀접한, 직접적인

d) Price-maintenance agreements

가격 유지 계약

under the Restrictive Trade Practices Acts 1956 and the *Resale Prices Act 1976.* Under s.26 of the 1976 Act, e.g., the supplier of goods is given a statutory cause of action, so that he may enforce against a person, not being a party to the contract of sale, a condition as to a minimum resale price.

카르텔 금지법
제품 공급자 / 법정소송사유(소권)
~에 대항해 주장하다, 부과하다
최저 재판매 가격

e) Assignment

권리의 양도

Assignment means transfer, and we consider here, under the heading "privity of contract", the law affecting the transfer of rights and liabilities to a third person who is not a party to the original contract.

이전
제목 / 영향을 주다
권리와 의무(책임)

The general rule is, that only persons who possess rights and liabilities under a contract are parties to it. But in certain circumstances, the contracting parties may drop out and others may take their places, thereby succeeding to the rights and liabilities. If one of the contracting parties dies, their rights and liabilities may pass to their personal representatives creating a legal assignment.

어떤 상황에서는
빠지다
그것에 의해
지나가다 / 대리인, 상속인

Liabilities under a contract cannot be assigned without the consent of the other party. They can only be assigned by *novation* which always requires the consent of the other party.

책임(의무) / 양도하다
동의
채권양수

Rights under a contract can normally be assigned, provided they are of a proprietary character. This means that, highly personal rights, e.g. those arising from a contract of service, cannot be assigned, except with the consent of the other party to the contract.

제공하다
소유권과 유사한
서비스 계약
~외에

***Example* — *Robson and Sharpe* v *Drummond (1831)* —:**

D hired a carriage from one Sharpe who undertook to paint it every year and keep it in repair. After three years Sharpe retired from his business and informed D that thereafter R would be responsible for the repairs. D refused to deal with R, and R sued on the agreement.

차량, 마차

Held: that D was entitled at law to refuse to deal with R, and further that Sharpe could not assign his liabilities under the contract without D's consent.

Diagram 37

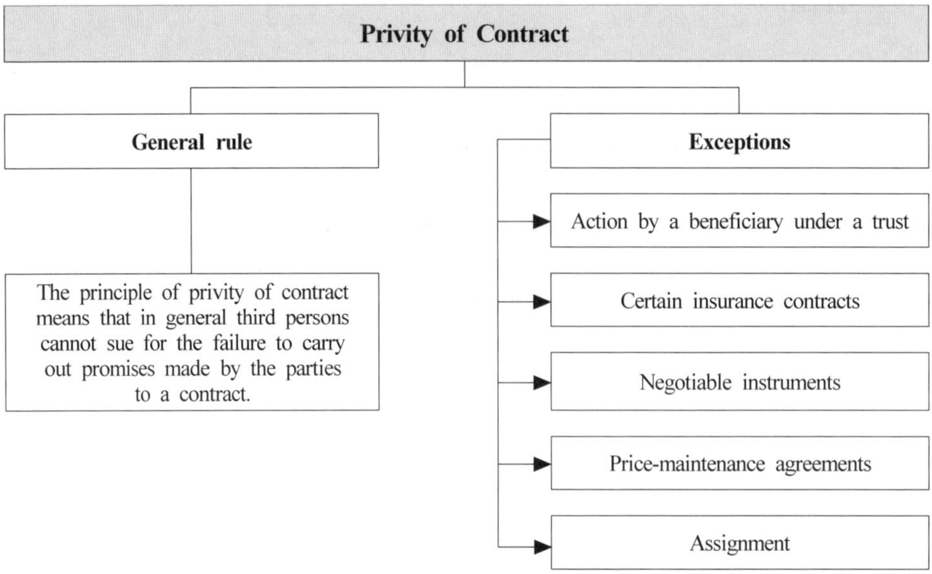

XIII. Further reading[1)]

Adams, Law for Business Students; *Applebey*, Contract Law*; Barker & Padfield*; *Beale, Bishop & Furmston,* Contract – Cases and Materials; *Beale/Hartkamp/Kötz/ Tallon* Cases, Materials and Text on Contract Law; *Blackstone's* Statutes on Contract, Tort & Restitution; *Bouder & Corns*, GCSE Law, Casebook; *Brown*, GCSE Law; *Cheshire, Fitfook & Firmstone's* Law of Contract; *Collins*, The Law of Contract; *Cracknell*, Contract (Cracknell's Law Student's Companion – cases and statutes); *Cooke/Oughton*, The Common Law of Obligations; *Denham*, Law – A Modern Introduction; *Dobson & Schmitthoff*, Business Law; *Duxbury*, Nutshells: Contract Law; *Elliot & Quinn*, Contract Law; *Geldart*, Introduction to English Law; *Harris*, An Introduction to Law; *James'* Introduction to English Law; *Jewell*, An Introduction to English Contract Law; *Koffmann/ Macdonald*, The Law of Contract; *Lyall*, An Introduction to British Law; *Poole*, Textbook on Contract Law, and:

1) Cf. footnote on p. 23.

Casebook on Contract Law, 5th ed.; *Richards*, Law of Contract, Harlow (Essex); *Sim & Scott's*, A Level English Law; *Smith*, J.C., The Law of Contract, and: A Casebook on Contract; *Smith & Keenan's*, English Law; *Stone*, Contract Law; *Templeman/Krishnan*, Obligations: Contract Law – Textbook – Revision Work Book –; *Templeman/Read*, Obligations: Contract Law – Casebook –; *Tayfoor*, Law Cartoons: Contract; *Treitel*, The Law of Contract.

Index

편역자 : **조익제**

독일변호사.
독일 최대의 지식재산권 전문로펌 Bardehle & Partner(뮌헨)에서 3년간 근무하는 동안, 독일 및 미국 의뢰인을 대리하여 상담과 송무를 진행하였다. 현재는 귀국하여 Lee International IP & Law Group(서울)에서 근무하고 있다. 국내유일의 미국 로스쿨인 한동국제법률대학원에서 비교특허법 등을 강의하였으며, 성균관대학교 법과대학원에서 독일의 송무경험을 바탕으로 한 민사소송법(특허소송관련) 박사논문을 준비중이다. 비교법적인 차원에서 영미법에 큰 관심을 가지고 있으며, 함께 배워가는 마음으로 영미법 시리즈를 소개하고 있다.

EADS의 Euro-Fighter 전투기 관련 특허침해소송, Siemens 상표분쟁 및 의약품 관련 국제 손해배상소송에서 Celltech 등 다국적 기업을 성공적으로 대리하였다.

기타 저서

- 표준 라이센스 계약(한-영판, 792쪽), 2004, 공저(파겐베르크, 가이슬러, 조익제)
- Leitfaden zum Koreanischen Patentrecht(독일어판, 한국특허법 매뉴얼), 2006

근무처

www.leeinternational.com, icho@leeinternational.com

조익제 변호사와 함께 영어로 읽는

영국 민사법 입문(1)

Introduction to English Civil Law

for Korean Speaking Lawyers and Law Students

2008년 1월 25일 초판1쇄 인쇄
2008년 2월 1일 초판1쇄 발행

편역자 조 익 제
발행인 고 준 영
발행처 **법 영 사**
(135-280) 서울시 강남구 대치동 611
전화 (501) 8898(대) FAX (501) 8895
등록 1987.11.5 제3-125호(윤)
Homepage : www.bubyoungsa.co.kr
E-mail : bypuco@chol.com

정가 15,000원

※ 저자와의 협의에 의하여 인지첨부를 생략함.
※ 본서는 ALPMANN SCHMIDT사와 본사와의 특약에 의해 독점 출판되었습니다.

ISBN 978-89-7032-243-8